Varieties

Varieties

ESSAYS BY
Jonathan Lieberson

WEIDENFELD & NICOLSON
NEW YORK

Published by Weidenfeld & Nicolson, New York
A Division of Wheatland Corporation
10 East 53rd Street
New York, NY 10022

Published in Canada by General Publishing Company, Ltd.

The following essays originally appeared in *The New York Review of Books:*
"Embarras de Richesse: The Life of Diana Vreeland," June 28, 1984; "What Is Hype?"
June 16, 1983; "Robert Wilson," April 11, 1985; "Diane Arbus," August 16, 1984;
"Oscar Levant," November 20, 1986; "Werner Erhard and est," April 5, 1979; "Isaiah
Berlin," March 6 and 20, 1980 (with portions from "Isaiah Berlin and the Limits of
Liberal Theory," *Salmagundi,* Summer 1982); "Karl Popper: Romantic Rationalist,"
November 18 and December 2, 1982 (which incorporates some remarks about the
work of P. K. Feyerabend that appeared in *The Journal of Philosophy,* 1977); "Is
Psychoanalysis a Science?" January 31, 1985; "Clifford Geertz: The Aims of Anthro-
pology," March 15, 1984; "The Silent Majority: Peasants in the Third World," October
22, 1981 (with portions from a longer review entitled "Peasant Values and Rural
Development," published by the Center for Policy Studies, The Population Council,
New York, 1981); "Too Many People? The History of the 'Population Explosion,' "
June 26, 1986 (with portions from the paper "Government Intervention in Fertility,"
co-authored with Dr. Bernard Berelson, which appeared in *Population and Devel-
opment Review,* vol. 5, no. 4 [December 1979], and portions from an essay entitled
"Morality and Population Policy," which appeared in *Population and Development
Review,* vol. 7, no. 1 [1981]).

The following essays originally appeared in *House and Garden*:
"The Psychology of Home and Decoration," November 1983; "Medieval Cookery,"
April 1984; "Escape from Esalen," October 1984.

"Sidney Morgenbesser" is reprinted from the introduction to Leigh S. Cauman, Isaac
Levi, Charles D. Parsons, and Robert Schwartz, *How Many Questions?: Essays in
Honor of Sidney Morgenbesser,* Indianapolis: Hackett, 1983.

Library of Congress Cataloging-in-Publication Data
Lieberson, Jonathan.
Varieties: essays.
I. Title.
AC8.L53   1987   081   87-8210
ISBN 1-55584-059-0

Manufactured in the United States of America
Designed by Irving Perkins Associates
First Edition
10 9 8 7 6 5 4 3 2 1

To B. and G.

Acknowledgments

I should like to thank Barbara Epstein and Shelley Wanger for their help in originally editing some of the pieces in this collection, and to offer thanks of a different order of magnitude to Robert Silvers, who commissioned the majority of these essays and who improved what I first showed him in diverse and fundamental ways. For information and advice in writing these pieces I should like to thank Joseph Alsop, Sir Isaiah Berlin, Dr. Paul Demeny, Professors Sidney Morgenbesser and Meyer Schapiro, and the late Professor Ernest Nagel. I must also thank Richard Howard and Mark Polizzotti for their assistance in translating passages from Paul Valéry; Richard Avedon; and Lord Weidenfeld. Lastly, I wish to record my gratitude to Lynn Nesbit and to my editor John Herman for their part in bringing out this volume.

Contents

Introduction   xi

PART ONE

Embarras de Richesse: The Life of Diana Vreeland   3
The Psychology of Home and Decoration   13
What Is Hype?   20
Medieval Cookery   29
Escape from Esalen   36
Robert Wilson   49
Diane Arbus   62
Oscar Levant   75
Werner Erhard and est   86

PART TWO

Sidney Morgenbesser   99
Isaiah Berlin   111
Karl Popper: Romantic Rationalist   148
Is Psychoanalysis a Science?   182
Paul Valéry   203

PART THREE

Clifford Geertz: The Aims of Anthropology 265

The Silent Majority: Peasants in the Third World 295

Too Many People? The History of the
"Population Explosion" 311

Introduction

The pieces collected here were written for several publications over the past decade and therefore possess less unity than they might have had they been written in relation to one another. Indeed, if there is any unity in them as they stand, I am not aware of it. Hence one of several reasons for naming the book as I have.

The first part of the book contains reviews of books of popular sociology and psychology, memoirs of unusual personalities and situations, and one or two pieces of travel criticism, the last belonging to a genre that is now nearly defunct, superseded by travel articles that are little more than uncontrolled declarations of enthusiasm. The rest of the book is mostly given to portraits of intellectuals and to discussion of some contemporary social and economic problems. How I came to write about these dispersed subjects is not easy to describe. Twenty years ago, when I first began to think about a career, I was a fixture in the sawdust-littered back room of Max's Kansas City, a restaurant in New York, where I could be found nearly any evening sitting on a hard bench, eating a spare meal of black bread and chick peas—all that I could afford—with fiery young painters and anorexic fashion models, one of whom, I recall, was born in Yorkshire and yet could not identify Winston Churchill. Few of these people could have been said to be profoundly absorbed in great literature or rational politics. Yet it should not be supposed that they did not take themselves seriously. More than once, a harrowing argument broke out and someone or other went home and killed himself. We were frank improbables, feverishly enthusiastic partisans of new ideas in the arts; our intellectual lives were agitated and embryonic, critical of everything yet somewhat too willing to try out any form of human experience. It was in this moral and emotional atmosphere that I first knew Diane Arbus and Andy Warhol and Diana Vreeland and others who were to become iconic figures of the period, and first took an interest in some of the subjects discussed in this book.

At the same time, I was a university student—and later a teacher—of academic philosophy (of all things), engaged in a ceaseless study of formal logic and later of scientific methods of thought generally. The impulse to become familiar with theoretical philosophy was much stronger among young people in those days than it is today, it seems to me; a *cachet* attached to the study of Hegel and Spinoza and Nietzsche; it seemed to represent a participation in a kind of counterculture of free speculation, and a rude gesture against the profit-and-loss thinking of the business world. In my case, philosophy provided more than a little relief, sometimes comic in its own way, from Max's Kansas City—and vice versa.

When I first began to write articles of the kind collected here, I hardly thought of myself as a "critic" of any kind, certainly not as that word has come to be used, for example, in the sense of a "food critic" or a "home furnishings critic," who terrifies everyone by delivering malicious verdicts about them. I instead imagined myself to be bringing ideas in the sciences or other specialized disciplines to people unfamiliar with them and trying to show the relations of these ideas to other ideas—those from which they developed or with which they are associated in popular imagination. I did not have any systematic idea of the world. It was, for me, a heap of problems and facts, full of exceptions to grand generalities. I deliberately failed to formulate large views about Art, Science, and Politics, or to replace one discarded theoretical system with a new one. I never imagined becoming a "professional philosopher."

At least two main questions are raised by the essays in Parts II and III. We constantly encounter problems—determining the atomic weights of elements, or the distance between planets, or the workings of a modern bureaucracy—that can be clarified by the methods of modern science, our best knowledge; and perhaps these methods can be extended to treat new kinds of difficulties, possibly even those that concern us most deeply— the dilemmas of our personal lives, or such questions as how to improve our national economy or make our legal system or our moral standards more rational. But what exactly is "science"? Several essays in the volume argue that no one has yet adequately described the proper scope of science or what is called its distinctive "method." We should not, it seems to me, expect any one to able to do so. Science is an open-ended variety of ways of describing aspects of reality, not a single rule or set of instructions. This means that the question of what can and cannot be described "scientifically" has no general answer and that it is not possible to assert dogmatically, for example, that anthropology or psychoanalysis is "not scientific" because it contravenes some rule that was once erroneously thought to be "definitive" of empirical science.

But although science is open, it has limits, and cannot be made the model of all rational human thought. If the essays in Part III have any common theme, it is that a variety of human problems resist solution by "social science" (as it is commonly described). A related point is made in the essay on the poet Valéry, where it is urged that the traditional conception of philosophy as (a mostly unsuccessful) "scientific" effort by philosophers to solve intransigent puzzles inherited from the ancient Greeks is misleading. There is something peculiar about philosophy conceived as an enterprise in which one sets out to solve problems that we have good reasons to suppose are insoluble. I argue that the invention and promotion of problems—and competition among philosophers—are as much essential features of philosophy as problem-solving, and that if this is so, the "nature" of philosophy is different from what many of us have been taught to suppose. Philosophy, of course, is only one sphere of thought in which we can see the great part played in human life by open and insoluble problems, problems that set a limit to the ambitions of our thought and that we must recognize for what they are, instead of naively assuming that an as-yet-unspecified "scientific method" will, sooner or later, scrub them away forever. Once we do so, we are also prepared to look sympathetically, as many of these essays do, on the kind of relativism and pluralism that acknowledges not just conflicts in our own chosen ideas, but also conflicts among the views of groups, cultures, patterns of thought, and moralities. And we may become sympathetic as well to the idea that it is necessary in all human life to choose among such alternatives without being able to resolve the theoretical conflicts that underlie them.

Part One

Embarras de Richesse: The Life of Diana Vreeland

Diana Vreeland, once the editor of *Harper's Bazaar* and then of *Vogue,* and now a curator at the Costume Institute of the Metropolitan Museum of Art, is a familiar figure to readers of fashion magazines. In recent years, because of her shrewdly maintained reputation and, more importantly, because of her transformation of the Costume Institute into a highly successful business enterprise through its annual exhibitions, she has been promoted by the press into an all-purpose *doyenne* of style who has outlived all rivals and who now imperiously renders opinions on contemporary life and manners. I vividly recall my first meeting with her. Like everyone else I was introduced not to her but to her long-nailed index finger, which she would point at one, extending it as a kind of barrier to trade. She was improbable in the extreme, sitting cross-legged, with erect spine, stroking the arch of one of her feet. She used theatrical gestures, stretching and kneading the air with her fingers and humming and purring in an authoritative manner if she agreed with something you had said. Her face resembled an Indian chief's. Her black hair looked as if it were made of concrete— hard enough, say, to repel a length of galvanized steel pipe.

She often interrupted her conversation to suck the smoke out of a Camel cigarette, leaving a jagged band of blood-colored lipstick around the unlit stem while holding it between her thumb and forefinger, the lit end facing her palm.

Her voice alternated between whispering, shouting, and between orating, exhorting, and tub-thumping. When she laughed, she slowly and deliberately intoned each "ha" of "ha-ha-ha," much, I imagined, as one of the denizens of Hogarth's *Gin Lane* might have done. Her walk was also unusual, almost exactly like the entrance of Bob Hope at a USO benefit—except when she took off her glasses, when she resembled instead a spider that had received ballet lessons. Between the humming and the purring and the shouting and whispering, the laughing and the odd walk, I must own that it crossed my mind that she was—not necessarily a "fake"—but immoderately artificial. I recalled the remark made about Max Beerbohm: "For God's sake, take off your face and reveal the mask underneath."

Her most distinctive trait was the strange telegraphic style in which she conveyed her thoughts: "too attractive . . . Nizam's son and all that . . . Versailles . . . Porthault." I often failed entirely to understand what she was talking about. When I asked her about an event that had taken place two nights earlier, she said something to the effect of "Oh, but it was extraordinary! We went up this sort of . . . and everyone had a tout petit splash of mmmmmmm . . . and we did a bit of this and a bit of that until we got to *I don't know where*, and I said something I can't recall to the official who was escorting us, blah, blah, blah . . . Of course I wouldn't be telling you this any more than you'd be telling me I don't know what . . . Oh, the HELL with it." When one could follow her, she often expressed curious opinions and terse formulations of occult knowledge, views like "Peanut butter is the greatest invention since Christianity," or "The Civil War was nothing compared to the smell of a San Diego orange." Her favorite author, she told me, was J. D. Salinger; and Liberace was "the greatest entertainer of all time"; while on vacation in Tunisia she learned of the death of Denys Finch Hatton, she said, from "the drums of Africa." I once heard her shriek on the phone to a friend of hers in Hong Kong: "If you're getting up at the crack of dawn, go out and buy some plates for me at one of the Russian Communistic shops."

She has now written her second book*—the first was a commentary on her favorite photographs called *Allure*. It purports to be her autobiography, but it is rather less than that and more like an Oriental pillow book, a series of haiku glimpses into the highly circumscribed world of fashion she has belonged to all her life. Depending on your point of view, it is likely to strike you as an *embarras de richesse* or vice versa.

Mrs. Vreeland was born Diana Dalziel in Paris. By her own account, her mother was an extravagant, hedonistic American who loved clothes and who entertained Diaghilev and Nijinsky and Ida Rubinstein. Mother and daughter did not get along very well: According to Mrs. Vreeland, "I was always her ugly little monster." Her father was a stout English stockbroker in the habit of saying "worse things happen at sea" if any unpleasantness occurred. Mrs. Vreeland witnessed the coronation of George V in 1911; three years later, she came with her family to the United States and was enrolled in the Brearley School in New York, although in retrospect she says, "I was looking for something Brearley couldn't offer." She therefore left it and entered dancing school, where she says she was taught by Fokine and others. In 1917 she and her sister were sent by their mother to Montana, for the reason, she says, that "during the night, there was an outbreak of infantile paralysis in Southampton." In Montana she met Buffalo Bill Cody and saw drunk men shoot each other to death. She "came out" in 1923, was blackballed from the Colony Club in New York City for being too "fast," and spent a great deal of time dancing with "gigolos."

In 1924 she met her future husband, T. Reed Vreeland, who

*Diana Vreeland, *D.V.*, George Plimpton and Christopher Hamphill, eds. (New York: Alfred A. Knopf, 1984).

was in the banking business, and they were married just after her mother was named as a corespondent in a divorce case; perhaps as a result, very few people came to their wedding. The Vreelands lived first in Albany, New York, and then in London. In 1937, when Mrs. Vreeland was in her thirties, the Vreelands returned to New York and she started to work at *Harper's Bazaar,* where she wrote a column entitled "Why Don't You?", which contained such advice as the following: "Why don't you rinse your blond child's hair in dead champagne, as they do in France? . . . Why don't you twist her pigtails around her ears like macaroons?" Mrs. Vreeland sketches her story up to the present, through her rise at *Harper's Bazaar* to editor in chief, then her tenure at *Vogue* in the Sixties, when her power was at its height, and finally her current job at the Metropolitan. There are also memories of her travels in Russia and Tunisia and of Munich and Budapest and Paris during the Thirties. ("I stayed at this ghastly hotel on the boulevard Haussmann with third-rate Indians in it. They were always strangling women across the court.") She has also included somewhat blurred portraits of friends such as Coco Chanel, the Duke and Duchess of Windsor, and Cole Porter.

This book is apparently designed to read as if it were "spoken" to a sympathetic, sophisticated visitor to Mrs. Vreeland's house, as when she says, "The Grand Hotel in Rome is attractive to me because of its divine concierge, Buzo. Do you know him?" Indeed, it seems to be little more than an artfully edited series of transcriptions from a tape recording. Perhaps this is preferable to what Mrs. Vreeland would have produced if she had written a book, but the policy of faithfully transcribing the rhythm and inflection of her spoken voice is not always an advantage. Here, for example, is her description of a Russian nobleman: "The Grand Duke Dimitri was *the* handsomest . . . the hang of his suits! His leg in a *boot!* Oh *God!* He was more interested in fishing and shooting—like all Russian men— but he was a beauty! Now, whether he killed Rasputin or not, who knows?"

* * *

Although there is rather too much in the book about half-forgotten society people, a number of Mrs. Vreeland's stories are about people and events that we would like to know more about from someone who knew or saw them at first hand. But unfortunately Mrs. Vreeland views history from an extraordinarily narrow perspective. Her focus is almost always on considerations of style and fashion. For example, although Isak Dinesen was "a great friend of mine" who came to tea "every Saturday afternoon," all we learn about her is what she ate and drank at these teas. She says that she saw Legs Diamond threaten a man at a speakeasy by patting the guns he wore under his coat—it is the "elegance of the gesture" that counts. What was Buffalo Bill Cody like? He "was essentially an entertainer. But what chic old Bill had! With his beard he looked like Edward VII, and he wore the fringed leather clothes that the hippies all wore in the sixties."

In Hitler's Germany, where she and her husband were vacationing, she says she pushed her way through a Nazi demonstration to get to her bath in time to make a concert. "We got through that evening all right," she says. "Actually, we were having the time of our lives. Every day we went out into the lovely, sweet-smelling countryside . . . having picnics and revisiting the castles of mad King Ludwig, which we could never see enough of." In the "pornographic museum" in Pompeii, where a part of the ancient city and the people in it are preserved exactly as they were when Vesuvius erupted, to which she had access through "a friend in the Mussolini government," she saw a slave making love to his mistress, frozen in time and space. She—and perhaps only she—noticed that "he wore the simplest sandal in the world. It had just *one* thong which went between the big toe and the one next to it, and *one* strap around the ankle attached to the heel." She had it copied and in her capacity as fashion magazine editor she introduced it to the American woman; it was, she says, "the Birth of the Thonged Sandal."

On at least one occasion, it seems, Mrs. Vreeland's preoccupation with clothes threatened to engulf her reason. During

the Phony War, on the eve of the most serious European crisis
of her lifetime, when the Vreelands were in Paris and were
urged to return to America, she chose to remain alone in Paris
to continue with her fittings. As she says, her husband knew
that it was futile to separate her from her clothes and shoes;
he "was a man with such a marvelous sense of . . . how women
are. He got on a ship with a lot of American friends leaving
France, and he left me behind." By her account, she finally
consented to leave when a friend begged her to take the "last
passenger ship with private cabins out of Europe." On her last
afternoon in Paris, with war impending, she walked down the
Champs-Elysées with a friend. "I'd just had my last fitting at
Chanel," she says. "I can remember exactly what I had on: a
little black moiré tailleur from Chanel, a little piece of black
lace wrapped around my head, and beautiful, absolutely exquisite black slippers like kid gloves." After the war, she returned at once to Paris and noticed that it had changed. "I
realized this when I went for my fittings. You don't know what
a part of life fittings once were. Remember I told you that
before the war I used to have three fittings on a *nightgown.*
. . . After the war you were no longer fitted for nightgowns."

Anyone seeking Mrs. Vreeland's opinions on the larger questions of life will be somewhat disappointed by this book. But
she has included dozens of observations about clothes, food,
health, colors, countries. If some of these can only be described
as little summaries of a lifetime of ignorance, in other places
she speaks with the cold analytical tone of La Rochefoucauld:
"The French are very generous if you offer them money."
There are lessons in behavioristic psychology: "It is a form of
anger if you can't control the foot . . . the *heavy tread* is a form
of anger." And sociological speculations: "The world will go
to lines of color—there's no question about it. It won't be just
the Africans . . . and it won't be just the Chinese—it will be
every part of the world that has any streak of color other than
white. The Western world will go." She has learned that "all
English are actors, and there are very few actors who are not

English." She provides a cure for hiccups and the advice to go
early in the morning to the dentist because "dealing with a
tired dentist is really very tough on you." Some of her remarks
achieve a kind of perfection of insignificance: "I'm crazy about
Indiana. So many people with style come from Indiana—not
that I can give you a long list, but it's true."

Mrs. Vreeland admits that she has a fondness for exaggeration; she says she has "always had a strong Kabuki streak."
And indeed she seems unable to qualify her appraisals of people
and events. When she went to Paris for a clothes collection,
"the whole of Chad" was at her hotel, and then a few years
later, "there was the whole of Africa—but I mean the *whole*
of Africa." She travels to Devonshire to see a tilting green and
"I've never seen anything so beautiful in my life"; on the previous page she says that "to me, a gauntlet is the most beautiful
thing," and later, that "the children of royalty . . . are always
the most beautiful children in the world." Her uncontrolled
enthusiasm and frequent use of gallicisms—"I knew," she writes,
"that we were heading toward *rien*"—make it easy to believe
she had a hand in the development of the style of expression
used in fashion magazines when they speak, for example, of
"the passion of cold cream" or claim that "the thrill of the
season is the little black *jupe*."

Such prose contributes to the impression one has after reading her book that while Mrs. Vreeland undoubtedly has led a
full life she has made it even fuller in the recounting. There is
a distinct flavor of monkeyshines in some of her stories. How,
for example, did she come to use a now famous singer as a
fashion model? As she tells it, she and her husband were staying
in Morocco, and one day, "on a little strip of beach between
Mohammadia and Rabat," there was a gust of wind and "a
piece of newspaper blew our way. It must have been from a
Czechoslovakian paper or something, because I couldn't read
the language—I know it wasn't Arabic, which, naturally, I read
fluently—but on the scrap of newspaper was a picture of this
perfectly *marvelous*-looking girl. It was Cher."

In another of her memories, she and her husband were stay-

ing at a hotel in Marseilles. Quite suddenly, the recently de-
posed king of Spain arrived with his entire retinue of servants,
courtiers, children, and so forth. The same evening, it so happened, the Vreelands and two others were invited to see the
red-light district of the city by the prefect of police, who sternly
warned them that the British consul disappeared off the face
of the earth some weeks before doing the same thing. According to her account, he asked them whether they were still
prepared to go. "Listen, can a duck swim? What the hell did
we care?" says Mrs. Vreeland. And so they took off and walked
through darkened alleys and squares, passing "these Pepe le
Mokos. The only thing you'd see was the ends of their cigarettes." They finally reached a brothel, where they were met
by the madam, "who was quite padded out and had a mous-
tache about the size of Adolphe Menjou's," and who took them
on a tour of the establishment: "We saw silver rooms, we saw
gold rooms, we saw rooms of mirrors . . . and then we went
into an enormous red-and-gold Edward VII ballroom with little
gold chairs all around and a band tuning up, led by this little
hunchback," who turned out to be "the most important musician in Marseilles." As Mrs. Vreeland says elsewhere in her
book, "now I *exaggerate*—always. And, of course, I'm terrible
on facts. But a good story . . . some of the *details* . . . are in
the imagination. I don't call this lying."

Even if Mrs. Vreeland may have invented or touched up
some of her past, at least she doesn't bother to stick to just
one myth about herself, and her book gains a certain charm
from her ability to blow the whistle on some of her own absurdities with an unexpected blunt remark and then to shift
comfortably to a quite different character. From some of the
things she says one might easily think of Mrs. Vreeland as
nothing but another woman of style and wealth, a sybarite like
her mother, who attends polo matches and dancing parties and
finds just about everything "totally great." In this mood, she
leaves everything to men; she is Odette de Crécy, a geisha.
Business recedes into the background almost as a hobby; she
lives only for fantasy.

But in the pages she devotes to her business career, there is
an unmistakable change in voice. Mrs. Vreeland becomes a
tough-talking magazine editor who says her lunch consisted of
a peanut butter and marmalade sandwich and a shot of Scotch,
and whose motto was "give 'em what they never knew they
wanted." In this mood she can write that fashion "was always
unreal to me." When in the Sixties she showed in *Vogue* a
photograph of a bare midriff and received complaints from
some readers, and was asked why she had run the picture, she
reports herself as having responded, "because I'm a reporter.
I know *news* when I see it! What are we talking about, for
Christ's sake—pleasing the bourgeoisie of North Dakota?" (Some
of her ideas, unlike this one, she admits "never reached the
general public," such as her decision "to lay an entire issue of
Vogue out backward, like a Japanese book, because that's how
I thought everyone looked at magazines.")

Odette de Crécy and Hildy Johnson do not quite fit together:
it is odd to hear Mrs. Vreeland denounce feminism and the
free press on one page of her book, and on another recount
how, when she failed to get a raise from the Hearst press lords
running *Harper's Bazaar,* she jumped to its competitor *Vogue*
because "they offered me a very large salary, an endless expense account . . . and Europe whenever I wanted to go." And
when Mrs. Vreeland narrates episodes in her life when she
tried to satisfy both her penchant for stylish fantasy and for
business, a bizarre effect is created that is uniquely hers. "I
was in the middle of my Dynel period then," she writes of one
phase of her career at *Vogue,* "one of the happiest periods of
my life, to tell you the truth, because I was *mad* about all the
things you could do with Dynel hair."

The "Dynel period" coincided with what Mrs. Vreeland calls
"the romantic years at *Vogue,*" when she organized a trip to
photograph a group of models in Tahiti. She was aware, she
says, that Gauguin had already painted the "big girls who sit
there with one flower in their hair," and so she chose, for
reasons she does not divulge, to send the group—models, photographer, hairdresser, Dynel—to Tahiti to photograph "the

most beautiful white horse with a long white tail on a pink beach—no little horse like a Gauguin, but a big romantic horse like the ones they have in a big way in Friesland in Northern *Holland,"* with the understanding that if the horse's tail was too short, Dynel could be used.

On its arrival the group was unable to find a Friesland horse in Tahiti, where there had apparently not been many horses at all in the previous century. Mrs. Vreeland thereupon communicated the terse instruction from New York to "fake it," and according to her, after three weeks of looking, and no doubt at considerable expense, they found an "ancient stallion" and pinned a section of Dynel hair to its tail. In the end, Mrs. Vreeland received a photograph, although she does not describe it, claiming that it is "too delicious for words." As she summarizes this curious episode, in words that could serve as a motto for her book: "I only take results. I've worked all my life on *results.* I didn't give a good goddamn if there were *no* horses in Tahiti—by God, we'd get some there, white ones, and get them outfitted with Dynel tails."

The Psychology of
Home and Decoration

For three years Joan Kron tried to discover the "meaning and purpose" of decorating, matters she feels have been ignored not only by the mass media but also by architects and decorators trained to look upon their work as purely "visual," and one of her aims was to see if social scientists have cast any light upon it. She believes they have: "To that perennial question: 'What's next in decorating?' " she says, "I would answer, what's next is not a style, or a color, or a look, but a *way of looking* at the home. I call it 'home-psych.' "* To read what follows this declaration is to be exposed to a true literary nightmare, a mixture of scientific conjecture, pseudoscience, cuteness, and *schlag* that beggars Maxwell Maltz's *PsychoCybernetics* and the collected works of Marabel Morgan.

Kron's book begins with a "conundrum." On the one hand, she says, we tend to "glorify and sentimentalize" the home. We "worship good taste" and spend $50 billion a year on furnishings. On the other hand, "decorating is loaded with bad

*Joan Kron, *Home-Psych: The Social Psychology of Home and Decoration* (New York: Clarkson N. Potter, 1983).

13

connotations. A preoccupation with it is considered trivial, narcissistic, materialistic, superficial" and "smacks of status-seeking." To those who find no genuine "conundrum" here, I must add that Kron's book is full of conundrums. Her explanation of our allegedly discordant attitudes can be stated quite briefly. Decorating the home, she claims, is not simply a "ruffle on reality," but "probably as close as one can get to a universal human activity—as significant and meaningful a human endeavor as mating or food-gathering or economic exchange." Decorating is "personalizing," "marking your environment to let people know where your boundaries begin and end and putting your personal stamp on a space and its contents." As she puts it in prose as engaging as that of a fashion-house press release, when you install your possessions in a place, "throw scarves over the lamps à la Scavullo to get the ambience *you* like, buy Miss Piggy mugs or *quel* other symbol (tennis racquet, Garfield the Cat, or hockey team) *you* identify with, make everything in your home conform to *your* standards of beauty and comfort, you are personalizing." It does seem to be going rather far by way of "personalizing" your home to actually buy a hockey team and put it there. Still, we roughly gather, in a nauseated sort of way, what Kron means when she writes that "without familiar things we feel disoriented, and our identities flicker and fade like ailing light bulbs."

But according to Kron "personalizing" is not merely a matter of "self-expression": "The furnishings of a home, the style of a house, and its landscape are all part of a system—a system of symbols. And every item in the system has meaning. Some objects have personal meanings, some have social meanings which change over time." We decorate our houses (and, according to Kron, especially our living rooms) not only to "express" ourselves (encouraged to do so as we have been in our day) but also to signify to others our success, our "status," our membership in groups. "Personality is a complex thing," says Kron, making an assertion that is constantly ignored in the social sciences. "If you think your passion for blue-and-white china, your affection for old quilts, or your affinity for shiny new furniture is an expression of your inner psyche and *nothing else,* you are mistaken. The personality of your house is related to factors *beyond* your biological uniqueness—variables such as your age, your sex, and most especially your social status." She sums up the matter in a crisp aphorism bound to find its way into any standard book of quotations: "In decorating matters, no man is an island. We are all part of some taste archipelago." In order to decorate sensibly we must find our "identity" and "a balance between the social and personal meanings of the home." But, Kron continues, this is not easy to do, and some "homemakers," fearful of pursuing the quest for self-identity to the bitter end, falter and succumb to "fear of furnishing" or even to "decorating interruptus," whereas others slavishly prostrate themselves before "celebrity decorators" who tyranically produce "environments" that their clients may not find pleasing.

These assertions are hardly secrets arduously wrested from nature by social scientists, yet since her book is meant to "open a dialogue" and to be rigorously objective, she unmercifully repeats and elaborates them in high-sounding language. An entire chapter on "Sex Role and Decorating Role" is little more than an extended treatment of the familiar theme that men and women have different "culturally determined" attitudes toward decorating; her chapter on "Home Cycles: What Time of Life Is This Place?" makes the same point about the old and the young. So far as I could tell, the only new information in the chapter entitled "Psyching Out Collecting" concerns Dolph Gotelli of northern California, the "foremost collector of Santa Claus iconography in the world," who discovered in a London doll museum his finest piece, a "hundred-year-old wind-up Santa that nods its head." Incidentally, Kron's explanation of how Gotelli noticed the object in a crowded museum is in my opinion one of the great anticlimaxes of modern literature. He did so, according to her, "by using the same highly developed discriminatory powers that an elephant uses to spot its favorite berries on the mukaita tree, that the koala uses to spot eucalyptus leaves, and that vegetarian animals use to select out their

preferred grasses, shoots, barks, leaves, seeds, fungi, and li-
chens." And what was this method? "He compared the physical
properties of the Santa at hand with Santas he had known."

"Some people don't start *or* finish personalizing because they
lack commitment to a relationship, a neighborhood, a job, or
a dwelling," says Kron, neatly covering all the bases and weak-
ening her claim to vacuity. Those who will turn hungrily to her
chapter "Psyching Out Collecting" for illumination will also
discover, among other things, that "two psychologists hypoth-
esized some years ago that commitment and decorating were
linked," although they will not learn who proposed the hypothesis or whether the hypothesis was tested, or if so, what
the results of the tests were. The chapter is mainly distinguished, in my view, for its second paragraph, a bittersweet
evocation of disquietude that recalls Turgenev: "Hundreds of
jonquils are beginning to bloom in the borders around Natalie
and Harvey's five-bedroom custom contemporary. But inside
the house, the living room is almost empty. Natalie and Harvey
have been seeing a marriage counselor for some time. The
problem is not sex or money or in-laws—the problem is furniture. For seven years Natalie has been unable to make any
but the most makeshift decorating decisions in the living room
and dining room."

With conclusions as thin as those Kron provides, it is not
clear that the years she spent reading "anthropology, sociology,
geography, economics, popular culture, market research, and
the relatively new field of environmental psychology" were
spent to good purpose. Most of the social scientific research
she cites is trivial, on the order of "comparing animals to hu-
mans is tricky" or open to doubt, like her claim that "most
human behavior can be explained" and the conclusion reached,
she says, by an unidentified "recent survey of our leisure activities": "Americans spend more time gardening than making
love." Several parts of her book are disfigured by pseudoscientific terms ("consumer topology," "achiever"), which, like
the bubbling retorts and dynamoelectric machines of old horror
films, are no doubt intended to lend atmosphere to the story,

or authority to judgments made in it, but which in the end only diminish their plausibility. My favorite among the social scientists quoted by Kron is Clare Cooper Marcus, who apparently speaks all but occasionally in worn-out idiom: "Just as an analyst must go through psychoanalysis [so as] not to lay his emotional trip on his patients, designers must understand their own biases and values and where they've come from in order not to lay them on their clients." At the very least, Kron could have substituted the expression "relate to" for the plainer "understand."

There is no doubt that Kron has read widely. She has found out, for example, that "Eskimos used to *lick* new acquisitions to cement the person/object relationship," although she maintains silence as to whether they still do, or whether the cemented objects could be pried off their tongues. She has read *Psycho-Decorating* by Margaret Harmon and *The Bathroom* by Alexander Kira, and she quotes Thoreau and Rousseau, Lévi-Strauss, Mary Douglas, Erving Goffman, Georg Simmel, Ernest Beaglehole, Mircea Eliade, and Norbert Elias, among others. Unfortunately, many of these quotations contribute very little to her argument. For example, nothing is added to a lengthy discussion of the deceitfulness that sometimes accompanies the photographing of houses and their contents for decorating magazines by quoting the following shattering *aperçu* from Ortega y Gasset: "The person portrayed and the portrait are two entirely different things."

Kron has also conducted what her publishers call "dozens of interviews with homemakers." She has turned up some interesting goofs in this way, like "Carmen, a student at the University of Hawaii," who is "perturbed that her roommate calls all the things she has on display 'junk': the cookie tins in which she stores her embroidery, the Bacardi bottles that remind her of parties past, the Confucius book her grandfather gave her, the worn quilt her grandmother made, the rock she found in Kona and painted to look like a wave, and the tennis ball canister she slammed a volley ball into and dented the first time she played tennis." One complaint I have about these

interviews is that Kron's eagerness to protect the confidentiality
of her informants leads her to identify them only by first name,
together with a brief descriptive clause. As a result, we learn
one thing from "Pamela, a California woman" and another from
"Carson, a 32-year-old hairdresser." In regular and unpitying
succession, these odd designations flit across the pages: "Raina,
a California art collector," "Carrie, a Pittsburgh mother,"
"Mavis, a Detroit woman," "Beverly, an intense, dark-haired
young woman": There is even someone inexplicably identified
only as "a 35-year-old veteran of the lotus position." The table
talk of "Rosebud, a young Virginia woman who owns a greet-
ing-cards shop" rivals that of Hazlitt: She tells Kron, " 'I always
wanted to show people, hey, I've got nice things.' "

There are other things in Kron's book that deserve attention.
It is good to learn, for example, that the chimes in Barry Gold-
water's Washington, D.C., condominium ring the Air Force
song and that "food consultant Barbara Kafka . . . offered a
course called 'Upward Mobility Through Lifestyle' at New York's
New School. Hardly anyone signed up." She makes the crisp
pronouncement that "you cannot decorate a room before you
know its gender," but does not identify the instruments needed
to making such a diagnosis. I cannot accept Kron's insistence
that in determining our "identity" we must ask ourselves such
questions as "Are you a blue person or a green person?" She
surely realizes that if anyone of her acquaintance was asked to
choose either alternative as his "identity," he would discharge
a scream or break into a run.

In her introduction to the book, Kron says that "*Home-Psych*
is beyond style." Why not simply admit that the book is written
in such a way that it is guaranteed to induce narcosis and violent
aversion by turns? For one thing, the exposition of her views
is undermined—and the book given an air of free association—
by her habit of sparing few details in describing decoration.
Whole pages seem to be devoted to skylights, beanbags, whirl-
pools, pillow shams, hanging plants, crushed velvet, shag rugs,
fur throws, hand-loomed shawls, and hearts-and-flowers wall-

paper. She also coins barbarisms like "status-tician" and verbs like "antique": "Sally, the folk art collector" and "her husband spend summer weekends at country auctions. They even send their children to camp in Maine so they can antique on the way up to attend Visiting Day. . . ." Perhaps what contributes most to the lethargic pace of the book is Kron's tendency to divide natural sentences into shorter (and usually unnatural) new ones, presumably because she thinks that we will not understand them otherwise: "Paula buys things that have meaning for her. Designs she considers innovative." *Home-Psych* is an ill-conceived. And indigestible jumble.

What Is Hype?

"People no longer do anything with respect to what they're doing," writes Steven Aronson, "they do everything with respect to that third eye, which is the eye of *People* magazine."* Our culture is "sorely menaced," he says, by what he calls "hype," "the merchandising of a product—be it an object, a person, or an idea—in an artificially engendered atmosphere of hysteria, in order to create a demand for it or to inflate such demand as already exists." Hype is a "conspiracy" against a gullible American public, "a force that makes a mockery of the human essence"; it debases our language and "manipulates taste as it vitiates our power to discriminate." These claims raise serious questions: Are our tastes as thoroughly influenced as Mr. Aronson suggests by a "conspiracy" of "hype"? What exactly is the part played by press agents and public-relations men, and in general by publicity and promotion, in determining our likes and dislikes, and even our conceptions of status and power?

Mr. Aronson tells us that his task is to inspect and "eviscer-

*Steven M. L. Aronson, *Hype* (New York: William Morrow, 1983).

ate" the phenomenon of hype. He sees the "hyping" of a career as a kind of contest: Behind the players eager to promote themselves, he says, there generally stands a "super" who manages, or somehow advances, their careers, usually with the help of publicists and promotional "representatives." Then there are what Aronson calls "referees" of the game, gossip columnists and others who dictate what is in, out, chic. Aronson claims to construct an "inductive model" of hype by offering the reader portraits of representative stars, supers, and referees.

His book begins with an account of how the fashion model Cheryl Tiegs became Middle America's sweetheart. There follows a series of chapters describing how the "What Becomes a Legend Most?" ad campaign for Blackglama mink resuscitated some older stars. Several chapters are devoted to "supers"—hairdressers like Kenneth, plastic surgeons (Dr. Thomas Rees and others), and publicists and agents (such as Irving Lazar, Herb Schmertz, and Bobby Zarem). The book describes self-promoters in architecture (such as Philip Johnson, Richard Meier, Robert Stern) and medicine (Dr. Denton Cooley). As for "referees," Aronson examines the careers of the restaurant owner Elaine, the food critic Mimi Sheraton, and the gossip columnist "Suzy." The book's last chapter is a portrait of the "empress of hype," the romance novelist Barbara Cartland.

Mr. Aronson is a skilled interviewer; he has a flair for inducing his subjects to hang themselves with a maximum of embarrassment. One unfortunate subject is the plastic surgeon Dr. Howard Bellin. He is the author of *Dr. Bellin's Beautiful You Book,* from which Aronson quotes such opinions as the following: "Eventually we may be able to develop an electrical device that can be worn at night to enlarge the chin and cheek bones, or even to provide additional height. Redesigning the entire body could be done by feeding personalized contour information into a computer." Bellin was recently sued by an abdominoplasty patient who charged that he had shifted her navel two and a half inches off center; a Manhattan court awarded her over three-quarters of a million dollars. Bellin tells Aronson that the belly-button episode "accomplished something I wanted very badly": His practice grew as a result of the publicity the suit created and his London tailors, Kilgour, French & Stanbury, mounted his "individual suit pattern" on its wall next to that of another celebrated client, Prince Michael of Kent.

Aronson has also extracted some choice statements from the architect Philip Johnson. Asked why a friend and colleague is successful, Johnson replies, "Chutzpah. He's a shit," and adds, "He wants to be the Philip Johnson of his generation." Later in the interview he claims that a well-known architectural historian's "greatest fault is that he isn't overenthusiastic about *me.*"

"More than any other public person in contemporary life," claims Aronson—one feels somewhat too generously—the tireless eighty-one-year-old Barbara Cartland "is synonymous with strenuous self-promotion, the prerequisite for acclaim in our time—a time in which every one of our ennobling values has been shaved down to one bald rubric: whether one is famous or not." Aronson describes how she started her career as a gossip columnist, then ran a hat shop, and how she became president of Britain's National Association for Health, which she used as an occasion to promote the Barbara Cartland "brain pill," "Celaton CH3 Tri-Plus." She takes seventy vitamin capsules a day and a special herb, about which she tells Aronson that "one man who took it lived to two hundred fifty-six—this has been authenticated by the Peking and French governments." She has recorded her favorite love songs with the Royal Philharmonic Orchestra, and has published more than one hundred novels including *The Vibration of Love, The Ghost Who Fell in Love,* and *The Prince and the Pekingese.*

When Aronson interviewed Cartland, she praised the skill of her daughter Lady Raine Spencer (stepmother of Princess Diana) at promoting Althorp, the Spencer family seat, through the sale of "rape whistles" decorated with pictures of the house. Asked whether Diana Spencer's marriage stimulated the sale of her books, she replied, "I don't honestly think it made any difference. Oh, maybe it gave a tiny push to my latest nonfiction, *Romantic Royal Marriage,* published on Charles and

Diana's wedding day. A nine-ninety-five trade paperback, one hundred twenty-eight pages with forty black-and-white photos and one hundred fifty color illustrations—you get a *lot* for your money." She seems to have liked the premier of India: "Indira is a very, very great friend of mine and I love her—I love her very, very much"; besides, "India's a divine country—everyone has such intense spiritual experiences because the air is so dry."

Back in New York, Aronson recounts how the fashion model Brooke Shields caught the skin of her stomach in the fly of her Calvin Klein jeans and despairingly rang up the designer for advice at 2 A.M. On a related subject, an apparel manufacturer tells Aronson: "I make Sasson jeans, I make Calvin Klein jeans, and I make Jordache jeans, and they're *all the same.*" We are told that Aristotle Onassis thought the Impressionists were so named because they wanted to make a big impression, and that a hairdresser, Maury Hopson, regards "mood synthesizing" as part of his job. Dr. Denton Cooley (who conducts his heart operations to the music of the Rolling Stones and has a tape deck built into one of his heart-lung machines) was asked by a movie star (who was in turn asked to play the surgeon in a film) whether he could attend one of his operations. The doctor consented, reached into the open chest of an infant patient, took out its palpitating heart, and placed it in the actor's palm. After hundreds of pages of such information, one feels the need for Mrs. Cartland's special herb.

Mr. Aronson likes very few people, and he indulges in rather too much heavy-handed vituperation and waspishness. Mocking Lillian Hellman for appearing in a Blackglama ad, and recalling the joke that she was subsequently mistaken by some for Bert Lahr or George Washington, he high-mindedly pursues the playwright's crime to the bitter end: "Would Madame Curie have succumbed to Blackglama's blandishments? Would Doris Lessing?" Referring to athletes who endorse products, he delivers a judgment that might have been uttered by Carlyle: "It's a pity when children worship heroes who themselves worship products." *Time* magazine once said of a photograph of Cheryl Tiegs wearing a transparent bathing suit, her "body is awesome, and her face is so fine and strong and unembarrassed that questions of taste do not arise." About this Aronson is prudishly severe, protesting that questions of taste do arise, for "we must remember for all practical purposes, this is a picture of a naked woman."

For the few subjects he likes, Aronson spares no fulsome commendation. Although according to Aronson, the hairdresser Kenneth is often dubbed an "artist"—even "Rembrandt of the Ringlets"—by the press, he thinks of himself as a humble servant; "publicity means nothing to Kenneth except as a source of business," and "he lives by his skill, not in his image." Aronson concludes warmly, "It is a quiet comfort to remember that, in the hype world of abhorrent exorbitance and odious disproportion, Kenneth remains proportionate." I read this passage several times before I gathered that we are not meant to believe that Kenneth's bodily parts capriciously alter their relative sizes. Mr. Aronson uses a special sense of the word "proportionate"; I have not been able to pin it down. In any case, we soon find that the food critic Mimi Sheraton is also "one of the few proportionate people in a multi-billion-dollar industry." She warns the public "against indiscriminately sucking the hype popsicles manufactured by the industry" that present-day eating has become. "Mimi *is* our guardian against food hype—just as proportionately as Kenneth is our guardian against hair hype." Public relations lost a proportionately great talent when Mr. Aronson chose to take up sociology.

His most extravagant praise, perhaps, is reserved for the gossip columnist Suzy, a "shrewd and deft referee of the social game." Her gossip is "delicious." Her life is "glamorous"; "unlike champagne when *it's* been around for a long time, Suzy's effervescence has never gone flat." Moreover, "Suzy dares to be ingenuous—after all, it's the behavior Americans are known the world over for—because she understands that we all live in the rush of connections to power." In her column of May 8, 1983, Suzy describes what sounds like a rush of this kind—a "super-glamorous" party given in a "fabulous townhouse" for the publication of Aronson's book. Among the

guests she lists Kenneth, Richard Meier, and Barbara Cartland's grandson, Viscount Lewisham. She writes, "Brendan
Gill allowed . . . that when the book came out, Steven Aronson
wouldn't have a friend left in this town. You wouldn't have
known it from the mob of the beautiful and the undamned who
pushed into Katherine Johnson's to see and be seen."

Aronson is of course right that press agents and public-relations
experts have debased language by ceaseless exaggeration and
inflation of this sort. "Perhaps it's too late," he writes, "to go
back to speaking plain, to speaking—as Emerson wrote—
straightforward American narrative." He thinks a culture cannot "possibly maintain a language" without "regulators of words"
such as "Hemingway and John O'Hara" of all people. However
this may be, his own book is written in the keyed-up style of
a press release, with one-word sentences and one-sentence paragraphs, often pretentious and occasionally unintelligible. Only
a regulator of words could write that a football player "gets
off on" appearing in an ad for fur or that people "luck out."
In Aronson's book, the patients of plastic surgeons have "cuts
and alterations made in the text of their flesh"; days are described as "electric" and "feisty"; public-relations agents "suck"
"pop platitudes" from the "tit of psychoanalysis"; a "hair bulletin" "zizzles" through the air; the British throne is described
as "an engorged organ of stupendous self-celebration." The
most curious description of all is that of an ad man's "pre-
sumption" as "uncircumcised."

Mr. Aronson writes that "thanks to today's license to billboard the secret side of public lives, gossip is more aggressive
than ever in making and breaking reputations, careers, mar-
riages, even governments," but, he hastily adds, he deplores
gossip and says that "to the seven deadly sins there should be
added an eighth: gossip at its most vicious." But Aronson's
own license to billboard the secret side of public lives allows
him to identify by name a New York editor who published
under a pseudonym a memoir of a sadomasochistic love affair,
to tell us that Queen Mother Frederika of Greece died while
her eyes were being lifted, to intimate that Dr. Herman Tar-

nower, who was shot by Jean Harris, was a practicing homosexual, and to disclose that Sophia Loren and Barbara Walters
had facelifts. In one voice, Aronson denounces gossip in a
superior tone of moral one-upmanship; in another, he broadcasts scandal that can only encourage other gossips to raise
their voices.

In a recent interview (conducted by himself in *Interview* magazine) Aronson claims that "what I've actually done is write a
kind of American ethnography—a more reliable ethnography,
it now seems, than Margaret Mead did in Samoa." But his
"ethnography" fails to give the analysis of "hype" that he prom-
ises. For one thing, his selection of subjects is skimpy, largely
omitting any mention of the phenomenon in the theater, the
movies, advertising, television, or literature. His explanation
of the alleged predominance of "hype" in our time is that "we
don't have the luxury the Greeks had of a set of gods firmly
in place. We want heroes and there are so few natural ones.
Perhaps that's why we have to keep inventing them—or rather,
having them hypecast for us." But something is missing here:
We have gone without the "luxury" he speaks of for many
hundreds of years, whereas "hype" is a relatively recent phenomenon.

Such vagueness is typical of Aronson's difficulty throughout
this book: For all its vehemence, his scorn has no clear object.
He does not adequately discriminate among the kinds of "hype"
or promotion he discusses—for example, between promotion
of an object or idea or person for the sake of profit and promotion simply for the sake of someone's vanity. In his introduction he says that "hype differs from advertising—which it
employs, along with public relations, as accomplices—in that
it is not directly paid for." Yet a few lines later he writes that
"perhaps the most nefarious feature of hype is that it is not
billboarded as a species of advertising and therefore enjoys
greater credibility." At times his book reads like a wholesale
condemnation of promotional advertising, on moral grounds,
as wasteful, tasteless, untruthful, etc. But he gives no persuasive arguments for such a claim, and it may be wondered whether

there are any, most unqualified attacks on advertising being seriously incomplete, like "blaming the waiters in restaurants for obesity," as a famous economist once said. Many passages in Aronson's book would lead one to think that he believes that press agents, publicists, and others have conspired to manipulate our tastes in an unprecedented fashion. Ours is "an age of hype," he says; hype has "come to fulfillment in our time"; "its inner workings are as invisible as its results are visible."

But if this is his view, it seems to me the opposite of the truth. I wonder whether the actual power and influence of publicists and promotional agents was not much more powerful a half-century ago—and precisely because it was less visible, more centralized, and less understood by the public. This was certainly the case in the movies in the days when men like Howard Dietz of MGM could shape the public personality of a star, when agents like Myron Selznick were "supers," and when gossip columnists like Hedda Hopper, Louella Parsons, and Walter Winchell "refereed" the game with little competition.

Today, on the other hand, we have all come to know more about how promotion and publicity really work; *People* and *Us* and similar magazines have made it understandable not just to a small or exclusive group of readers but to millions of supermarket consumers. Teachers and housewives and high-school students know today how people can buy their way onto best-dressed lists and enter "society," or how publicists can help get records "on the charts." Today "publicity" and "exposure" have become something like a popular commodity; the paths to celebrity are more numerous, partly because the gossip industry has been expanded (and made freer) by internal competition, so that every branch of industry—not just "entertainment"—has its gossip columnists and promoters. This process probably began in recent years when fashion designers like Calvin Klein began to treat themselves, and to be treated by others, as "stars" in their own right, and the whole machinery of celebrity used previously only in films, theater, television, and the recording industry was transposed onto fashion. Now it has been extended to include nearly everything else one can imagine—interior decoration, Wall Street, government (the presidency), real estate, the writing of novels, even the world of publicists themselves.

The effect of these changes could be that, *contra* Aronson's fears of a successful "conspiracy" of hype organized against us, we may be freer to distrust (or accept) publicity because its internal mechanisms themselves are better understood and publicized. And, although no one really knows how to find out whether this is so or not, perhaps as a result we are quicker to exercise our consumer sovereignty and detect promotional inflation and its products—such as people who are "famous for being famous"—when we see it. As Joseph E. Levine says in an interview in Aronson's book: "Today you can beat the shit out of a picture—drums, parades—and the public still won't come."

In parts of his book, Aronson seems to allow that hype solely for business purposes is acceptable, as in the case of Kenneth. But how are such cases to be distinguished from the hype Aronson loathes? After all, by his admission, a line in a gossip column or even adverse publicity might secure more patients for the coarse Dr. Bellin, and thus promote business. One begins to suspect that the true subject of Aronson's book is his own dislike of people he takes to be vulgar and pushy and his preference for those he thinks are not. Unfortunately the way he describes them both makes them indistinguishable.

This is an oddly self-refuting book: Written in the style of the gossip it is intended to combat, and advancing exaggerated and unsubstantiated theses, it is more an instance of hype (as Aronson defines it) than an exposé of it. And the tone, in turn morally ferocious and unctuous, in which it discusses the members of the world it evokes prompts the impression that its author is undecided between the desire to repudiate his subject and the longing to be installed as its arbiter.

Medieval Cookery

LIVE FROG AND TURTLE PIE

Ingredients

Prepare the largest pie shell and top lid which your pastry pans
    and oven will accommodate
A "spring-mold pan" or one allowing easy removal of the pie
    crust is best to use
Butter for greasing baking pan
2 or more cups of dried beans or such a "heavy" cereal as Grape-
    Nuts
Live tethered birds or frogs or turtles or wind-up animals
2 egg yolks
½ teaspoon cinnamon

Method

1. Preheat oven to 425°.
2. Very lightly grease the large pie pan, then dust with flour.
3. Reserving sufficient dough for a top crust, press in a reasonably
   thick bottom pie crust.
4. Fill the pie shell with dried beans, or other reusable filler, to
   weight down the crust as it bakes to avoid bubbling. Apply
   and carefully seal the upper crust to the lower.

5. Glaze with egg yolk mixed with cinnamon.
6. Bake 40 minutes at 425° or until golden brown.
7. When cool, carefully gain access to the bottom crust and cut a large hole—three- to four-inch diameter—through which remove all bean or cereal filler, reserving the piece of cut crust.
8. Into the well-cooled shell, insert the live or wind-up animals immediately before serving. If possible, replace the pastry cut so as to "close the hole." (I have not been able to do so; but the medieval cooks apparently could.)
9. Scrupulously carefully, cut around the circumference of the crust at time of serving, about one-quarter way around the pie. Equally gently, cut toward the center, taking extreme care not to touch the animals (or mechanical toys). Lift out upper crust portion.
10. The birds or frogs will happily "liberate" themselves on the table in order to amaze and amuse the feasters.
11. This pie makes a dramatic finale to a formal feast.

—from *Fabulous Feasts:*
Medieval Cookery and Ceremony
by Madeleine Pelner Cosman

One evening some years ago, I sat in the dining room of a talkative French woman living in New York and shook my head for perhaps the twentieth time that night to remain awake during her unceasing flow of talk. Praised by her friends as a gifted cook, she had on this occasion apparently decided to provide me with an account of her latest enthusiasm, the Crusades, instead of dinner; it was past midnight, and, unlike her, I was nearly insensible from the macroalcoholic diet we had observed for the past four hours. Finally I broke into her description and croaked a remark I was to regret bitterly, something like, "Gee, I wonder what the food those kids had at home must have tasted like." Although my weakness allowed me to say it only in a whisper, the remark had a dynamic effect on Juliette Mensonge. Sitting bolt upright and widening her eyes, she said that curiously enough, she too had been absorbed in the very same question since she was a young girl. Moreover, she knew others—many others—who would like to see it (or rather taste it) answered. Among these, she said, were her friends Dr. Reiman, a lapsed Jungian analyst who had managed to confine his practice to the exorcism of demons in reflective show-business folk, and his wife, a practicing analyst, and also a certain Professor Badolini, an Italian medievalist engaged in research at a city college. These people could be gathered together with ease. Why not form a little club, as it were, of medieval food tasters? Why not create afresh the music and tastes and smells of a medieval feast? Why not meet weekly? Why not let her arrange the entire business? With ill-considered generosity I nodded agreement and ran gasping into the street in search of an open pizza parlor.

On an evening some weeks later, I was greeted at Juliette's door by Dr. Reiman, a large, jovial man who good-naturedly pooh-poohed my surprise on finding him wearing a brocade cape and pointed slippers, dress that somewhat clashed with the cigarillo hanging from his lips. His wife, similarly attired, was a handsome woman who was seated beneath an elaborate baldachin (cleverly made out of grocery boxes stapled to the wall). Juliette, she said, had been working on tonight's meal for days and had been worried that the unusual orders she had placed with the butchers, fish vendors, and apothecaries would be delayed. She was interrupted by the sound of raised voices in the kitchen exchanging maledictions in Italian, followed by the abrupt entrance of Professor Badolini, an energetic little man, carrying some aluminum plates and goblets to the table. After greeting me, he rolled his eyes and looked at the kitchen; he had just been in there with Juliette, he whispered in imperfect English, and she had disputed his program for the presentation of the courses. But who was the medievalist, he or she? Was it not he who had designed the costumes that he and the others were wearing? And why, he said, pointing a crooked finger at me, had I not worn mine?

The professor's disputation fortunately soon gave way to the commencement of the feast ceremony. Although musicians were not available, someone had brought a record of medieval and Renaissance music, and to a great flourish of drums and trumpets, the kitchen door opened and Juliette entered carrying a large tureen. She had worked a startling transformation of her usual appearance, and wore a high-waisted velvet gown and train; after pausing to boot aside some orange rinds that lay in the kitchen doorway, she bowed gracefully to allow her head-gear—a conical hat and veil that resembled a giant ice-cream cone placed upside down on her head—to pass through the arch.

"This soup hasn't been eaten since 1500," Juliette said ambiguously when we were all seated and she removed the lid of the tureen and began to stir its greenish, lumpy contents with a wooden spoon. "It's a spiced broth that was a favorite of Louis the Bald of France," she cheerily continued. "I had to convince the butcher and other people I called that I was not mad in order to get the ingredients." It was the professor who posed the urgent question on all our minds as Juliette handed us our portions: "The ingredients, these are which?" As Juliette crisply enumerated them—pickled goat, snipe, sneezewort, duck feet, truelove, licorice—our faces grew paler; and no one paid any attention to Mrs. Reiman's plaintive suggestion, unfortunately directed at me, that truelove was a well-known aphrodisiac in the Dark Ages. As we turned our spoons around and around in the soup, fearful of tasting, some appalling component—a fishhead, a tusk, or so I recall thinking at the time, a frog—would rise to the surface, linger on the edge of the spoon, and then slither back into the slop. "Hurry up and get on with it, for God's sake," Juliette urged. "We have ten more courses to go. I'll clean up while Professor Badolini shows you how to play some medieval games of chance."

Some of us, I am afraid, felt that we had already played one medieval game of chance too many and were engaged in devising a pretext for leaving, but it was no use. Announced by a drum roll and fanfare, another course, swan-neck pudding, was brought to the table, and then others, each more ghastly than its predecessor: boar's head, bear stomach stuffed with ginger, spiced liver of whale on a bed of seaweed.

The conversation during the feast, to be frank, was disappointing, even though our inhibitions had been annihilated by Dr. Reiman's ever greater ministrations of malmsey, the greatest of which he reserved for his own goblet. For a while, only he spoke, but he soon revealed himself to be a staggering bore whose reminiscences of hydrotherapy and Bad Kissingen, which he punctuated with a particular hee-haw laugh, reduced the rest of us to despair. By the eighth course, we had fallen into a profound silence, each of us staring at our food with glassy-eyed bovine concentration.

Though we did not talk much, there was an unspoken oppression we all felt. We had tried to please our hostess by eating the food on our plates and hailing each new course with cheers or praise. Our cries were so bleary and insincere, however, that they produced the unintended effect of releasing a strain of sadism in her. By the end of the third course, Juliette had changed into a Dickens workhouse overseer and would stand over each of us until we had finished our portions. This policy was not only impolite; it was having visibly deleterious effects, especially on the professor.

I had earlier caught him only pretending to enjoy the almonds dyed black in sheep's blood that Juliette assured us was a delicacy of the Dark Ages; it was plain to see he was not really swallowing them at all, but concealing them in his cheek, like a chipmunk. I saw in his frightened eyes that he knew I knew his secret, but a sense of fraternity arose between us when my reassuring nod told him that I would not snitch on him. But later his condition, exacerbated by Juliette's constant force-feeding, worsened. He seemed to withdraw from our company entirely, and his face froze into the awful smile worn by the subjects of wind-tunnel experiments. We had been given to understand that his scholarly specialty was the study of drainage systems (and more generally the disposal of garbage) in medieval cities; and it is just possible that he was speculating on the irony that he had had to travel to this room, in a center of late capitalism like New York City, in order to get a taste of what he had been investigating for many years through secondhand sources. However this may be, his silence so alarmed us that when Juliette was out of the room I encouraged the Reimans to loosen his tie and to throw his uneaten food out the window. Unfortunately, the windows had been screwed shut, possibly in anticipation of this jacquerie. If I had not been able to dispose of a great deal of the uneaten food (and much of my own) by feeding it to Juliette's terrier puppy, something dreadful might have occurred.

This makeshift proved impossible to employ in the case of the dessert, advertised by Juliette as the apple doucettes or tarts favored by generations of English kings, for the puppy had been taken by its mistress into the kitchen, from which we heard a strange mixture of low-pitched snarls, cooings, and imprecations. The tarts seemed to have been baked for hundreds of years to acquire the consistency of trilobites, so that they were at once too hard to be chewed and too large to be swallowed whole. In the end we were forced to create an "accident" by upsetting with our feet the tray on which they were served, and then sitting back in silence as we watched them hit the floor and turn in numerous revolutions until they clattered to a rest. Fortunately, Juliette was feverishly at work during this mutiny on the final and most ambitious course of the evening, so that the matter was never discussed.

On the other hand, the colossal pastry structure she rolled out on a sideboard a half-hour later was subsequently the topic of wide discussion in "food circles" for years: A four-foot-tall "subtlety," or edible sculpture, it was a remarkably lifelike pastry model of a large dog, with glazed cherry eyes, hazelnut nails, and exquisitely delicate pastry paws, hocks, and withers. At a loss for the usual servile compliments and full with feelings we could not express, we stood around it in silence for many minutes. What followed this exhibition, however, is somewhat indistinct in my memory. I think that the job of cutting the pie fell to the professor, but in any case before he had a chance to do so, we heard a faint scratching sound, and then, with a tremendous centrifugal force, the entire affair exploded and the puppy that had been inserted in it was not only "liberated" but had sunk its fangs into the professor's hand. As a shrill pipe tune wailed in the background, the pup trampled the subtlety to dust, and then flew up and down the table, upsetting goblets and overturning oil and spice vessels; soon, he was so thoroughly soaked in oil that he was as difficult to hold down as a live water snake. The firmest impression I have of the cataclysm is of Juliette, her conical hat askew, appealing for assistance to Mrs. Reiman, who sat giggling over an upset tankard of pomegranate wine. I would have liked to have participated in the melee in one fashion or another, but as I shouted to my hostess above the din, it was nearly midnight and I was late for an eye examination. I later heard that the destruction lasted deep into the night and was as extensive as that of the Battle of Crécy.

Despite this setback, Juliette's reputation as a medieval cook grew, at least to the extent that freelance ambulance drivers were said to park in front of her apartment house to pick up the emergency cases they expected would sooner or later be carried from her dinner parties. The original members of the medieval feast club, it seems, were never asked again; obviously we knew too much. But now, thanks to Mrs. Cosman's recipe, I know even more. Juliette's "live dog" pie failed because she had not been able (any more than Mrs. Cosman had) to "close the hole" of the pastry and thus had allowed the dog to "liberate" itself prematurely. If there's any lesson to be drawn from all of this, I suppose it is that those who wish to recapture the culinary past and who venture beyond grilled bear or sweet-and-sour seal stew aren't really playing with a full deck.

Escape from Esalen

Pushing aside a complimentary tray of passion-fruit slices, I threw myself down on the bed of my room in the inn, reputedly the most luxurious hotel in Big Sur, and asked myself how so banal a conjunction of circumstances could have soured a holiday trip. The flight from New York had been marred by my seatmate, a California business executive of enormous girth, whose buttresses of bacon spilled over the armrest onto me, and who, after marinating himself in Scotch, fell into a deep sleep, punctuated by slurred off-color dream phrases, during the projection of a James Bond thriller. We were seated to the extreme left of the screen, and almost under it, so that I could only view the screen by craning my neck and looking past him. Unfortunately, near the climax of the film, he turned in his sleep with a protracted gurgle, and now faced me so closely that our noses would have touched—they did once—had I not leaned far to my left. In order to see the film, I had to run the risk of his awakening to find me staring directly into his massive face. Apart from this circumstance, and although the airline staff behaved, contrary to the implication carried by the name of the carrier, in a thoroughly disorganized fashion, the rest of

36

the flight was without incident. Indeed, the biggest nonevent of all was the nonarrival of my luggage in San Francisco, a trifling affair I had to neglect in order to sprint the length of the airport to make a connecting flight to Monterey. A picturesque surprise greeted me when I ran panting onto the runway to catch it, for what I saw was not a plane at all, but what looked like a laundry basket held in the beak of a listless pterodactyl. Stepping into the contraption, I saw that in fact it was an ancient reconnaissance six-seater, in the charge of two teenagers, one of whom was boning up on an airway manual held upside down. The flight operations—an absurd description of the fiddling they did with the knobs, buttons, and pedals at their disposal—certainly sent color into the cheeks of the passengers: For some forty minutes the plane passed through a series of nauseating lurches and abrupt descents into air pockets, each of which was accompanied, as in a church responsory, by moans from the passengers as pitiful as those in the "Dies Irae" of Verdi's *Requiem*.

The inn (really a cluster of fancy dormitories perched on a hill), where I arrived a gibbering wreck some hours later, had been described to me as surpassing in luxury any similar institution in northern California. How wildly irresponsible this speculation was came home to me with peculiar force after my first interview with the desk clerk, a pretty blonde whose empty eyes and toneless manner of speech suggested a lifetime spent strung out on hypnotic drugs among the Frisbee crowd. She told me that I would be able to pay for my room only by credit card, provided that I furnish identification in the form of a driver's license together with information about the make and year of my automobile. When I explained to her that I neither used credit cards nor drove a car, but offered to pay by personal check backed up by my passport, she unconvincingly suppressed a giggle at my antiquated preference for impeccable New York banks and official government documents over so-called "credit" cards, symptoms of all that is misguided in our economic way of life.

In any case, the matter disposed of after a half-hour debate that drew attention from other guests by its ferocity and invective, I went on to explain that my luggage had been orphaned. "I have no fresh changes, you see," I said airily, "so will you send the presser or the room boy for the clothes I am wearing, and also the waiter, as I'll be dining in my room tonight in about an hour. . . ." Interrupting me curtly, the clerk said that the inn had no presser, no room boy, no laundry services of any kind, and no room service; if I wished, some slices of passion fruit or a jug of spring water could be sent to my room, but for a meal I would have to go to the hotel restaurant. "There it is," she said, pointing out the window to a speck on the top of the next mountain range and easily a forty-minute walk away, "but it won't be open for another two hours and since it's Saturday night, you won't get a reservation there for another two hours after that." I subsisted the rest of the afternoon by clawing open bananas pilfered from the hotel lobby.

At eight that evening, smoothing down my disheveled city clothes, I set out on the "scenic" walk the hotel had constructed to the restaurant. It proved to be an endlessly long and winding path through a forest, with funny little fake dead ends and rickety bridges over dried-up streams. The deeper I went into the forest the more each step I took grew palpable with tension. I imagined the ghosts of murderous lumberjacks whose trade had been displaced when the hotel was built leering at me through broken branches; at every turn in the path I saw the outline of a puma ready to dispatch me. When I reached the restaurant, a glass-and-wood affair typical of northern California, I was spooked, compulsively dusting pine needles off my shoulders and disengaging burrs from my trouser legs, which may explain why the headwaiter seated me in a distant corner of the room, under a giant wooden beam and near the source of the inevitable recorded harp arrangements of Ravel and Satie. So fearful was I of not securing another reservation for the next 24 hours that I spent many hours in this seat, alarming other guests by my gluttony and stuffing buns and rolls into my jacket. It was pleasant enough, save for one irritating feature of the place. Each waiter I encountered there had cultivated the same strange fear of making an assertion. No matter how trivial the information that I requested, it was conveyed to me in an interrogative. I would ask, "How is the veal cooked?" and I would be told, "On the barbecue?" "Where is the bar?" would be answered by "Down the hall?" I have since learned that this curious affectation has been superseded in some parts of California by the practice of responding to a question by repeating it, so that the answer to "Where is the wine list?" is "Where is the wine list?" thus ensuring that no information whatsoever is passed.

After my first day at the inn, I wearied of writing letters home and wearing earplugs at the swimming pool to drown out the laughter of debauched singles gamboling in the hot tubs nearby, and decided it was time to explore the countryside. I had planned to rent a bicycle, but no service of this kind existed in Big Sur. I next considered a car and driver. This, too, appeared unavailable until after much effort I discovered a limousine service in distant Santa Clara. The car I was provided with, however—an immense silver Cadillac with circular portholes—was not ideally suited to the rustic terrain of Big Sur or its pockmarked roads, and when I was driven in it to places of interest such as state parks or nearby towns I was ogled by passersby. Perhaps, noting my rumpled suit and distracted look, they assumed that I was a presidential candidate who had lost his way, but as that sight must be fairly common to them, the explanation could not be a complete one.

My first call in the Cadillac was at a celebrated local hangout called Nepenthe, a restaurant where I settled myself into a crowd of T-shirted, bearded cats with potbellies and their women, many of whom took after Boadicea in appearance. We all sat there munching carrots and scooping up garbanzo beans, for the most part in silence, although occasionally a recording of bell music would be played or some comment from one of the couples, like "Play it cool, Goldilocks," would be heard. Everyone was exceedingly gentle, and even the bee that circled my ambrosiaburger retreated gracefully when he realized that I would not share it willingly. And the Druid wearing large amounts of wooden jewelry and a Navaho blanket who approached me and softly inquired whether I was a member of "the healing community" begged off on her own initiative when I replied that I subscribed in every detail to the therapeutic approach of Fritz Kunkel.

The next day we drove to Carmel—a show-town with expensive stores selling, it seemed, mostly bread—and then on to Monterey, which, if possible, appeared to have surpassed its earlier efforts to ensnare tourists. Within moments of alighting from the car, I was swept into a noisome sea of corpulent psychiatrists and unreconstructed bohemians on Fisherman's Wharf. We inspected (as if with a group mind) little clay lobsters, scrimshaw work, and statues of bullwhackers; smiled idiotically at a flea-bitten trained monkey snatching dollar bills from us; threw tidbits to jaded performing sea lions and pelicans; stared at piles of bug-eyed rock cod and dried blowfish. Although one can tire rapidly of bleached wood, sandpipers, and flattened cypresses, the Seventeen-Mile Drive outside Monterey and more generally the coastline highway from it to Big Sur struck me as splendid as ever. As one leaves Monterey, with its mansions and golf courses, the road takes one through large, brilliantly green fields that stretch almost to the water line, and everywhere there is light and color and the smell of the sea. Then the road climbs and passes through more green fields, some of them thick with horses and sheep, which overlook a turbulent sea out of which huge piles of rock rise abruptly; the effect is rather like that of the western Irish coast. As it nears Big Sur, the road climbs even more and soon is nothing but a thin strip of pavement cut into the rock of the mountain, with high cliffs on one side and bottomless pits on the other, marked by diabolical twists and hairpin turns, giving the motorist frightening and startling views of tremendous expanses. I regret to say that amidst all this beauty I was torn by the conflicting impulses to throw myself out the window, on the one hand, and on the other to press myself to the door of the car nearest the inside of the road. And in addition, a disquieting suspicion arose within me that my driver, who had already displayed difficulties in driving the Cadillac through the twists in the road, was slowly becoming hypnotized by the vast expanses ahead of him and would soon plunge the car into the sea. To ensure that he was on the ball, I periodically shouted at him at the top of my voice to ignore the passing spectacles.

If I was afflicted with vertigo that afternoon, a more complicated strain of the same condition affected me the following day. I had always dreamed of visiting Esalen, the famous "human potential" institute located nearby my hotel. Unfortunately, on ringing up I was told that a rockslide blocked the road linking me to it, and that if I wished to visit, I could only do so between six at night and six in the morning, when the highway workers repairing the road were not at their posts, and that I should then have to cross the slide by foot, a distance of about a mile. My enthusiasm to see Esalen suffocated the voices of reason, and I arranged with my driver to drop me at my end of the slide at 6 A.M., and with an official of the Institute to meet me at the other end shortly thereafter.

It was still dark when I started my way across the slide the next day. At first, I inched along, hugging the mountainside, every so often coming with a start against a bulldozer or a road sign warning of danger. Twice I took the wrong path and walked perilously close to the edge of a cliff, leaping back when I heard the sound of waves hundreds of feet below me. Midway across, my ears picked up something that turned my blood to ice. The wind had dislodged a handful of pebbles from the mountainside above me, and they skipped down over the larger rocks. As I was for all purposes blind in the darkness, I had no way of checking my immediate conjecture that this signified the beginning of another, more extensive and devastating rockslide. Electrified by fear, I doubled my efforts to reach the other side and began to scurry across the path in little steps like a Chinese peasant, my body bent almost double and my hands tracing the ground to ensure my safety. In doing all this, however, I neglected to consider what effect the previous night's dense fog might have had on the consistency of the soil at the places where the workers had plowed it with their bulldozers. At one point I sank with a piercing yell to my knees in mud and imagined that I was about to drop all the way down the mountain into Davy Jones's locker. Fortunately, the light had begun to break and I made out a tree root, which I used to help me reach firmer soil, where I lay for a few minutes recovering my strength. Then, in the dimness, I saw a shape that lightened my heart: Another human being was crossing the slide in the same direction as I was going. Except that he was an old, white-haired man who carried some sort of staff, I shall never know who he was, for despite my friendly cries he took no notice whatsoever of me; perhaps, as was later suggested to me, he was a Zen monk walking to the Tassajara monastery down the coast. In any case, despite his cold reception, I followed him and made it to the other side, where I met my contact from Esalen. Within minutes after I stepped into her car, we drove into the gate of the Institute, a compound of houses located on a strip of land between the Santa Lucia Mountains and the sea.

To describe Esalen as devoted to research into "human potential" utterly fails to convey the staggering number and variety of its activities. For this one must turn to a document that was placed in my hand on arrival, and which is one of the most absorbing I have ever read: the Esalen catalogue of January-June 1984. According to it, just a few of the methods for exploring the central questions of life offered by Esalen are: "psychosynthesis," "holonomic integration" (which employs "evocative music, controlled breathing, facilitative body work, and mandala drawing"), "the hypnotic approaches of Dr. Milton H. Erickson," "hypnosis for health maintenance," "bioenergetics," "group rituals," "Hawaiian Huna" (an ancient mystical teaching of Polynesia), "modern kundalini research," "singing Gestalt therapy," "hot seat" encounter groups, "neo-Reichian emotional release," and ways "to get release from chronic pain and tension" such as "Moshe Feldenkrais' awareness work, Lauren Berry's joint work, deep tissue as taught by Ida Rolf, and the trigger point work of John St. John." One can visit the Esalen hot springs on a weeknight (open, however, I was told, to the public only from 1 to 5 A.M.), or attend a weekend seminar, or stay for longer periods of time as a resident or student.

Although once one has been exposed to the Esalen catalogue it is difficult to put down, the descriptions in it of courses offered by the Institute present some unusual problems of interpretation. One weekend course, entitled "Exorcising the Demon 'Should,' " is described in part as follows: "Within each of us there lives a demon—our own personal critic—whose greatest joy comes from criticizing, denigrating, and destroying every experience we have . . . this demon, who commands us to be who we aren't in order to satisfy someone we can never satisfy, is the demon that we will seek to exorcise during the weekend." The price is $230, quite a bargain in light of the far greater price paid in similar efforts by Rimbaud or the Marquis de Sade. The promises made by other courses are not as easy to pin down. A course, also carrying the price tag of $230, called "Zen and the Art of Fly Fishing," is described as "a combination of practical instruction, visualization, physical exercise, and guided fantasy"; it argues that "there is a focus and subtlety of movement in fly fishing akin to Eastern meditative disciplines. The possibility always exists of entering the trout's world. In fly fishing, the trout are the teachers," a claim which suggests underwater tutorials, taught by Disney-like professor fishes wearing spectacles.

Pitiless Teutonic rigor is implied in the following course, entitled "Polarity Massage" ($230): "The Esalen mineral baths will be the classroom for exploring and learning by experience the basic concepts of polarity body work through the medium of massage. Emphasis will be on the dynamics of living anatomy and polarity energy balancing methods as implemented in the course of complete, full-body massage." And one course that would seem to require a stern hand if it is not to degenerate into hanky-panky claims to introduce "a new way of seeing the body, using eyes, nose, throat, hands, ears, and hara," the last-named being "an energy center located two fingers below the navel." The course description that sent thought balloons with question marks in them gliding over my head was "Shamanic Healing, Journeying, and the Afterlife Experience: Basic and Intermediate Shamanic Practice" ($680). In it, "with the aid of traditional sonic-driving and dancing methods, the group will engage in archetypical exercises and rituals practiced by North and South American Indian shamans to awaken dormant human capabilities and forgotten connections with the powers of nature. Practice will include shamanic journeys to both the Lower- and Upper-worlds for knowledge and power, work with animal and plant powers, divination, clairvoyance, and shamanic methods of healing." In addition, "there will be an introduction to the Ghost Dance method and to shamanic ways of exploring the afterlife experience"; participants are invited to "bring drums and rattles." The faculty conducting these seminars and workshops contains many unusual personalities, including a specialist in "personal applications of video," the founder of the "Gestalt Fool Theater Family of San Francisco," a writer "with earlier careers as homemaker and fiber artist," and someone called "Hareesh," crisply described as "interested in alternative nutritional programs." A tenure-track faculty member is Jezariah Canyon Munyer, who teaches a course entitled "Miracles of Infancy" ($230) with his parents; he is one year old.

Inflamed by expectations of witnessing some of these activities during my visit to Esalen, I was distressed to find that none of them were being currently offered, and that because of the rockslide I was doomed to spend twelve hours in what can only be described as a peculiar mixture of a singles resort and a lunatic asylum. This impression was suggested to me by my first sight of residents at the Institute, a wiry, bearded old man out of John Brown's gang jogging painfully down a hillside path in the company of two laughing young women wearing waist-length hair and feather earrings, and it was confirmed by my encounters with others, equally arresting: a tall, head-nodding man who had just been to Findhorn, in Scotland, a "community" where he had been taught to speak with affection to cabbages and roses in order to make them grow, and where, he assured me, astonishing results had occurred; an earnest, bespectacled woman who had vowed never to use the word "I," and who hugged whomever she was with before taking leave; two elderly ladies in jumpsuits, sitting motionlessly and staring pop-eyed at the sea, then vigorously stripping off the suits and surrendering themselves to the sun; a woman who skipped down a hill singing coloratura exercises in half-voice, and then stopped, took a breath, and erupted into some deafening spectacular high notes; a man who said, "I have too many cars in my emotional garage."

I attended lunch in the mess hall of the Institute in a crowd full of saintly faces and uplifted voices; declining an offer of some malodorous organic stew, I confined myself to a stubby glass of low-fat milk, until I observed that the glass was caked with filth and in a lightning move surreptitiously bleached a nearby cactus plant with the tainted liquid. After lunch, I elected to take a massage near the hot springs from one of Esalen's celebrated massage team. The scene that greeted me when I arrived there did not differ appreciably from that found in a typical Fifties nudist colony brochure: a number of senior citizens (including some Wagnerian Rhinemaidens with braids) frolicking in outdoor stone tubs and tossing medicine balls back and forth, splendidly unashamed of their liver spots, giant bellies, and floppy udders. It would have been instructive to take a leisurely survey of the behavior but the sulfurous odors rising from the springs forced me to turn away.

My masseuse I guessed to be in her mid-forties, a vigorous apostle of health, who wore only a pair of sunglasses and a towel around her waist. To my delight, she posed not a single question to me and set to work immediately. Midway through the massage, however, while I was lying face down, I noticed to my surprise that her towel had crumpled to the floor below me. Thinking that her devotion to her work made her forgetful of such details, I was about to inform her when I felt my own towel gently disengaged from my body and tossed to the floor, so that both of us were fully exposed to the meditating grandmothers I had seen earlier on the cliff above the bathhouse. Her soothing fingers soon made me semiconscious, however, and I would have remained so were it not for an unforeseen incident. A masseur who had been working over a mountain of flesh of indeterminate sex on the next sunning table decided to take this time to retail his spiritual autobiography in a voice that could be heard at San Simeon some fifty miles down the coast. At first I tried to dismiss him as a mere phenomenon in space and time, of no enduring significance, but I was unable to sustain this attitude and began to listen. It seemed that he had recently discovered through painful self-analysis that he had never really been born. As he pounded and remolded the creature beneath him, he told us that he was following a new "discipline" called "rebirthing therapy," moreover of the "wet" sort that involved his being dragged in large basins of warm water and then, with great ceremony, lifted like a neonate into the world. He subscribed, he continued, to a rigorous retraining of his character and each day would write on his wrist a guiding thought like "purify yourself," and his teachers had assigned him exercises to test his powers of forming and re-forming "relationships," one of which required that he spend exactly sixty minutes in a bar with a woman. No doubt in a desperate effort to cut him off, the entity under his care stirred to life and twisted helplessly about on the mat. "Shhhhh," the masseur cooed, firmly holding him down, "muscles have memories. My deep tissue work may be reviving them. I may touch your foot and a memory of your childhood may return. You may cry, you may get angry. Here is a pillow to scream into." When my own massage was over, and I was leaving, I looked back at him: He was now violently kneading the flesh of his client, whose face was buried in the pillow, and repeating the words, "Externalize! Verbalize! Externalize! . . ."

According to the catalogue's scarcely intelligible description, Gestalt practice is "a form—nonanalytic, noncoercive, nonjudgmental—evolving out of the work of Fritz Perls, relating that work to ways of personal clearing and development both ancient and modern," and one of the highlights of my visit was

that of attending a Gestalt encounter group led by one of Esalen's founders, Richard Price. A "hot seat" session, in which
Price "facilitated" the catharsis of whoever chose to sit on a
designated pillow near him, it was one of the very silliest events
I have ever seen. The pillow was immediately occupied by a
Texan woman of about twenty. Within a minute, as if on cue,
she released a thin, low wail, which I took to be a malfunction
of the air-conditioning unit until it changed suddenly into an
ear-splitting shriek. This in turn subsided and the low wail,
suggestive of the smoke-intoxicated cries of the Pythian priest-
ess at Delphi, returned. Then she began to mutter: "No, Daddy,
no! Find someone your own age to play with!" words of
unmistakable significance that electrified the fraternity sitting
cross-legged around her. When she then shouted these words
fortissimo for about ten minutes thereafter, Price intervened
and asked her what "age-space" she was "in." "Six," she snapped
back, eliciting gasps of admiration and envy from her audience,
many of whom were eager to follow her in the hot seat and
were perhaps less skilled at pinpointing the date of traumatic
memories. "Tell Daddy you are afraid of him," Price suggested, and she did. "Now tell Daddy you need and want him,"
and she did. "And now alternate, experiment: Say to Daddy,
'I want you,' 'I hate you,' 'I need you,' 'I don't need you.' 'I
hate you.'" Then he placed his forearm against her knees
(which at this stage were brought up to her chin in the manner
of one of the inmates at Charenton) and asked her to "externalize" her predicament by first pushing his arm away and then
drawing it close to her. In time, she produced a library of
memories of such staggering dullness that it gradually became
clear as day that her original complaint against Daddy had just
been thrown in for glamour and that the real bone she wanted
to pick with him was that he failed to adopt a "nonjudgmental"
approach to her academic studies. Sensing that I had been taken
in by a consummate con-artist (or two) and noting with delight
that the dials on my watch nearly signified the hour of my
departure, I stood up to leave; as I did so, the Texan woman
was reciting on Price's instruction pat little phrases like "I can

get attention from you without feeling pushed" to the men in the room, each by turn, and was presently murmuring it coquettishly to a young man who, I had heard earlier, had recently been the target of a missile of hot food thrown by a man with whose wife he had been dallying. Soon I was being driven through the Institute compound on the way back to the rockslide, and was once more ankle-deep in mud as I journeyed to meet the Cadillac on the other side. The moment I was out of view of the delegation that had driven me to the slide, I hurled the handfuls of promotional literature they had pressed on me into the sea with a sobbing laugh. Funny how one can summon the full force of one's personality to get things done without the aid of juice fasts or afterlife experiences.

Robert Wilson

Since 1976, when *Einstein on the Beach,* written with the composer Philip Glass, was performed at the Metropolitan Opera, Robert Wilson has acquired a reputation as an all-around showman, a hip, Texan Wagner who produces enormous, expensive "intermedia" spectacles in Europe and is followed by swooning disciples and donors. Few people had seen his work, however, until *Einstein* was revived in late 1984 at the Brooklyn Academy of Music's "Next Wave" series. And only travelers to Europe were familiar with the ambitious work that Wilson had been preparing for the past six years, entitled *The CIVIL warS: a tree is best measured when it is down.* Conceived as an "opera" combining the contributions of artists from six countries, including Philip Glass and the East German playwright Heiner Müller and a pop musician, David Byrne of the group Talking Heads, *The CIVIL warS* has five immense acts and lasts twelve hours. For the opera's thirteen intermissions, Wilson has created what he calls "knee plays," the "joints" of the opera; these usually consist, as far as I can see, of a small group of actors performing simple actions such as holding up an arm or standing up and sitting down. It has yet to be produced in its entirety, although portions of it have been seen in Rotterdam, Tokyo, Cologne, Marseilles, and Rome. At one point, it was hoped that the entire work might be performed with an all-star cast, including David Bowie and Hildegard Behrens, as part of the 1984 Olympic Arts Festival in Los Angeles, but the $2.5 million needed for three performances could not be raised. In late February 1985 the American Repertory Theater in Cambridge produced under Wilson's direction the opera's "German" section, a part of the opera that Wilson thinks can be seen on its own. Written in part with Heiner Müller, an East German whose plays are popular among the West German avant-garde, the segment of the opera consists of Scene E from Act III and Scene A from Act IV, both of which have previously been produced only in Cologne, and the epilogue of Act IV, which was also seen in Rome.

What is *The CIVIL warS* about? In a booklet issued for this production, Wilson says the work began as "an exploration of the American Civil War, the Industrial Revolution, and Matthew Brady's photography. Then I began thinking about the whole last half of the nineteenth century: Jules Verne, the opening up of the East to the West, Commodore Perry and the black ships going to Japan." The title, he says, refers not so much to the American Civil War as to all civil wars, to "historical confrontations, not necessarily violent, which comment on man's long journey towards brotherhood." That is why he "capitalized CIVIL and the plural of warS."

Wilson has a broad and somewhat arbitrary notion of civil war. As it turns out, most of the German section of his opera is about Frederick the Great, the enlightened despot of Sans Souci and the founder of modern Prussia. Wilson and Müller present a succession of incidents from Frederick's life, from a fight with his autocratic father (who disliked his dandyism and his friendship with another man, Katte, and forced Frederick to witness Katte's execution as a deserter from the army) to his death. As Wilson explains, "Act IV, Scene A of this play begins with Frederick the Great as a young man standing up to his father, separating from his father, and eventually becoming king. I took it as a prototype of a world family." The separation between father and son is a form of civil war, he says; indeed, "how the soldier puts his sock on before marching off to battle is a civil war; even a child learning to tie his shoe could be considered a civil war."

The incidents from Frederick's life are portrayed at great length by Wilson in short scenes involving twenty-six actors, often in conjunction with film montages on a large screen showing mug shots of ordinary people, swimming turtles, flying eagles. The overall effect is to suggest that Frederick became a tough, militaristic ruler; and by showing us archival footage of the bullet-ridden ruins of the Reichstag in the Second World War, Wilson reminds us that Hitler shot himself in his underground bunker before a portrait of Frederick. The texts for the production were written by Müller and Wilson and include extracts from Racine, Hölderlin, Shakespeare, Kafka, Goethe, and Frederick's own writings. In the epilogue to Act IV, a huge white owl perched on a tree recites Hopi Indian prophecies to actors representing King Lear and Abraham Lincoln. Under the circumstances, the ART felt it wise to append to the booklet distributed to the audience a statement that "Robert Wilson's theatrical technique represents a significant departure from customary forms of dramatic storytelling. Events rarely occur in sequence and follow no discernible causal pattern. Like a dream or a hallucination, the action of a Wilson 'play' takes shape, dissolves, overlaps, fragments, and reforms. Two or three 'stories' may be told simultaneously, using characters drawn from different historical epochs, from different geographical locations."

Wilson is one of the most imaginative people working in the theater; he has an eye for arresting images and a remarkable sense of how to use light, color, form, volume to create them. For example, in an interview in *Theatre* magazine (1983), Wilson explained that he had been asked by the Wagner family to come to Bayreuth to direct *Parsifal*. The production did not come off, but Wilson had already thought through the imagery of his production. "There's no house curtain," he said. "Instead there's a curtain of light. Then a wall of water with the beams of light coming vertically across. Eventually a lake appears at the back and that's the prelude. The whole piece is in blue. Gurnemanz appears here at the downstage edge of the lake." Elsewhere in the opera, he would use

> a great disk of light that moves on stage from the side and an iceberg floating upstage. Eventually the disk of light settles on the center of the lake. Parsifal stands downstage watching with his back to the audience the way the audience watches it. I don't have the knights or any of that. Amfortas is carried out in his litter and he goes into the iceberg and takes out an Egyptian box. Inside is a clear glass chalice which is shaped like an X.

At the end of the second act, "Klingsor throws his spear at Parsifal. Here it's a rod of light. The scene is all back painted and at the moment Parsifal picks up the glowing rod we turn on all the lights from behind and everything appears in cold black and white like a skeleton."

The CIVIL warS is full of remarkable images. In the Cambridge production, a woman "scribe" wearing a conical hat and a costume of wrinkled cloth walked out onto the stage with a giant pencil strapped across her shoulder; then, looking like a John Tenniel drawing for *Alice in Wonderland,* she walked briskly up a ramp built over the orchestra section of the theater followed by a man wearing a gas mask and dressed entirely in black. In another scene, seven faces with grotesque death-mask makeup created by Wilson pop up out of trapdoors in the orchestra. In the epilogue to Act IV, an extremely tall and thin Abraham Lincoln enters from the right of the stage. Perhaps twenty feet tall, his stovepipe hat seeming to brush the top of the proscenium arch, he walks slowly across the stage, then falls backward even more slowly and floats on his side on the left.

Wilson has also created elegant props: a pointed hat with a tiny light bulb affixed to its tip, wooden chairs with square frames for backs; a wooden horse on which Frederick rocks back and forth while wearing a Japanese mask. If one looks at the drawings and photographs of three-dimensional models of the sets Wilson has created for other parts of *The CIVIL warS*[1] one will find further evidence of Wilson's flair for creating visual impressions. In Act I, for example, the "World's Tallest Woman" enters stage right carrying a tiny man in her palm; in Act II, eleven pairs of feet appear just below the top of the stage; thereafter, historical characters like Mata Hari and Karl Marx move vertically up and down the stage. In Act III, ten Lincolns are shown lying in hospital beds. (In the exhibition catalogue one finds photographs of the extraordinary pieces of furniture Wilson has made for his other productions: a flying bench made of wire mesh; a chair made of galvanized pipe, and another draped with crumpled sheets of lead.)

But in *The CIVIL warS,* as in *Einstein on the Beach,* one is constantly struck by the impression that Wilson does not really know what to do with his images once he has presented them. He never joins them successfully to each other so that their aesthetic values can accumulate or develop; more often than not, one feels that the oblique and wispy spoken texts and stage movements that follow their first appearance could be cut without much being lost. The images are not used in an effective collaboration with music, dance, or text; in Wilson's productions, these tend to provide either a pale background for the images or else to interfere, in an irritating and pretentious way, with our appreciation of them. We never really learn much about the American Civil War, or about Frederick the Great or Einstein. Wilson's "subject matter" and titles seem arbitrarily chosen to illustrate vague ideas about the menace of technology, the evils of violence, and popular myths of fame and power. Parts of *Einstein* might just as well have been titled *Edison* (one of Wilson's other productions) and what I saw of *The CIVIL warS* might have been titled *The Life and Times of Joseph Stalin,* another work by Wilson.

[1]These may be seen in the catalogue of an exhibition of Wilson's work at the Contemporary Arts Center in Cincinnati that was organized by Robert Stearns in 1980, reissued as *Robert Wilson: The Theatre of Images* (New York: Harper & Row, 1984).

The German section of *The CIVIL warS* is, however, more coherent and consecutive than *Einstein,* in which the actors moved about like somnambulists or puppets, reciting banal snippets of conversation from daily life, such as "Have you found it yet? No, I haven't found it yet. I'll just have to keep looking," or counting, "1-2-3; 1-2-3-4." The music by Philip Glass was anesthetic, like Oriental bell music. What stayed in the mind after leaving the theater was images—a slowly descending white line bisecting the black backdrop of the stage; a ring of light hovering over whirligig dancers; a solid bar of light being lifted slowly into the flies.

In *The CIVIL warS* Wilson has used a greater variety of theatrical effects. The scene from Act III, for example, with which the production in Cambridge begins, shows us a band of Civil War soldiers at reveille. The setting is a camp of pitched tents as in a Brady or Houghton photograph. All that occurs is that the soldiers wake up, get dressed, drink coffee, hum a song, and march out. After the others have gone, a soldier mounts a rock or tree stump to stand watch. Wilson has him mount the platform as slowly as possible, so that we can see the phase of each act he performs; the effect is like watching a sequence of Muybridge photos. Once he is fully standing, the soldier waits and very slowly scans the horizon from side to side. In a second, he snaps his head in the direction of a noise only he has heard then the lights are shut off. The entire scene is effective, even though the actors were mostly Harvard undergraduates who did not always move with the disciplined economy Wilson can sometimes achieve with his actors.

Moreover, in *The CIVIL warS* Wilson has been much more successful than in *Einstein* in showing his humorous or whimsical side, which owes not a little to vaudeville and cabaret. He brings on a woman chewing a cigar who tells a story about the difficulties of getting her car repaired; a second woman stands nearby extravagantly chewing gum and wiggling her hips. The scene is not really funny; it relies on a kind of music-hall or burlesque humor, and we laugh only because the types are so exaggerated. In an earlier scene, a giant bullet-shaped spaceship lands on the stage in a cloud of smoke and then ascends, leaving behind two enormous grappling bears. The audience was so relieved by the presence of such a circus effect in a long evening of often unintelligible juxtapositions of texts and images that it laughed nervously and uproariously at the bears (as it did later at the cigar woman). After Wilson had presented two or three more such broad effects, the audience seemed to await more of them as eagerly as other audiences await the leaps of Baryshnikov. Wilson obliged them, but sometimes in overly camp episodes, as when the mother of Frederick mouths the bass melody of Schubert's *Erlkönig,* or when the penis of Abraham Lincoln—the arm of the hidden actor propelling the Lincoln statue—takes a curtain call.

But the same difficulties that arose with Wilson's earlier work were present in *The CIVIL warS.* If he seeks the effect of a dream or a hallucination, as the program claims, he cannot supply the continuity that underlies such states of mind. One also felt that Wilson failed again to incorporate the music and language into his work, to make the aesthetic force of his images work effectively with either. The music for the German section of *The CIVIL warS* was composed largely by Hans Peter Kuhn, a German composer whose music resembles that of Glass— notes played on what appeared to be an electronically amplified organ and held for long periods or combined with other notes in simple chords and arpeggios. The texts written or chosen by Müller and Wilson were at times as foolish as those of *Einstein.* The soldiers in Act III say to each other "yeah," "ha," and "hunh," or "I don't care what it means," and their voices are carried by microphones distributed through the audience, so that we constantly felt we were being addressed by the person sitting next to us. The woman with the giant pencil repeats over and over again the words "Stone Scissors Paper. Stone Sharpens Scissors Scissors Cuts Paper Paper Wraps Stone," a contribution of Heiner Müller. The death masks in the orchestra chant "american motors, american capitals, american control" and "ibm forever/never [repeated seven times] dream of selling ibm" and other sophomoric patter.

As with *Einstein* people in the audience began to walk out, some of them just at the moment an actor on the stage was saying the words, "oh stay by me and go you not / for my heart is the loveliest spot." Those of us who stayed were as relieved when Wilson and Müller had actors recite Racine and Shakespeare (even if we did not understand why) as we were by the monologue of the cigar woman. The problem was to understand why Wilson, who has a brilliant visual imagination and a superb sense of timing, and who knows how both to interest and to please audiences, should have felt obliged, as he has in the past, to hold on to his images until they become tedious and to accompany them with soporific music and words no more interesting than those used in a Senate filibuster.

Part of the answer lies in Wilson's idea of what theater should be and do, an idea which seems to have arisen from an early concern with children's therapy. In Texas, where he was born in 1941, Wilson was cured of a speech impediment by Mrs. Byrd Hoffman, a dancer and teacher then in her seventies. She succeeded in doing so, he has said, by giving him exercises to "release tension," so that "by relaxing and taking my time" he overcame the disability. Mrs. Hoffman was "amazing because she never taught a technique, she never gave me a way to approach it, it was more that I discovered it on my own."

Wilson became an adherent of this kind of therapeutic work and produced children's theater at the University of Texas. When he arrived in New York, he took a job as consultant to the New York City Board of Education and Department of Welfare and subsequently became a special instructor in the public schools. He was also a consultant with Head Start and organized theatrical works with other disabled people, including iron lung patients. Stefan Brecht, the son of Bertolt Brecht, who has worked with Wilson as an actor and written a long book about the development of Wilson's "theater of images"— a book at once acute and somewhat nutty—says that Wilson's "therapeutic work with children judged retarded, autistic, or mentally impaired, often with apparently organic deficiencies or lacking in coordination," was the source of his theatrical ideas.

Wilson, he says, "seems to have focused on getting them to do simple things on the principle that this activation by fostering their bodily self-awareness and giving them self-assurance would generalize into a general mental activation."[2] Wilson tried to overcome the disabilities of these children by constant repetition of simple movements. At some point, Brecht writes, "he got into similar work with more or less normal, functioning repressed adults: awareness sessions. The general point seems to have been to start people doing things for the sake of doing them, naturally expressive of their individuality."

Another kind of influence on Wilson's idea of the theater arose from his exposure to the experimental dance and theater of the early Sixties, when he was a painter and student of architecture at Pratt Institute. Wilson speaks more explicitly about the influence of children's therapy on his theater productions than he does about the influence of other artists, but much of his work recalls the experimental "painters' theater" of the early Sixties, largely created by painters and attended mostly by people in the art world. This form of theater was influenced by the "action painting" of the abstract expressionists, such as Jackson Pollock, whose paintings were held to be expressive of emotion and intuition and were also thought to be the records of movements and actions, and by the collages of Kurt Schwitters. It was also influenced by the musical theory John Cage taught at the New School in the Fifties, which owed much to Dadaism. Cage sought to exploit indeterminacy and chance in composing his music, and to present unrelated events at the same time. He extended his view to visual and other arts, and, as musical adviser to Merce Cunningham's dance company, had a part in the creation of Cunningham's spare dances, which often had no "story" or "characters" and which also were sometimes organized by chance methods.

[2]Stefan Brecht, *The Theatre of Visions: Robert Wilson* (Frankfurt: Suhrkamp Verlag, 1978), p. 212.

Cage also influenced Allan Kaprow and others in the art world—such as the painters Robert Rauschenberg, Claes Oldenburg, and Jim Dine—who created the "assemblages" and "environments" which led to the "happenings" of the Sixties. Kaprow and others intended that happenings would avoid what they felt to be the artificial devices of traditional theater, such as its emphasis on plot, or development, or exposition, or indeed "acting," but especially the subordination of the theater to the text. In happenings, language was used in a different way from that of traditional theater; for example, actors spoke ad-lib or used words chosen randomly and repeated them many times. The creators of happenings often gave up the idea of the "stage" and the proscenium arch and tried to include audiences in their spectacles, sometimes abusing them and trying to shock them out of their cultural assumptions by presenting them with startling juxtapositions of images and movements. Brecht quotes an early collaborator of Wilson's who claims that Wilson was "influenced a lot" by Cage.

In 1970, Wilson started a foundation and a school named after his old teacher, the Byrd Hoffman School for Byrds, made up of amateurs who were taken with Wilson's ideas and who performed in his early plays. In these productions Wilson seems to have tried to combine the emphasis on therapy and "nonverbal communication" he had promoted in his work with children with some of the ideas of the "painters' theater." The theater would be a form of "communication" similar to the relations he was able to have with the children he instructed; he would communicate with us as he had with them, through "images," not words. As he said in an interview published in the program, "most theatre that we see today is thought about in terms of the word, the text. Everything is subservient to the text: the actors' gestures, the lighting, the decor, the costumes—everything is there to interpret, or to comment on, or to illustrate the text. . . . In my theatre, what we see is as important as what we hear."

Wilson's idea was to try to increase our "awareness" by freeing our imagination through images and by showing ordinary people, not performers, doing simple things and having "authentic experiences." Furthermore, he wished to do so in such a way that the theater would be a place where the audience would be able to think in unexpected ways and to meditate. Unlike that of a play on Broadway, the audience, he said, would be able to "choose" what to see. *The CIVIL warS,* for example, "tells many stories, some of them simultaneous, and *you* put them together, probably after you go home." Time is needed if the audience is to turn inward and to reflect on itself: "Most theater deals with speeded-up time, but I use the kind of natural time in which it takes the sun to set, a cloud to change, a day to dawn. I give you time to reflect, to meditate about other things than those happening on the stage."[3]

This therapeutic conception of theater is shared by Heiner Müller, who Wilson claims was important to him because "for the first time I had a collaboration with someone that dealt with language in terms of pictures." Müller claims that theater should be what has been called "a laboratory for the social imagination." It should, he says, "mobilize imagination," which in all industrial societies, "the German Democratic Republic included," is "throttled." He claims that "the worst experience I had during my stay in the United States was a film I saw called *Fantasia,* by Disney. . . . The most barbaric thing about this film, something I learned later, was that almost every American child between the ages of six and eight gets to view it. Which means that these people will never again be able to hear specific works by Beethoven, Bach, Handel, Tchaikovsky, etc., without seeing the Disney figures and images. The horrifying thing for me in this is the occupation of the imagination by clichés and images which will never go away: the use of images to prevent the having of experiences." The theater, by contrast, should present images that unsettle the imagination and prevent it from hardening.[4]

[3]*The New York Times,* December 2, 1984, Arts & Leisure, p. 5.
[4]Heiner Müller, *Hamlet-machine* (New York: Performing Arts Journal Publications, 1984), p. 138.

The emphasis in Wilson's work on slowed-down action, on repetition, on "natural" body movement in "natural" time; the preference he has for working with composers like Glass and Kuhn, or writers like Müller, who treat music and language as he treats images; his insistence that audiences be able to "choose" what they see in the theater and that they have time in which to meditate: all this seems to derive from his therapeutic conception of theater. More often than not, however, the analogy between children's therapy and theater betrays Wilson into absurdities, conferring virtue on repetitiousness and tedium and diminishing the aesthetic force of his images by encouraging him to hold them longer than they can bear. Is there in any case any reason to believe that ordinary adults benefit from Wilson's theater in the way he intends? Are his images therapeutic? Indeed, does it matter whether they are?

Most of Wilson's audience, I suspect, are drawn to him because they know that he is among the few living theater directors and producers who have any new ideas. They see about them the stirring of ashes: Broadway revivals of older plays and imports from England of sentimental and expensive musicals, unsuccessful "adaptations" of old movies. They hear in teenage dance music the 1950s *réchauffé*. Many of them are willing to follow Wilson and to suspend the conventions of narrative, plot, and character. But they soon find, I think, that he offers no coherent alternative to traditional theater. They are startled and fascinated by the visual surface of his work and by the unusual juxtapositions of images and characters he creates, in which, say, Charlie Chaplin might meet the Nibelungs. They enjoy his bears and music-hall effects. But after a short while, I suspect, they begin to think about their medical bills, or to doze, or they parade up and down the lobby of the theater. It is not clear how, when they get home, they are to go about "putting together" the "stories" Wilson has shown them. Nor is there much reason to believe that the kinds of images Müller speaks of prevent the "throttling" of imagination any more than *Fantasia* or that our imaginations are as susceptible to the deadening effects of popular culture as he supposes. Audiences, moreover, "choose" what to see and how to direct their attention in Broadway theaters no less than in Wilson's operas.

Not only is the analogy between theater and therapy that is implicit in Wilson's work strained, the idea of theater it supports is ill-suited to Wilson's real gifts, which are for conceiving visual forms and are not easily placed at the service of an external purpose like therapy. He has a cool aesthetic temperament, which expresses itself in precise, architectural décor and imagery; he is at his best in using light and staging and his splendid furniture and other props to create such visual effects. His talent is for the fantastic and the bizarre, not the natural and redemptive. When he strays from the use of these gifts, when he uses shallow, incoherent texts, his work becomes pretentious and awkward. He has been straying, however, for some time now and the result is one riveting flop after another.

Diane Arbus

The photographer Diane Arbus was born in 1923 in New York and forty-eight years later killed herself in her apartment in an artists' community in the same city. Her parents, David and Gertrude Nemerov, were well-to-do Jews whose fortune derived from Russeks, a fur and clothing store which Gertrude's father had founded, and with which David was associated, first as a window dresser, then as merchandising director, and finally as president and chairman of the board. Together with her sister and her brother, Howard, who was to become a well-known poet, Diane grew up in a tight, closed, snobbish world of the newly rich, in which she was alternately petted and ignored by her parents, ordered to wear white gloves by her nanny while walking in the park, and confined in an enormous, lonely apartment on Central Park West. Patricia Bosworth's account of Arbus's childhood is the best part of her book: She manages to convey something of the pretensions and mannerisms of the Nemerovs, and in her portrayal of David Nemerov, a vain and charming, but fundamentally hard, businessman, she introduces us to a person who at times seems far more interesting than Diane Arbus.[1]

Nemerov sent his children to progressive schools such as the Ethical Culture School and Fieldston, where they were bound to develop aspirations to do other in life than assist him at Russeks or become businessmen's wives like Gertrude; and yet, when they did so, he complained and was not readily available for help. According to Howard Nemerov, his poetry was probably never read by his father. When David Nemerov retired from Russeks and took up painting as a hobby, and subsequently mounted a show and managed not only to sell most of his paintings to Seventh Avenue associates but also to earn a notice in *Time* magazine, he told his son (who was by this time in his late thirties), "You see? An artist can be successful at making money." He was able to provide his children with opportunities, but, as with many other self-made men, the occasional pride he felt in them appears to have been always tinctured with a certain resentment and competitiveness, as well as with a reluctance to let them develop in their own way—attitudes that were almost certain to produce in them at once a lack of self-esteem and an arrogant and neurotic perfectionism. Both Diane and Howard suffered periodically from deep depressions, as did their mother, who herself had come from a background not entirely unlike theirs.

An intelligent, shy girl, Diane did not escape her parents' world easily: Unlike her brother and sister, who married gentiles, she married Allan Arbus, the nephew of David Nemerov's predecessor as president of Russeks, who resembled her enough that they were at times confused for brother and sister. The Arbuses opened a photographic studio with Nemerov's help—he characteristically promised at first to buy them their camera equipment and then subsequently reversed himself and ended up paying only for some of it—and photographed advertise-

[1] Patricia Bosworth, *Diane Arbus: A Biography* (New York: Alfred A. Knopf, 1984).

ments for Russeks; in time, they became fairly successful, and worked for such magazines as *Glamour* and *Seventeen*. The two worked well together—Allan was the photographer and Diane the "stylist," conceiving the idea of a shooting and arranging the clothes, makeup, and accessories of the models—but both of them disliked commercial photography and wished to do other things, he to become an actor and she to pursue her interest in "serious" photography. In this she was subsequently encouraged by the photographer Lisette Model, who was known for her photographs of drunks and beggars and other "grotesques." In 1957 the Arbuses broke up their business partnership in order to promote their separate interests and somewhat later their marriage collapsed. They remained friends, however, and Diane tried to make money from her photographs in order to help Allan support their two daughters and herself.

Although Bosworth is at pains to point out that Diane Arbus took a good many fashion photographs and portraits of celebrities in order to make money, it is her arresting photographs of unusual subjects that made her famous. She told Model that she wished to photograph what is "evil." She photographed (or wished to photograph) child prostitutes, copulating dogs, midgets, morgues, "Sealo the Seal Boy, who had hands growing out of his shoulders," a woman who trained herself to eat and sleep under water, cats in fancy dress, dwarfs and giants, a man who collected string for twenty years, transvestites and hermaphrodites, hydrocephalics and retardates, "a man who said he was Joan Crawford." Some of the safer of her photographs were published in *Harper's Bazaar* when its art director was the late Marvin Israel, who in a sense replaced Allan Arbus as the dominant male influence in Arbus's life. In 1967 the New Documents show at the Museum of Modern Art, organized by John Szarkowski, introduced her work to a wider public.

Some years before the New Documents show, however, she had fallen ill with hepatitis, which had been aggravated by a regime of antidepressants and birth control pills, and it took years for her to recover from it. In 1969, when she was divorced from Allan Arbus and he moved to California and her daughters began to lead lives of their own, she found herself alone and fearful of growing old. Her depressions grew more frequent. She complained to friends that she may have succeeded as an "artist" but still had few assignments that brought in money. She tried to put together a portfolio of her work: it sold only three copies, to friends. In 1971 she committed suicide, to which she apparently thought we all have a "right." The following year she was the first American photographer to be exhibited at the Venice Biennale.

Bosworth explains in the preface to her book that although Arbus's brother, sister, and mother agreed to provide information and otherwise cooperate with her in writing it, her former husband, daughters, and several others, such as Marvin Israel, refused to do so. This perhaps explains to some extent why the first part of the book, when Bosworth has at hand the reminiscences of Arbus's family, is so interesting, whereas the latter parts are little more than a succession of details and incidents of dubious provenance, with very little of larger significance brought out. This part of the book constantly gives the impression that she is not up to her subject and neither knows enough about Arbus nor has sufficient critical equipment to help us appreciate her work.

One feels in these later sections of her book that Bosworth has simply filled in the gaps in her evidence with speculations of her own and with lurid and upsetting hearsay about Arbus—which she supplies liberally—even though the sole possible justification for telling us, for example, that Arbus was bisexual, or attended orgies, is the contribution such stories might make to the kind of rounded portrait she utterly fails to provide. A pall of smut hangs over the book: Everything about Arbus is painted in black and gray; she emerges a midnight figure, brooding and morbid and sexually perverse, slightly absurd as she runs about asking her friends if they know any "battered people" or "freaks" she can photograph.

Bosworth also employs some questionable journalistic methods in the later parts of the book. She frequently makes statements about Arbus's character that she fails to confirm with anything like adequate evidence. She boldly states that Diane "said" something or other, but when we turn to her footnotes we discover that the evidence that she did so is nothing more than one of her informants' memories after decades of an afternoon spent together or a breakfast. "Diane's sexual fantasies," we are told, "were dark and perverse. She once confided that she envied a girlfriend who'd been raped," but we are never told to whom she confided this or when. Bosworth mentions other "friends" of Arbus, unnamed or furnished with pseudonyms, who seem to be nothing but mouthpieces for her own speculations.

She writes, for example, that the Arbuses permitted themselves marital infidelities and openly discussed them between themselves and their close friends. But it appears that when Allan Arbus fell in love with an actress, their marriage collapsed. Why did this happen? There is no clear answer in the book, but some light is thrown on the matter when Bosworth introduces the pseudonymous "Cheech McKensie" (better, I suppose, than Ken McCheechie), who says that Diane phoned her during the critical period when the marriage was deteriorating and asked to see her. "Cheech" says that Diane met her at "the baths on Monroe Street," where "we sat fully clothed in the steam on the stairs and there were elderly Jewish women surrounding us" while "Diane poured her heart out to me." The burden of Diane's confession was that while she felt her own infidelities were "unimportant," she felt betrayed when Allan fell in love. The scene ends improbably when, in Cheech's words, Diane "took out her camera and began snapping away at the women lolling around in their sheets," as if "she were trying to kill them with her camera." Recall that they were in a steam bath: What sort of camera did she use to "kill" her subjects? What kinds of photographs resulted from this episode? Such questions are not pursued by Bosworth.

This kind of anecdote is characteristic of the sloppy way in which the book has been produced. It is also full of repetitions and of ill-composed sentences such as the following: "Avedon recommended her for a lucrative advertising job to photograph a new camera in her own particular way." Characters are mentioned many pages before we are told who they are and how they figured in Arbus's life. Words appear in different spellings on different pages. An article on Arbus is listed on one page as having appeared in 1978 and on another in 1971. An estate is described as "shambling," a woman has a "smelly waddle"; even Bosworth's accounts of vivid incidents are marred by her use of words like "grungy" and "funky."

Marvin Israel wrote about Arbus that "whatever she was and whatever she said she was, was in some sense disguised," and the job of her biographer would seem to be to break through these disguises and try to give a coherent account of her personality, but Bosworth presents so many separate pieces of evidence that incline one to different and often opposite conclusions that after reading her book one really has no clear view of Arbus's character at all. Bosworth seems at times to see Arbus as something of a "liberated woman" *avant la lettre,* who was brought up to be nothing but a wife and mother but who was driven by artistic impulses to escape the suffocating and pretentious world of her parents and to force her way into the "male club" of commercial photography, in which she was at times unjustly paid less than her male colleagues.

Despite her tiny, frail appearance, Bosworth suggests, Arbus could be tough and competitive; she worked hard to get ahead, and occasionally used dishonest methods to do so. Thus, although Bosworth says in one place that Arbus was worried about obtaining releases from her subjects "since it touched on a photographer's moral responsibility" and quotes her defending herself against the charge that her pictures are cruel by claiming that her subjects "wanted to have their pictures taken," she also shows us that Arbus lied in order to get some of her photographs, assuring her subjects that her pictures were for her portfolio only and then publishing them. She quotes Arbus's sister as saying that Diane took photographs she knew were "sensationalistic. She said she'd taken them that way deliberately. She was determined to make more money so Al-

Ian wouldn't have to give her so much—she thought notorious pictures were one way of getting more assignments."

Several of Arbus's subjects are reported by Bosworth as claiming that she would ask them to pose for her and would then wait and wait until their pose fell away and they looked strained and uncomfortable, at which time she would suddenly snap their picture. Even one of her offbeat subjects could tell what she was up to: "Cora Pratt," a New England woman who occasionally dressed up in dreadful clothes and wore enormous false teeth, and who in doing so assumed the personality of a blundering, nutty practical joker, told Bosworth that "Diane Arbus was awful nice to me. Sweet. . . . But before she left she asked me a couple of times was I really sincere about having these two people inside myself? I kept telling her I was sincere, but I guess she didn't believe me because I didn't end up at her show in the Museum of Modern Art."

One curious episode in Bosworth's book concerns the author Germaine Greer, who had been on a book tour in New York in 1971 and who consented to be photographed in her hotel room by Arbus. Her initial impression of Arbus, she told Bosworth, was that of "a delicate little girl," but "all of a sudden she knelt on the bed and hung over me with this wide-angle lens staring me in the face. . . . It developed into a sort of duel between us, because I *resisted* being photographed like that—close up with all my pores and lines showing! She kept asking me all sorts of personal questions, and I became aware that she would only shoot when my face was showing tension or concern or boredom or annoyance . . . but because she was a woman I didn't tell her to fuck off. If she'd been a man, I'd have kicked her in the balls."

On the other hand, Bosworth also says that Arbus was certainly not a feminist and was somewhat contemptuous of feminists; she told a reporter that "a woman spends the first block of her life looking for a husband and learning to be a wife and mother," and she felt, according to Bosworth, "an aching sense of worthlessness" after her husband's departure. Moreover, says Bosworth, "she knew she had an advantage on the job in the company of men. In the beginning she was ignored, but even after she got better known she could still get away with a lot of things a man couldn't. She'd appear insecure about her equipment; she couldn't always load film into a camera; she'd flirt. 'I'd stop at nothing to get the picture I wanted,' she told one of her students. . . . 'And being a woman helped.' " Unjust social arrangements seem to have had little to do with Arbus's success or failure as a photographer, however, especially since, as Bosworth says, "by 1970—liberated by the Pill, feminism, and federal funding—women artists in general were starting to be self-supporting" and Arbus deliberately chose a "different route" from that of other women artists, creating "detached and impenetrable" work and refusing to be called a "woman artist."

Bosworth does not make much effort to explain these conflicting aspects of Arbus's character. More seriously, her midnight view of her subject, with its focus on masturbation and orgies, leaves out or underemphasizes what seem to me important features. While it is perhaps absurd to speculate too much about her character in light of Israel's words, mentioned earlier, it seems that Arbus thought of herself as set apart from society at large by special gifts. From her own words and those of her close colleagues, we know that she saw her photography as part of the wider ambition of acquiring courage and self-knowledge: By entering the worlds of her oddities and photographing them she felt she challenged the fears she had acquired in her protected childhood. Tracking, pursuing, and pinning down her peculiar subjects evidently thrilled her and were seen by her as a part of a daring game, more valuable in the playing than in her photographs; she thought of her camera as a talisman that protected her from the dangers she encountered in getting her photographs. She was, she said, a "spy" who could "figure" herself into any situation and who had "some slight corner on something about the quality of things" so that "there are things which nobody would see unless I photographed them."

While young she had written that she wished to be "a great

sad artist": She believed this involved a life of risks and poverty. Art could not be "rewarded" with money; fashion could not be "art." Indeed, she seems to have been ashamed of making money and she was careless about handling it, as her father had been. In nearly everything she says about herself in the collected interviews and tape-recorded remarks that her daughter and Marvin Israel put together after her death there are exhalations of an inarticulate and poetic atmosphere of mind that she must have acquired at the progressive schools she attended and that no doubt gave rise to this romantic, magical, and somewhat aristocratic conception of the artist.[2]

There is also in Arbus—what Bosworth does not mention— a dry and restrained, whimsical sense of humor that is not a little self-conscious and literary and that does not always quite succeed. In one of her earliest photographic essays, which first appeared in *Harper's Bazaar* and was later reprinted with additions in *Infinity,* there are some clear examples of this humor, together with ample evidence of that careless and romantic tendency I have mentioned. "These are," she says of her subjects, "six singular people who appear like metaphors somewhere further out than we do, beckoned, not driven, invented by belief, author and hero of a real dream by which our courage and cunning are tested and tried; so that we may wonder all over again what is veritable and inevitable and possible and what it is to become whoever we may be."[3] What are we, and how have we become what we are? We have constructed ourselves, she thinks, and we could have been different.

Her camera is a moral instrument that will show us just a few of the infinite possible paths of self-development. In the descriptions she appends to her photographs that follow, of a man who has been tattooed 306 times, or a humorous old tramp who describes himself as Uncle Sam and wears a red, white,

---

[2]See *Diane Arbus: An Aperture Monograph* (New York:Aperture/The Museum of Modern Art, 1971).

[3]See *Infinity,* vol. 2 (February 1962).

and blue satin suit, there is no feeling at all that she is setting out to depict freaks. We get instead the impression that she is offering an amused appreciation of people who have chosen to adopt unusual patterns of life; she rather enjoys these characters, we feel, in the way she enjoyed, as Bosworth notes, reading Edith Sitwell's descriptions of English eccentrics or Lewis Carroll, and indeed there is a fairy-tale atmosphere in some of her descriptions of her pictures. One of her subjects calls himself a prince and lives in a "bejewelled, encrusted, embellished and bedizened 6 by 9 ft. room on 48th Street." He says he is the "rightful Hereditary claimant to the Throne of the Byzantine Eastern Roman Empire" and that

> if his Empire were restored to him, he would model its Constitution after that of the United States with the additional proviso of Absolute Power for the Emperor, but he does not seek this destiny, preferring to live quietly as he does, enjoying the nightly society of his friends in the 57th Street Automat. He has prudently avoided venturing near Constantinople, the hereditary Capital of the Empire, where several of his ancestors were assassinated.

The tattooed man is described in the way one might introduce a character in a children's story: He "has so much more than enough of women that he treats them with a devastating coolness. . . . They often promise to marry him if he will erase his tattoos so whenever he wants to break off with a girl he gets another." Another of her subjects, a mulatto male impersonator, is a figure in an allegory: She was accused of being a man in women's clothing and admits "wryly that most people would figure they'd had enough, just being a mulatto, and would be content to sit on the racial fence without climbing astride the sexual one." Somewhat like Dr. Watson, Arbus gives each of her subjects a title, like "The Marked Man" or, in the case of the male impersonator, Miss Storme de Larverie, "The Lady Who Appears to Be a Gentleman."

Arbus's photographs cannot be for us what they were for

viewers in the Sixties, when they first appeared, and were interpreted against standards developed in a cultural mood strikingly different from ours. But how do they stand up today? Bosworth's book contains no more satisfactory an account or appraisal of Arbus's photography than of her character. The background of Arbus's style, she says, lay in the reaction of photographers like Robert Frank and others to the classical style of Edward Steichen, with its emphasis on "tonal quality," composition, and fine printing. Arbus, she says, combined the radical "snapshot aesthetic" of Frank with "heroic portraiture," producing work she describes in such terms as "intimate and creepy" or "grotesque and defiantly spiritual." Arbus's "central concern," she continues, was "focused on the nature of being alone and our pitiful range of attempted defenses against it." Arbus, she thinks, sought to reveal the private faces of her subjects, and in order to arrive at this truth she developed a "self-conscious collaborative" approach "in which subject and photographer reveal themselves to the camera as to each other." She repeatedly quotes sources who tell her, for example, that Arbus "stripped away everything to the thing itself" and "stripped away all artiness."

This is a popular interpretation of Arbus, but it is not convincing. Whether or not Arbus practiced a self-conscious collaboration with her subjects, the photographs themselves seem neither to reveal the "truth" about their subjects (let alone about their author, who remains entirely mysterious) nor to escape "artiness." With their black borders and stark, brightly lit subjects, they have a cold, dead elegance that seems studied and artificial; a self-conscious artistic sensibility seems to obtrude excessively into these pictures, as if their creator were still, to some extent, arranging the models and their makeup and accessories. The whimsical tendency I mentioned earlier that touches her work in places seems to have hardened in her later work, in which she seems to be preoccupied with marginal patterns of life and with rendering the familiar strange, so that while these later photographs of course show true aspects of their subjects, as all photographs in a sense do, they are no more truthful than a district attorney's speech that emphasizes some truths in order to distort others. Nor do they always serve the moral function she thought her work could serve, for in many cases they do not broaden our moral imagination or faithfully describe the variety of human experience.

It is instructive to put Arbus's work alongside that of a photographer she greatly admired, Weegee, who worked for New York tabloids in the 1930s and 1940s and who later moved to Hollywood, where he made "photocaricatures" using kaleidoscopic lenses. Weegee's subjects are similar to Arbus's—he shows us drunks, corpses, transvestites, people sleeping on park benches in the summer, children picking at their noses—but there is nothing morbid or remote about his pictures; they are thrilling and vulgar. He has a sense of humor. Arbus's mannered, static snapshots show people detached from their ordinary circumstances like entomological specimens, whereas Weegee's subjects, whether they be girls imploring their favorite movie stars for autographs at a premiere or members of a crowd staring at a murder victim, some laughing and others crying, are always shown in the midst of their lives, absorbed in their misfortunes or happiness. He has, moreover, a way of inducing in us a feeling for their fears and impulses and expectations, whereas Arbus's work is unable to do this: her photographs call too much attention to her; one is too much reminded that her success as a photographer consists in her "figuring" herself into a strange situation and too much invited to ask how she did it; her photographs seem merely to announce her successes to us.

The temperament that informs Weegee's photographs seems coarse, unsentimental, but also enthusiastic; he is drawn to any manifestation of life—fist fights, car accidents, rehearsals at the opera, riots, Harlem masquerade parties; he is wild for money, cigars, whores, and careless about "releases." He will do anything for a photograph, and tells us in his autobiography that he once dressed up as a hospital orderly to get into the room of a dying gangster with his camera.[4] Yet this temperament, one feels, is more generous than Arbus's and can take in more of the fullness and the constant features of life than hers can. Her work, by contrast, is chaste, icy, stylized; there is something life-denying, at any rate not quite human, about it that prevents it from being altogether first-rate.

[4]See *Weegee by Weegee* (New York: Da Capo Press, 1975). Da Capo Press republished his *Naked City* and *Weegee's People* in paperback in the spring of 1985.

Oscar Levant

For those who like to take things to extremes, Oscar Levant was a hero. Before he died in 1972, he had completed a great arc of self-destruction that ruined his career as a pianist, and a radio and film star, and that had put him into a series of hospitals to be treated for drug addiction and mental illness. In his last years, he often appeared on television, where he boasted of his "boss-hating attitude" and impertinence, and gained a reputation for insulting his hosts and sponsors. His impertinence extended into his private relations—or perhaps it originated there—in a remarkable way. When his ex-wife married the theater owner Arthur Loew, he telephoned them at 2 A.M. on their wedding night and asked her, "What's playing at Loew's State tonight and when does the feature go on?" His phobias and superstitions were carefully recorded by his friends. They knew of streets he refused to walk on because of the bad associations they evoked, and how he would run out of a room if he saw Scriabin's music on the piano. Pigeons flying west, a discarded Butterfinger's wrapper, or more than two extinguished cigarettes in an ashtray were evil signs for him. His great friend S. N. Behrman described him as "a character who, if he did not exist, could not be imagined."

This was certainly true of his appearance. When I first met him at his house in Beverly Hills, he looked as if he had just undergone a police interrogation. His face was puffy, pockmarked, with threatening black eyebrows and an exceedingly wide mouth. He shuffled his large body around the room as if he were looking for a place to sleep, and then crumbled onto a long sofa. I don't recall that he said very much except to explain that he had been in a sanitarium for the past few months. But every so often he would break into half a smile—thereby revealing cigarette-stained teeth and becoming even more unattractive—and mutter an authoritative appraisal of his situation: "My home is a nice place to visit, but I'd sure hate to live here."

Levant wrote three books, parts of which are well worth the efforts of an enterprising publisher to bring together in a single volume. The first and best of these, *A Smattering of Ignorance*, published in 1940, recounts his early career as a composer and pianist, as well as his friendships with George Gershwin and Harpo Marx. He was born in Pittsburgh in 1906. He not only learned very early to play the piano but also to play different kinds of music, so that although he acquired a classical training he was able to make money playing with dance bands. He also wrote popular songs, some of which, like "Blame It on My Youth," a ballad with a somewhat indecisive melody, were hits. He tells us in a memoir entitled "Leaves of Trash" that when he came to New York in the late Twenties to play the piano with dance bands he fell in with a set of Broadway showgirls, gangsters, and songwriters. The songwriters, he says, would gather around the pianos in publishers' offices to play new songs like Billy Rose's "Love Is Like a Punch in the Nose" or Gershwin's "There's More to a Kiss Than a . . ." (followed by the sound of three kissing smacks). He saw so much of Joe Adonis, Frank Costello, and other gangsters that he later complained that Senator Kefauver "ruined my social life."

During this time, however, he continued to study music composition with the hope of one day composing distinctively American music. But this, he explains, was very difficult to do in the Twenties. His friend George Gershwin held out a hope, as did Aaron Copland, but, he says,

American music itself was in complete disrepute. It is questionable, indeed, if disrepute is the right word—there was no public awareness that such music existed. From time to time and for purely chauvinistic reasons, some pseudo-American work might be produced for a Washington's Birthday or an Independence Day program, but it was, invariably, ideologically hyphenated: German-American, as in the case of Chadwick and Hadley, Scandinavian-American, as MacDowell's, French-American (Loeffler and Griffes), and even in the lighter species, Irish-German-American, as Victor Herbert's.

(He tells us elsewhere his opinion of Herbert. When a publisher asked him whether he could be induced to write a biography of Herbert, he replied, "Write one? I couldn't even read one.")

There were no important critics, he says, to promote the cause of young composers like Carl Ruggles or Henry Cowell or Edgar Varèse. Many of these young men felt obliged to go abroad to study music and when they returned they were "dislocated." With the exception of Serge Koussevitzky, who, Oscar says, was "unparalleled in the performance of Russian music, whether it is by Mussorgsky, Rimsky-Korsakov, Strauss, Wagner, or Aaron Copland," orchestras did not wish to play their music. The League of Composers, founded by Copland and others in 1923, did something to further American music, but Oscar found the policies of the league impractical. At the American Music Festival at Yaddo in 1932, when Copland spoke to composers of the need to impose a system of fees for performance rights on orchestras, choral organizations, and even recitalists using American material, Oscar found it "paradoxical" that composers should be demanding fees when conductors and audiences did not want to play or hear their music. Although he had been asked to the festival by Copland to play his sonatina for piano, Levant felt like an "interloper from

Broadway." "The air was full of jeers for everything and everyone outside the closed shop of those present," he wrote, and one of the pieces performed, a string quartet by Marc Blitzstein, was made up of slow movements and reminded him of "a meal consisting entirely of stained glass, with different dressings." He abruptly left Yaddo, instructing the cabdriver, "To the next festival, please!"

Levant remained eager to compose and even went so far as to study with Arnold Schoenberg in the Thirties, when Schoenberg was teaching music at UCLA and Levant was visiting Harpo Marx in Hollywood. Schoenberg was haughty, distant. His command of English was imperfect—when Levant told him that the twelve-tone system did not work for him, he responded, "That's the beauty of it—it never works!"—and his life was continually marked by absurd collisions between the customs and manners of Vienna and those of MGM, the Farmer's Market, and Hollywood Boulevard. He allowed himself to be asked by Irving Thalberg to write the music for *The Good Earth,* but when he demanded too much—a colossal fee, together with the understanding that the characters played by Paul Muni and Luise Rainer communicate in the *Sprechgesang* of *Erwartung* and *Pierrot lunaire*—the offer was withdrawn.

When Levant induced Harpo Marx to ask Schoenberg to dinner, he was surprised to find that the other guests were Beatrice Lillie and Fanny Brice. "To make conversation," he writes, "Brice inquired what 'hits' Schoenberg had written; and after dinner she kept coaxing Schoenberg with 'C'mon professor, play us a tune.' I never found out whether she expected him to provide her with a successor to 'My Man' or possibly a comedy song like 'I'm an Indian.' " Oscar felt *déraciné* in Los Angeles, too, especially so when a movie producer announced to him that "the greatest piece of music ever written is *Humoreske,*" or when a woman seated next to him at a dinner party told him: "I prefer your Schnabel to your Beethoven."

Schoenberg was imperious—Oscar calls their relationship "exchanging his ideas with him"—but he also seems to have wanted to help. Levant says that Schoenberg asked him to become his assistant at UCLA, but he refused. When he wrote a string quartet in 1937, Schoenberg tried to interest the conductor Otto Klemperer in it by having it performed in his own house. "The first movement," Levant writes,

> went quite well. After the opening of the second movement, a four-note ostinato, Schoenberg interrupted the players and said to me didactically, "Those four notes should be played by a bassoon." As he had been very aware of the contents of my quartet, this came as an unnecessary intrusion. The performance was aborted by a heated debate about true string writing. Schoenberg pointed out that Mozart's string quartets were unsurpassed in conception—he maintained that the Brahms quartets, although musically beyond cavil, nevertheless were composed for two pianos first, and then transcribed into string writing. These polemics about orchestral composition were further illustrated by Schoenberg's contention that Ravel, who was still alive and had a special fame as a brilliant orchestrator, wrote first for piano and then orchestrated. In the meantime, because of this discussion, my string quartet was completely abandoned.

Schoenberg tried to interest Klemperer in Oscar's work on a second occasion. The conductor was asked to the house of Schoenberg's friend Salka Viertel, and at a prearranged time Schoenberg asked Oscar to play his piano concerto. It was, Oscar writes, "the opportunity that would have meant so much to me." Inexplicably, he says, he sat at the piano and played "When Irish Eyes Are Smiling."

While in Hollywood, Levant tried to make money by writing music for films like *Charlie Chan at the Opera,* but, for reasons he makes clear, he dropped this career very quickly. In the Thirties, he explains, the pay taken home by a composer was determined by the number of minutes of music used by the producer. Film music was written according to unvarying formulas and had to fit into categories like "main titles" or "inserts." Oscar writes that all train music was based on Honegger's *Pacific 231.* Carousel music was derived from the fair scene in Stravinsky's *Petrouchka,* and walks in the garden from Delius. There were, he says, "several species of fog music":

Ordinary fogs were "Ravel-Debussy, with the element of the latter derived from his *Fêtes*" (the muted trumpets); special kinds of fogs, "for prison breaks or bank robberies," draw on "a few of the recondite figurations from Dukas's *L'Apprenti Sorcier.*"

Composers like Alfred Newman, Max Steiner, and Erich Korngold competed to write the most memorable "main titles." These were typically, he writes, "a harp glissando, ascending-scale passages for the violins—fortissimo—as well as for the woodwinds, all topped by a cymbal clash on the first beat, after which, grandiose tuttis." Different composers with entirely different skills and musical knowledge worked on the same films, and often the result made little sense. Levant describes a montage which was supposed to show how a singer (played by Jeanette MacDonald) became a great star by presenting in rapid succession opera bills from Monte Carlo, Berlin, Paris, Budapest, Covent Garden. The musical background, however, contained themes from *The Barber of Seville, Tristan, Don Giovanni,* and *Der Rosenkavalier,* "suggesting that MacDonald could sing anything from Isolde to Violetta, from Rosina to Donna Anna." Again, he says that "it was with more than a slight feeling of surprise that I listened to the pattern of Ravel's 'La Valse' as the background to a brilliant treatment of a Cole Porter song in *Rosalie.*"

Fortunately, Oscar found great success as a concert pianist in the Forties. After Gershwin died in 1937, Levant became widely known as an interpreter of the *Rhapsody in Blue* and the *Concerto in F.* Around this time, too, he was invited to join the "experts" panel on the radio program *Information Please.* He displayed a prodigious knowledge of music and sports, and after some of the jokes he made on the program were reported in the press, he realized that his "impertinence had become a salable product." He suggested to Schoenberg that he write a piano concerto, which the composer (but not Oscar) apparently understood as a commission—Schoenberg, Oscar writes, may have inserted an anagram of Oscar's name in the tone row of the composition. Levant says he did not perform the piece because he wasn't "prepared" for it, but it seems that in the end he did pay for it. He later recorded Schoenberg's *Six Pieces for Piano*, but he was so concerned to play the last chord as Schoenberg had intended—*pianissimo piano*—that no sound emerged at all and the record was never released.

During the late Forties and early Fifties, he found his largest audiences in films, the most famous of which were musicals like *An American in Paris, Rhapsody in Blue, The Band Wagon,* and *The Barkleys of Broadway.* In these and other films he usually played an impudent sidekick of the male lead. These characters conveniently combined the talents Oscar possessed in life. It must be obvious to anyone who saw these films that he had no appreciable talent as an actor. He therefore was usually given only two things to do: play short, spectacular pieces like the *Sabre Dance* and make insulting remarks, most of which he wrote himself. When a girl annoyed him, he would say, "What I like about you is that you are unfettered by the slavery of talent." Or he would tell a rich man what he had said when he was introduced to the banker Eugene Meyer: "I'd like to trade trust funds with you." These characters were so implausible that some of the producers of his movies explained them by saying that he was playing himself.

To keep up with an onerous schedule of movies, concerts, radio programs, he began to take pills, and a little while later, after he suffered a heart attack, he became addicted to phenobarbital and Demerol. His concert career languished. He was increasingly bored by concerts, he writes: "It is not only the same uniform of white tie and tails, the same inadequate instruments, the same unperceptive audiences—but it is the all-embracing boredom of the act." When he was given an unfavorable review by a well-known Chicago music critic, he rang her up and thanked her, saying that he loathed appearing in public and could use her review to cancel the rest of his tour. (He canceled performances so often that he said that he could send out a flyer announcing that he was "open for a limited number of cancellations.") In Washington, he was accused by a local critic of indulging in "impudent raillery" during his performance with some young people sitting in a box.

In the summer of 1952, he lost his coordination during a performance at the Lewisohn Stadium in New York. (He attributed this to "unbearable neurotic hysteria which included a psychogenic paralysis.") Around the same time, he was thrown out of the musicians' union for snubbing its chief, James Petrillo, who wanted him to back the union in a local dispute. The following year he had a nervous breakdown and entered the first of a succession of hospitals and sanitariums. Doctors there made him withdraw from Demerol—synthetic heroin—in solitary confinement; at another hospital, doctors gave him shock treatments to overcome depression. Whenever he was released from one of these hospitals, he would at once start to take drugs again. His wife would implore all the doctors she knew to refuse him prescriptions. But one doctor would call at his house while she was asleep and administer injections of Demerol in his parked car. When she caught him, he claimed that his Hippocratic principles forbade him from refusing the call from someone in need.

In 1956 Oscar was able to return to public life and to appear on a television show in Los Angeles. Before he went on, he writes, he would take "five Dexedrines and—as a balance and check—ten milligrams of Thorazine." Insanely elated, he would insult his sponsors and guests. He was thrown off the program for his comment on the marriage, by a rabbi, of Marilyn Monroe and Arthur Miller. "Now that Marilyn Monroe is kosher," he said, "Arthur Miller can eat her." He then had a second nervous breakdown and did not appear on television until a year and a half later, when he was given his own show, a talk show on which writers and actors and politicians would be interviewed by him and questions from the audience read aloud by his wife. "This is Oscar Levant," he would announce, "who has made insanity America's favorite hobby. My show is now syndicated. It goes to the Menninger Clinic in Topeka, Bellevue in New York, and the psychiatric ward at Mt. Sinai in Los Angeles." He called the show *Disgrace the Nation*.

In his last years, Levant managed to create a ghastly new metier. He had "retired five times"—as a pianist, a composer, a radio and film star, and an author (although he was to write two more books). He now succeeded as a "personality" on television by making jokes about his drug addiction and his declining mental and physical health. In appearances with Jack Paar, Merv Griffin, and other talk-show hosts he presented himself as a Hollywood Philoctetes enumerating the sufferings his talents had imposed on him. In the second and third books he wrote, *The Memoirs of an Amnesiac* and *The Unimportance of Being Oscar,* he wrote more and more about himself and increasingly so in the tone of a nightclub comedian. These later books are little more than compendiums of neurotic one-liners and inconclusive stories about famous people he has known. The theme of self-loathing is the leitmotif. "I've been doing archaeological research and have discovered my own remains," he writes, and "the results may be found in the ensuing pages." He "lacks no failing." A weekend with him, he says, causes neurosis in others. Recording machines hang up on him. When asked as a child what he wanted to be when he grew up, he replied, "an orphan." Nightclub jokes crowd the pages of these books. Zsa Zsa Gabor's "conversation is faster than her mind." He knew Doris Day "before she became a virgin." Leonard Bernstein "uses music as an accompaniment to his conducting."

Like the creator of a television situation comedy, he develops in his last books a series of skits about his home life. He says that he sleeps twenty hours a day and never leaves the bedroom, where he reads the London *Observer* and succeeded in discovering the origin of the expression "fudge" in Disraeli's "Remarks on the Navy." He indulges in mock hatred of his wife, who keeps drugs from him. She poisoned one of his daughters against him, he writes, by writing nasty notes and swallowing them during pregnancy. The secret of his marriage, he says, is that "neither of us can stand me." (All marriage, in any case, is "a triumph of habit over hatred.") He is enslaved by complicated rules and prohibitions. He admits, for example, that

"I never smoke a cigarette when there is a commercial with an umbrella in a closed room."

These rites and superstitions seemed to have become so demanding and complicated that he barely had time for his family, not to mention his work. He will not allow a lemon on his table, he writes, and has become frightened by "the bottled anger and rapelike aggressiveness of Coca-Cola." Dressing and preparing for sleep each has numerological significance. When he enters his bathroom, "I put the index fingers of both hands on the slit of the door and silently count to eight. I repeat this once more. On my exit, I also do this twice." When he takes off trousers or pajama pants, "the count is eight. But when I lie down on my bed, I lean my head to one side of my pillow and silently count to five twice." When he turns on water faucets, "I tap each faucet with both hands eight times before I draw the water. After I've finished, I tap each of them again eight times. I also recite a silent prayer. It goes: Good luck, bad luck, good luck, Romain Gary, Christopher Isherwood, and Krishna Menon." He realizes these exercises are pure superstition, but he feels comforted by them, and no psychiatrist or psychoanalyst has been able to induce him to surrender them. He even believes there is a reason for him not to give them up. They are, he says, the only physical exercise he takes.

Levant's rudeness was often embarrassing. He was constantly crying out for attention from his wife, his doctors, his critics, his television and film audiences. Yet there was something endearing and honorable about him. He was honest. His self-dislike was the result of measuring himself against a high standard. He knew his musical compositions, for example, had no humor, "no light, no transparency"—and that he had allowed his talents to atrophy. He knew, too, that he had lost interest in whatever profession brought him success. (Success, he explained, made him feel "guilty"—so much so that whenever he watched a courtroom drama on television and the accused was asked to stand, he did so.) Whenever he was contemptuous of others his comments usually carried some point. And when he brought others down with him, they rarely fell as low as he did. He observed that Judy Garland took almost as many pills as he did; if they had married, he said, "she would have given birth to a sleeping pill instead of a child—we could have named it Barb-Iturate." But he was just as hard on himself. It was characteristic of him to cite in one of his books the transcript of an exchange he had with Jack Paar, who asked him, "Did it ever occur to you, dear old friend, that a lot of your trouble or illness may just be in your mind?" He replied, "What a place for it to be!"

Werner Erhard and est

After viewing the discarded crutches, eyeglasses, ear trumpets, and other paraphernalia at Lourdes, Anatole France is said to have inquired: "What—no wooden legs?" One could ask a similar question about the cures promised by most self-help books—of frustrations, bad tempers, unsatisfactory orgasms, migraines, insomnia, and other symptoms of the unhappy mind. Their "rules" for a happier life are generally no more helpful or inspiring to the unhappy man than a diet of tap water to an alcoholic. The writing in most of them, moreover, is appalling: formularized zest, officious enthusiasm, kiddy talk.

Yet these works are some of the places to look if you wish to find expression, however crude, of popular attitudes to classical questions of ethics and human conduct. One might think that trained professional philosophers—many of whose precursors were the first self-help exponents—would take an interest in these books, but professional philosophers and self-help authors usually occupy noncommunicating compartments. Philosophers tend to see themselves as on a frontier of thought; if their work makes "progress" in their field, they think, it will sooner or later filter down to the multitude. Self-help writers, in turn, usually try to point to practical results of their ideas. They no longer seek or even welcome, if they once did, the cooperation of philosophers and turn for approval instead to athletes and film stars.

The result of all this is disconcerting: philosophers in effect abandon the field of popular philosophical discussion to irresponsible simplifiers; conversely, the latter proceed with ever-increasing confidence but without the benefit of rigorous criticism. Perhaps the last exemplar in this country of a great philosopher who discussed self-help methods with care was William James, who once expressed the hope that philosophy would get as close to problems of life as realistic novels. Of course, it may be argued that no other man of such distinction has lent his support to such undistinguished currents of thought. The content of self-help literature, after all, has not changed much since the nineteenth-century evangelical "mind-cure" movements James discussed with such naive sympathy. These movements promoted "fore-thought vs. fear-thought," urged us to "get in tune with the infinite," or (the counsel of the "Don't worry!" sect) to repeat while dressing for the day the words "Youth, Health, Vigor!"

At first, then, it seems fortunate that William Warren Bartley III should have chosen to record and appraise the life and work of Werner Erhard, founder of one of the more successful self-help trainings, est (erhard seminars training).[1] Bartley's lucid and penetrating work in philosophy and the history of ideas has advanced our understanding, especially of the work of the philosopher Karl Popper and the influence of the Vienna School reform movement of the 1920s on the "middle" Wittgenstein, and he would seem an ideally judicious interpreter. Unfortunately, as we shall see, Bartley leaves behind his philosophical training when addressing problems that challenge the coher-

---

[1]William Warren Bartley III, *Werner Erhard: The Transformation of a Man, The Founding of est* (New York: Clarkson N. Potter, 1979).

ence or worth of est. But the book is nevertheless instructive. It is also attractively written, never shrill or unduly proselytizing, and it avoids the hysteria and tribalism that usually accompany the early years of movements like est.

The book is at once a biography of Erhard and an account of the history of his ideas up to the present state. Its subject is indeed, to use Bartley's word, "improbable." A self-confessed impostor and liar, Erhard is a former car salesman and business executive. He was born in Philadelphia in 1935. In 1960 he left his wife and their four children and changed his name from Jack Rosenberg to Jack Frost, then to his present one, a compound of the first name of the German physicist Heisenberg and the last name of the ex-chancellor. "Appropriating" someone else's car and securing new driver's licenses for himself and a girlfriend (who had also changed her name), he headed with her for the West Coast. There he worked for the sales department of a magazine and organized, among other things, an all-woman sales staff.

To augment his knowledge of business motivation, he took up what he called "disciplines": the self-image psychocybernetics of the plastic surgeon Maxwell Maltz, hypnosis, "the familiar mind over matter experiments—the control of pain and bleeding, telepathy, those things." He also became interested in "human potential" psychologies, "abilitism," the martial arts, Zen (under the tutelage of Alan Watts), gestalt and encounter training. At one time, Erhard has claimed (in a grotesque formulation), he was "into von Neumann and Einstein." The Dale Carnegie course, with its charm school elocution lessons, captured him in 1967; he learned there that he "had no problem turning other people on."

But Erhard had in addition to these "disciplines" the advantage of periodic revelations. On a beach at Atlantic City, of all places, he "became the universe." Later, like Moses, he had some "conversations with God." Finally, on a freeway in California—"somewhere between Corte Madera and the Golden Gate Bridge," Bartley adds portentously—he became "transformed." In Erhard's words this event did not happen in time and space. . . . What happened had no form. . . . I realized that I knew nothing—I realized that I knew everything. All the things that I had ever heard and read, and all those hours of practice, suddenly fell into place. . . . I saw that there were no hidden meanings, that everything was just the way it is, and that I was already all right. . . . It *was* all right; it always had been all right; it always would be all right—no matter what happened. I didn't just think this: suddenly I *knew* it. . . . I no longer thought of myself as the person named Werner Erhard. . . . There was no longer any need to try to be Werner Erhard and not to be Jack Rosenberg.

After this convulsive experience, Erhard began "est," bringing together his calling to "transform" others and his considerable business skills. At last, Bartley concludes in his picaresque narrative, "Werner" had become a "complete" human being.

Bartley's account of the est training and theory may be summed up briefly. The training is not so much a therapy as "a contribution to the ecology of consciousness." It is "a new form of participatory theater" that incorporates Socratic method, which he describes as "the artful interrogation that is midwife at the birth of consciousness." Lasting sixty hours and costing about $300, the training begins when one submits oneself to the instructions and questioning of a Socratic trainer; est early earned a reputation as "no piss training" since you cannot go to the bathroom (or, for that matter, eat or sleep) unless the trainer says so. The aim of the training is to cultivate "aliveness" and capacity for "experience" by leading you through a "process" whereby a "siege" is laid on what est calls "Mind."

To est, Mind is "uncorrected cybernetic machinery," a self-perpetuating "program"; it is unfree, for it is "attached" or "positional." It promotes a "life plan" indicating how one's energies are to be distributed, and is enslaved by fixed beliefs and values. Mind only makes you become more and more what you always have been. "Re-programming" Mind by changing fixed beliefs and plans cannot produce what est wants for you: You might become a better plumber or a more famous singer, but you will not be "satisfied." Satisfaction can come only through a "transcendence" of Mind, a face-lift of the spirit, and to set up the conditions under which this upheaval can occur is the point of the training. By transcending or "confronting" Mind, you are ready to face the radical choice whether or not to "identify with Self," whether or not to be "transformed."

But what is "Self"? It is something abstract, neither mine nor yours, the source of change, the part of us that is free (although it is strictly speaking no *part* of us). "If you come from the Self," if you create in yourself what happened to Erhard on the freeway, you become "complete"; you "get the secret," as Werner says, "that life is already together and what you have to experience is experiencing it being together," that "the striving to put it together is a denial of the truth that is already together and that further striving keeps you from getting it together." Unless you "identify with Self," I heard Erhard say recently in a public appearance, "you don't feel OK inside because you haven't experienced your OKness."

The process of breaking down Mind and Belief—in est jargon, of "*getting* that there's nothing to be got" (so that if you don't "get it," you got it)—is said to be an arduous task, potentially brutal and humiliating; toward the end of the training, Bartley says, the inner life of the trainees may be so disturbed that "their very clothes exude the stench of congested thought." Erhard wants everyone to take the training, and he has begun it in prisons, prepared special versions of it for children, created a complicated network of *après*-est "graduate" events, and sponsored educational programs (such as the Werner Erhard Charitable Foundation). Driving from city to city in a Mercedes with the license plate reading "SO WUT," "Werner" is rapidly expanding his multimillion-dollar consciousness corporation.

There can be no doubt that Erhard is a remarkable man— his mother says "he could sell you City Hall"—or that Bartley is smitten with him. Werner is "the embodiment of American Will," "the Johnny Appleseed of consciousness," "a man who seemed at once like a child, and Merlin-like, an immensely old and wise man." These rubbishy assertions are matched by Erhard's preface to the book, in which he quotes (as does Bartley) a remark from Kierkegaard's *Journals*: "What our age needs is education. And so this is what happened: God chose a man who also needed to be educated, and educated him *privatissime,* so that he might be able to teach others from his own experience." Erhard adds, "And God did take me and educate me—unconventionally and *very* privately." The teaching that resulted from this education is also unconventional and unfortunately often so private as to be unintelligible. As Bartley brings them one by one to our attention, Erhard's numerous dicta—"nationalism, which increases positionality, is an *epistemological* disaster"; "belief is a disease"; "it is a law of mind that you become what you resist"; "I came here because I didn't go to the place next door" (said to his anxious family upon reuniting with them after a twelve-year estrangement), etc.—gradually become almost unendurable. Instead of the rogue genius Bartley takes him to be, he begins to sound and act more like a yogic Felix Krull.

Some people seem to find practical value in the est training.[2] A priest says that after the training "the 'supposed to' is gone from my life. . . . I *got* that I am satisfied with being the way I am." A young graduate is now at last able to let her hair grow naturally. Another graduate says that "I saw that letting go of life, relinquishing control, was the answer." Even young children and teens who have taken the ten-day "live-in" course assume a Merlin-like keenness: an eight-year-old graduate, seeing his mother in an emotional quandary, astonished her by saying, "You're being the victim, Mom." It is claimed that the lives of many people are flooded with sunshine after they have fully digested Werner's claim that "I happen to think you are perfect exactly the way you are."

The question of how to awaken one's energies for facing up to life is logically separable from the question of what to do with them once they are awake and of what, if anything, con-

---

[2]For the following reactions to the est training (and others), see Adelaide Bry, *60 Hours That Transform Your Life* (New York: Harper & Row, 1976).

stitutes improvement or construction. What does one *do* with all this aliveness and enthusiasm? This question is moral: Which direction should I take? Should I try to imitate Jesus or Henry Ford or Lenin? Should I try to master a specific task? Should I try to make money or retreat from the marketplace? Should I go back to sleep?

Est claims only the modest task of waking us up, and to this end weekends with Werner may not be lost. But the theory behind est, the rationale for awakening, seems to me full of illusions. What could possibly be implied by the claim that we are perfect as we are? It seems to imply that once we've had our awakening no further efforts are wanted, no more evidence needs to be accumulated, no intelligent vigilance over our acts, no further choices are required.

All that is needed is that we experience what is already there: "Life," says Werner, "works when you choose what you've got. Actually what you've got is what you chose even if you don't know it. To move on, choose what you've got." But aliveness in itself is certainly no more the aim of life than physical fitness or mental alertness. What of those people who are "experiencing" unavoidable sufferings, diseases, or unhappy love affairs? As an anodyne to the undesirable, est endorses the strange theory—borrowed from Scientology—that if you experience anything deeply enough and re-create it in imagination, it will disappear. If this were so, Werner himself would be plucked out of existence by his more imaginative detractors.

If we are indeed perfect, then "self-help" becomes no more than self-congratulation. It seems that having discovered that no "discipline" worked for him, Erhard concluded that no discipline could work at all. Having discovered that some belief can stiffen into dogmatism, he concluded that all belief is corrupt. He correctly sees that all ordered life and intellectual activity require a "position," a core of perceived truths, but he concludes that Mind (as he defines it) should be "transcended." He thus lapses into that species of philosophical hypochondria that finds safety in the compensatory fantasy of a Big Self outside space and time, a riskless paradise of tranquillity where we are no longer vulnerable. His is not the first fantasy of its kind to have been created, but it is no more logically cogent in Erhard's computer terminology than it is in the far more elevated discourse of the Buddhists or Stoics, Epictetus or Schopenhauer.

Bartley is indeed, as the book jacket declares, a member of the Werner Erhard Charitable Foundation. He does not bother to examine certain important metaphysical questions that naturally arise upon inspection of the est theory of Mind and Self. For example: Mind is personal and unfree. Self is impersonal and free. But if training ideally leads you to decide to "identify with Self," who's the *you* at the moment of choice? If it is the "you" we are all familiar with, who actually exists in space-time, isn't the choice as unfree and out of our control as any other "Mind-state"? If it is the transcendent "Self" that is deciding to identify with itself, then who in particular undertook the training and benefited from it?

Nor does Bartley acknowledge the transparent implication that the est theory has no moral spine. The great moral issue for all those who wish to improve themselves is the discovery of ways of marshaling their capacities, enlarging their sensitivities, and introducing intelligent control, direction, and significance into their lives. Est, on the other hand, substitutes for this work an abusive and upsetting training together with sterile generalities about Perfection and the Self. Morality requires a position, but having a "position" is condemned by est as "coming from the Mind-State." As Bartley reports the est view, "Right action is contextually determined behavior; wrong action is determined by position." "Contextually determined behavior" is behavior that is "appropriate," that "follows the Tao," that does what is "fitting." But what standard governs what is "fitting" when you have to decide, say, whether to go to war or not? The answer is that "any standard of fittingness" is "a recipe for a lie," that "to carry over 'standards of appropriateness' or 'conventions' or 'proprieties' from one moment to another is to fail to complete one moment and to set up a barrier to experiencing the next moment," to "become stuck in a position." "Appropriate action is not doing anything: it is neither submitting nor resisting—nor 'doing nothing' "; "it is just being there."

In other words, whether or not it is murder to boil an egg, say, or immoral to engage in ruthless business competition depends, in est language, "on where you're coming from," the "context" or "situation" as you see it. The rational discipline of criticizing standards, improving techniques of making choices, building a better moral view upon painfully agreed-upon fundamentals—this entire program yields before the Tao, "the demands of the context." One can only wonder how many of Werner Erhard's graduate students know how distant this philosophy is from what was required of him to become the entrepreneur they all admire. Whatever the training many accomplish, the est theory encourages one to become a kind of fool, a Zen harlequin, "nonjudgmental" and nonevaluative, favoring a relativistic stupor over science and argument, cynically distrusting all "abstractions" and general rules, collapsing with self-conscious laughter at double-talk and Oriental riddles.

A final question: How could a highly competent professional philosopher like Bartley fall for this? One possible reason presents itself if we examine the consistent working out of the view of his major philosophical influence, Karl Popper. Although, as we shall see in a later chapter, Popper professes to supply us with a "critical rationalism" that will define the sphere of "objective reason," he ends up by drawing it so narrowly that most of life and nearly all choices of any consequence—moral or otherwise—escape critical control, and we are left to follow our subjective inclinations wherever they lead. Instead of locating features of the surrounding circumstances that could provide a basis for rational criteria of choice (even if dependent on the context) he stands frozen at the crucial point, suffering from logical qualms about "induction."

Perhaps it is a satisfaction to est's devotees—Professor Bartley, Valerie Harper, John Denver, and others—to be able to claim that even the best of modern philosophy has been forced to recognize the truth of ancient relativistic wisdom. If so, this seems to me a preposterous short-cut to self-justification. But Bartley's book best serves to remind us that a professional philosopher who participates in popular discussions of self-help philosophy risks neglecting his responsibilities if he uncritically promotes claptrap solutions like est's to philosophical problems. Bartley's book does far too little to dispel the popular misconception that these problems either are of no importance at all or else can be easily and harmlessly avoided.

Part Two

Sidney Morgenbesser

The philosopher Sidney Morgenbesser once fell into a conversation with a literary critic, greatly respected in his time and now dead, a man who, unlike Morgenbesser, was uneasy about his Jewishness, and who hinted that he preferred not to write or talk much about Jewish matters. After he heard yet another expression of this attitude from the critic at an academic meeting, Morgenbesser paused for a moment, searching for a phrase that would sum up his view of the man, and then said to him, "I see that your motto is 'Incognito ergo sum'!"

The tale reminds one of the analytic cast, the impulse to disembowel bombast, the tendency to disclose serious opinions in indirect, usually jocose, ways, which characterize Morgenbesser's mind. It is perhaps less well known than other stories about him, such as the one about his listening to a linguistic philosopher propound the thesis that double affirmatives are not used as negatives in any known language and piping up from the back of the lecture hall, "Yeah, yeah." It is certainly less well known than Morgenbesser's question to a psychiatrist who had argued at an academic conference that mental disease is a myth: "Doctor, since you don't think there is any mental illness, do you think it's all in the mind?" He once told me that the great problem of the age was the conflict between science and theology, a problem he expressed by the question, "Are there Jews on other planets?"

When I first encountered Morgenbesser in the late Sixties, I knew only somewhat forbidding facts about him, for example, that Bertrand Russell had called him one of the cleverest young men he had met on one of his trips to the United States. Then there were rumors that Morgenbesser had undergone the arduous training necessary to become a rabbi, but, upon passing these tests, had abruptly given up the rabbinate to study philosophy. It was, therefore, a relief to find that there was little intimidating about him when we would occasionally meet in a *Lokal* he found congenial to high philosophical discourse, the fetid center counter of the Chock Full O'Nuts on Broadway at 116th Street, a place he treated in those days as a kind of village café—much as he called the stationer's down the block "the candy store"—and where one could often find him sitting in front of a ziggurat of textbooks, discussing economics, politics, philosophy, and baseball history by turns.

To many of his philosophy students, I am sure, his humor provided a release from the pomposities and stiffness of much of philosophy. At times, his humor seemed almost a way of doing philosophy, as when in those apocalyptic days, he responded to the sharp demand of a student radical whether he believed Mao's Law of Contradiction with the terse "I do and I do not." At all times, Morgenbesser's humor encouraged one to suppose that it was possible to be a philosopher and not become a stuffed shirt or a disembodied idea. For example, I learned early on that Morgenbesser had his own extended family of philosophers. "Hermeneutics," he told me, was his uncle from New Jersey; "Sui Generis" was a celebrated Chinese philosopher with a prolific school. Everyone knew that Gilbert Ryle, in his *Concept of Mind,* had described the Cartesian view of the mind as that of a "ghost in the machine"; for Morgenbesser, a brilliant but dry, hyperprecise logician from Princeton was "the machine in the ghost." Then there was the man whom

Morgenbesser called "the quantum philosopher": "You can't figure out him and his position simultaneously." There were other remarks that endeared Morgenbesser to one. He once told B. F. Skinner that the error of behaviorism is that it assumes "you can't be anthropomorphic about human beings." When he learned that a student, completing her doctoral dissertation under Albert Hofstadter, had complained of writer's block and was advised by Hofstadter to do as he did, "let the material take over" and "do the job for you," Morgenbesser shouted to Hofstadter down a crowded hall, "Albert! I hear you're being written by a book!" When a man on a Long Island beach shouted across to him, "Hey, buddy, what time is it?" he shouted back: "Where I am, or where you are?" And who else would have parodied the vogue of interdisciplinary courses by asking what one could learn from a course in torts and concerti—or by urging that a joint course in philosophy and engineering be offered, entitled "The Abstract and the Concrete." Writers often feel, to invert and transpose a celebrated remark of Cyril Connolly's, that inside every thin article is a fat one wildly signaling to be let out. It might be argued that inside every bit of effective philosophical humor is a thesis that could be expressed in an orderly sequence of paragraphs accompanied by footnotes and references. In a reversal of Wittgenstein's proposal to write a book of philosophy consisting entirely of jokes, a different type of talent could have, no doubt, written many of Morgenbesser's jokes as elaborate articles in philosophical journals.

Morgenbesser's humor does not compete, but coexists, with a profound seriousness about philosophy; indeed, perhaps neither of these two traits could have been refined to the high degree they possess in Morgenbesser without the influence of the other. His seriousness has made him a moral animateur among his students and friends. It is wonderfully displayed in his teaching. Morgenbesser will sit at the end of a seminar table, his glasses posed on the middle of his nose, his hair awry, his hands clutching the sides of his chair, his demeanor alert and restless. A traditional philosophical question will be stated, but, he will ask, is it really a problem in the first place? Why? For whom? At Morgenbesser's hands, philosophical problems rapidly cease to resemble the boxed-off, tidy textbook quandaries familiar to the novice. Rather, they are shown to be open, perhaps permanently so, and bound up with each other in intricate ways. Answers to them are shown to be almost always incomplete and constrained by exceptions, counterexamples, complexities. Indeed, to many the general effect of a Morgenbesser class is that of witnessing the building of an elaborate structure of doubts and complications. A question concerning the "nature" of physical objects—for example, are they solid, substantial entities or merely figments of mental constructions?—will be introduced with the aid of commonsense illustrations; he will then bring to bear a number of traditional views: realist, idealist, subjectivist, "Critical Realist," and so on, comparing and contrasting them all the while. The discussion, though fascinating, can become complicated: A Lockean doctrine of substance, let us say, will be criticized as *seeming* to conflict with some finding of modern science, but then Morgenbesser will argue that it *might* be interpreted so that it does not. A Kantian, he will show, would argue thesis *A* in response to the classical doctrine, and a Jamesian or Bergsonian, thesis *B*; these two views are incompatible, but *some* pragmatists have a modest thesis *C*—which may or may not conflict with *A*—but which is certainly incompatible with view *D,* which Professor *E,* in an article one can for the most part ignore in the current *Journal of Philosophy,* does not see is only *one* interpretation that can be assigned to *A.* After a couple of hours of this, one may no longer know what one believes or believe what one knows. Knots are untied by Morgenbesser, to be sure, but frequently the remaining bits of rope are retied into a new knot before the class is over. No one generates uncertainty about what one believes more skillfully than Morgenbesser: He is a toxic for the intellectually arrogant, a godsend for the constitutionally skeptical. He once told me that he was waiting in line in a *bodega* on the Lower East Side when a furious commotion occurred. The man directly in front of him in the line—a rabbi—was badgering the counterman with a series of questions: "Why did you give me the *right* change? Why didn't you give me the *wrong* change?" The counterman was bewildered at first, but began to conclude that the rabbi thought he was dishonest. When Sidney intervened to avert violence, the rabbi protested that he had done nothing wrong: He was only trying to "teach the value of unexpected questions," he said. Morgenbesser's method of questioning occasionally has a similar effect.

But Morgenbesser is not the Socratic teacher multiplying criticisms and doubts beyond necessity. Nor is he what Sidney Hook once described as Morris R. Cohen's teaching ideal, a "sanitation engineer sent into the world to free students' minds of intellectual rubbish." Though he does not impose upon his students a body of doctrine, he does aim to teach them how to argue; he does convey a body of attitudes, or rather attitudes about attitudes and beliefs, attitudes about how to form—or discard—attitudes and beliefs. He can eviscerate a pupil with a comment like "Your thesis has form but no content." When I first took courses with him, I was warned by well-intentioned senior philosophy students to beware certain telltale signs of impending disaster, to watch in particular for phrases like "Let me see if I understand your thesis." These, I was given to understand, were invariably augurs of a public exhibition, conducted by Morgenbesser, of some poor unfortunate's intellectual annihilation. Was there not some kind of legal redress, I would wonder as I often underwent this kind of trial, to insulate a student from this kind of humiliation? There are several kinds of teacher, and Morgenbesser is among the very few who have compelled many students to think for themselves; he has even succeeded at times in bruising what Veblen called the "trained incapacity" of scholars in the academy.

In and out of the classroom, Morgenbesser is the most distinguishing of men, in the tradition of A. O. Lovejoy and C. D. Broad. He will never be content with a dualism if a septet of distinctions is around, and if one is not around, he can invent it. I do not know how long this has been so, but 7 seems to be his favorite number for enumerating the senses of a term: "There are at least seven things meant by the term 'theory,' " he will say; "May I draw your attention to at least seven senses of the word 'privacy'?" His attachment to the number 7 rivals that of Hegel or Peirce or Vico to the number 3. At a claustrophobic seminar at Columbia—a guest mandarin was present to dissect some conundra—I watched Morgenbesser furiously scribble down the cardinal numbers from 1 to 7 on his commentator's scratch pad; small matter that the speaker had not yet opened his mouth.

This preoccupation with the collection and cross-fertilization of distinctions may have a sevenfold cause. One might be a suspicion that if enough distinctions are drawn, most of the traditional problems of philosophy that once tormented us can be shown to be confused and may therefore subsequently vanish like punctured balloons. But if, as he would say, Morgenbesser ever did believe something like this, I do not think he does so today. Certainly the problems that exercised him the most—the nature of human choice, the freedom of the will, the nature of scientific explanation, and in particular the philosophical problems arising from reflection on the theories and methods of the social sciences—instead of disappearing have been rejuvenated or at any rate kept alive by his scrupulous reformulations of them. If he were to write down his mature reflections on these problems, together with the flotilla of distinctions he has created over the years to express them, I feel sure that those philosophers who herald the imminent "death" of philosophy would be chastened.

Does Morgenbesser have any positive philosophical beliefs and concerns? He will ask you rhetorically, "Do you know how many revolutions in philosophy I have seen?" and then enumerate them like a hotel manager ticking off available rooms in off-season. It is difficult to believe that he has ever been taken in by any specific creed, philosophical or other. He is too incredulous—although he is also skeptical of his skepticism. But he is strongly committed to certain values. He is deeply concerned with social justice, and with the human need to belong to a group and to share values with its members. He strongly believes that philosophy can be an instrument of assistance in clarifying these subjects and practical problems involving them. He frequently comments on political questions and their resolution, and refuses to rule out in principle a dose of "radical," structural, political, and economic change as a solution to persistent social ailments in our society. Perhaps he has had since his youth a fascination with Marxism, but his discussions of this subject today are so full of rococo criticism that no one blames him when he says he has recently had "a declining rate of interest in Marxism." This reminds me, incidentally, of his excellent idea of a lecture devoted to Marx and Spencer. One must imagine a prestigious British university on the first day of term: The musty classroom would gradually fill up, the bell would ring, the idealistic youths would dutifully extract from their satchels their bibliographies on the two thinkers. Then the lecturer, clad in stiff academic gown, would mount the podium and gravely declaim in measured periods: "The store was founded in 1871, when capital was made available to the Marks family through the intercession of a justly renowned financier. . . ."

Morgenbesser is not a systematic philosopher. No one is more aware than he that philosophy is frequently fantasy, indifferent to prosaic fact and intoxicated by the desire to install some one-sided principle as the governing law of the universe. He is not against system in principle, but he has devoted much time to protesting against theorizing and systematizing where it is not necessary. "To explain why a man slipped on a banana peel," he once wrote, "we do not need a general theory of slipping"; in another place he said that "no one thinks that accidents are explained by accidental laws." Furthermore, he thinks that the universe rarely conforms to the sort of simplified theory that philosophers have traditionally constructed; many of our best efforts, he believes, lie in clarifying what we are looking for and why, and in patiently reminding ourselves of the things that may have slipped through the nets of our theories, the exceptions, the multiple "ways" the world can be.

We need, he thinks, to respect the conclusions and methods of the special sciences, to develop careful habits of inference and inquiry—and habits for breaking and remaking these habits should new evidence lead us to question the old ones. Pure reason, the idol of philosophers of centuries past, is likely to get us nowhere.

Morgenbesser is skeptical about many things, but he does not subscribe to the skeptic's quest for uncertainty. Although he does not employ a primitive razor like that of the logical positivists, he does ask us to eschew certain old-fashioned skeptical problems. This is especially true of efforts to provide extensive and indiscriminate justifications of our beliefs and opinions. Reminding us of common sense and ordinary life, he argues that many propositions do not require justification in a great variety of situations. We are certain that there is an Atlantic Ocean; who seriously doubts that they were once younger than they are now, or that they have a mother?

Speaking of mothers, Morgenbesser typically refers to members of his family when reminding us of what we would say and do in ordinary life. I have heard that when he visited Oxford some years ago, his mother became such a familiar hypothetical figure that local philosophers acquired the habit of asking, when interpreting some especially intransigent formulation, "But what would Sidney's mother say?" much as, generations before, Cook Wilson and H. A. Prichard would appeal to the judgment of their postmen and bakers.

It is rewarding to read Morgenbesser's various essays in philosophy, baroque, even forbidding, as they may seem. A first reading generally leaves one with the impression that one has passed through a jungle of distinctions. But a second or third reading reveals a structure and an argument one had not noticed before. In nearly all these essays, some spurious dualism or problem is unmasked or discredited. But Morgenbesser conceives his work not just as clearing away dead wood, or "explaining away," but also as elucidating genuine problems that might be confronted by scientists and others in their continuing inquiries; it is a process of analysis which might just as well be entitled "explaining toward" a more adequate view of the issues. For example, in his article, "The Realist-Instrumentalist Controversy," he attempts to make sense of a conflict that has bedeviled philosophers since the birth of modern science and perhaps before, roughly, whether scientific theories describe entities in the world or are merely devices for calculating observable phenomena. Is this a genuine conflict? Apart from criticizing paradoxical interpretations of realist and instrumentalist theses, Morgenbesser's answer is that the conflict is not between two opposing doctrines, but between approaches that are mutually reinforcing, and it is not unfair to say that the method he employs in reaching this conclusion is one like that of the Scholastics, of discovering the truth by drawing distinctions and assigning everything its proper realm. Along the way he draws many illuminating distinctions, especially concerning the notions of "theory."

Developing points he articulated long before the current vogue for "paradigms" and "research programs," he argues that a central sense of the term "theory" in science refers to "sentences or semi-sentences which indicate the type of laws that [a] given discipline might develop," "sentences which though lawlike do not function as principles from which the relevant laws are to be derived," but with which they are "in accord." For example, the germ theory of disease simply claims that every disease is caused by *some* germ, but doesn't say which; the discovery that tuberculosis is caused by the tubercle bacillus is in "accord" with the germ theory, but does not follow logically from it. These higher-level theories he calls "theories for" a discipline, not theories "in a discipline," and he provides a penetrating discussion of their function in scientific inquiry, a discussion that is still useful as a corrective to some current debates on the subject.

Again, in his "Imperialism: Some Preliminary Distinctions," a paper which originated as a talk before the Society for Philosophy and Public Affairs (of which he was a founding member), he sought to clarify this central concept in political science and economics and to remove some of the "moral confusion" that envelops contemporary discussion in international affairs. Characteristically, he notes that there is no perfectly general theory of imperialism, and no need for one, and that we must distinguish among its many senses if we are to use the term responsibly. As in the paper on realism and instrumentalism, Morgenbesser employs the analytic apparatus and terminology of much contemporary philosophy. But his distinctions are designed not to clear up puzzles, or as exercises in cleverness, or as semantic rules in a "language" of science or politics, but rather, to provide guidance to current investigations and debates among scientists and among politicians and policy-makers.

In other papers, he has written extensively on such questions as whether the concepts and methods of the social sciences resemble, or ought to resemble, those of the natural sciences, whether the aim of the social sciences is to discover laws, whether the central social sciences are reducible to natural ones; he has discussed such topics as the "deductive-nomological" model of scientific explanation, the part played by what he calls lawlike sentences, lawful sentences, and laws in the sciences, and the debate among methodological individualists, proponents of psychologism, and methodological holists in the social sciences. Behind much of this work lies his conviction that philosophical analysis and theory can speak to human questions and that social science might have a part to play in improving our practices and institutions.

For Morgenbesser, science is an activity undertaken by investigators held together by common traditions, interests, and values—a genuine "community"—from which all of us have much to learn about conducting our lives and solving disputes. It is a problem-solving community whose members "share higher-order attitudes about beliefs and attitudes to revise them in light of the objections to them brought by others." Science is "distinguished by cooperative and shared work or at least by institutionalized methods of communication of results and criticism, methods which have resulted not in chaos, but in the miracle of modern science." For him, "it is by using as paradigmatic the techniques that the scientist has institutionalized for the justification of belief that we can suggest techniques for the justification of attitude. And it is by firmly entrenching liberal and democratic habits that we facilitate the functioning of a free society in which science best flourishes."

When questioned on the matter of influences on his thought, Morgenbesser will tell you that the great influences on him have been John Dewey, the prophet Jeremiah, and Joe DiMaggio. As the remark is no doubt intended to suggest, there are tensions in Morgenbesser. One of these is that on the one hand, he does indeed seek to discuss problems and issues that have arisen in actual inquiries that demand clarification; he does want to discuss current problems, for he thinks that philosophy should be an instrument assisting us in criticizing, articulating, clarifying, and supplying alternatives to our current identities, ideologies, and social and political and economic institutions. But on the other hand, there is in him as well a fascination with questions and issues for their own sake, with reflection uninhibited and undisturbed by questions of application. In the latter mood, he has devoted himself to problems that, it can be argued, philosophers like Dewey would not have pursued for five minutes. It is not accidental that the critical influences on Morgenbesser included not only such thinkers as Dewey and Ernest Nagel, but also philosophers as detached from ordinary human problems and life as G. E. Moore and Nelson Goodman.

Morgenbesser may not publish as often as some other philosophers, but he certainly does talk a good deal, and he attends numerous academic conferences—even though, as he will tell you, he is a follower of Heraclitus and will not step into the same conference twice. It is in his talk that Morgenbesser's influence has been felt most—an influence that is never adequately conveyed in lists of academic degrees and honors. His metier is the disciplined conversation, disciplined especially, since it must be onerous for this most spontaneously amusing of men to resist painting the dull truth in exciting but misleading pigments. But there is a stabilizing sobriety that lies behind his mercurial surface: Seriousness and a caution that is sometimes mistaken for procrastination define his intellectual tone as much as do his puns and flights of fantasy.

There are some facts about Sidney Morgenbesser I shall claim to know in the commonsense fashion celebrated by G. E. Moore. He is suffused with a love of philosophy; it is not merely a game or a profession for him. He is a man of decency and sweetness. He has a Protean capacity for imaginative sympathetic understanding and identification, and is drawn to people and ideas of every variety. He has helped many students, friends, and colleagues by offering them his ideas, his books, his advice, and his professional and moral guidance. He is not in the least self-dramatizing or eccentric. One might be tempted to say that he recalls Spinoza, the saintly Jewish bachelor, but this would be pitifully unjust to Morgenbesser's contumacious sportiveness, which allows him to do what Spinoza never did, philosophize and yet avoid the usual transformation of the philosopher into a walking theorem. Sidney Morgenbesser, I must own, somehow reminds me of a combination of Spinoza and the late Groucho Marx. The metaphysician or psychologist may judge for himself the likelihood of such a combination. I can only assert that it has been embodied for over threescore years in a man who haunts the "candy stores" of Morningside Heights.

Isaiah Berlin

Edmund Wilson once described Isaiah Berlin as "an extraordinary Oxford don, who left Russia at the age of eight and has a sort of double Russian-and-British personality. The combination is uncanny but fascinating." But even these words from such a usually restrained source fail to do justice to the variety of gifts of this civilized and widely admired man who at one time or another has been a philosopher, a political theorist, an acute practical analyst of American and European politics, a historian of ideas, a biographer of Marx and translator of Turgenev, an active and influential participant in Jewish affairs, a longtime director of the Royal Opera House, a founder of Wolfson College at Oxford, and President of the British Academy. Those who have been in his presence have witnessed his intellectual gaiety; he is a learned and justly celebrated conversationalist, a man who enlarges the lives of his colleagues, his students, his friends.

The four volumes of Isaiah Berlin's collected essays and other writings that have appeared under the editorship of Henry

This essay was co-written with Sidney Morgenbesser.

111

Hardy should dispel the persistent myth that he has not found much time for scholarly writing among his many activities and that his work consists largely of critical and fragmentary occasional pieces that have no collective shape and express no single point of view. Berlin, as these volumes show, is an imaginative philosopher and historian of ideas who has repeatedly reminded us not to underestimate the influence of abstract ideas in human affairs, however harmless such ideas may appear when detached from their historical settings and microscopically analyzed by philosophers. He has reminded us that we cannot live without explaining the world to ourselves; that such explanations always rest on a conception of what is and can be; that whether we know it or not, insofar as we care about ideas at all, we are all participants in debates once familiar only to coteries of intellectuals.

Berlin sees his task as one of contributing to our self-knowledge by exhuming, clarifying, and criticizing the main ideas and values that lie behind our current conceptions of ourselves—of understanding historically whence we came and how we came to be where we are now, thereby diminishing the dangers of being at the mercy of unexamined beliefs. This task requires rare psychological sensitivity, the capacity to enter into the consciousness of men far removed in space and time, and Berlin discharges it with grace and skill in his essays in the history of ideas.[1]

Berlin's portraits of thinkers from Machiavelli to Sorel are neither chronicles nor exegetical exercises; he approaches ideas as incarnated in the men who conceived them; his subjects are never mere vehicles. Berlin is thoroughly at home with ideas in their personal and emotional, social or cultural embodiments—whether his subject is a fanatical reactionary like Joseph de Maistre or a fastidious dandy like Benjamin Disraeli, he manages to achieve an astonishing directness of contact with it.

[1]Isaiah Berlin, *Against the Current: Essays in the History of Ideas* (New York: Viking, 1980).

His intellectual preoccupations and gifts of imaginative reconstruction are brought together in these essays on men who dissented from shallow views of human nature: the ambiguous Machiavelli, the heroic and profound scholar Vico, the celebrated savant Montesquieu, as well as lesser-known men, eccentric fanatics like Georges Sorel and J. G. Hamann, and the gentle visionary Moses Hess. Berlin appreciates how all these men were treated by their contemporaries, more often than not, as "immovable, isolated rocks with their absurd appearance of seeking to arrest or deflect the central current." All of them struggled with, or timidly grasped, or celebrated human freedom and the diversity of human values and patterns of life.

I

According to Isaiah Berlin, one of the deepest assumptions of Western political thought, found in Plato and scarcely questioned since, is "the conviction that there exist true, immutable, universal, timeless objective values, valid for all men, everywhere, at all times; that these values are at least in principle realizable, whether or not human beings are, or have been, or even will be, capable of realizing them on earth; that these values form a coherent system, a harmony which, conceived in social terms, constitutes the perfect society."

We may desire, for example, both expensive missiles to protect "national security" and freedom from burdensome taxation; an excellent secondary educational system for all but not an admissions policy which overlooks merit or the effects of past discrimination; equal rights for all but not unwanted neighbors. These conflicting sentiments are expressions of more abstract values we prize—justice, freedom, happiness, security, loyalty. It is a common conviction (or hope) that these conflicts are apparent, that our various values can be somehow harmoniously realized—or at least ranked in importance—perhaps by the efforts of some especially clever thinker, a politician or religious savior or sociologist, or by the use of some method, scientific or philosophical, or some technological invention.

This conviction is familiar enough, but is it true? Berlin thinks that it is not, and his criticism of it is expressed—as so often in his work—through inspection of the ideas of the historical figures he believes were especially prominent in undermining it. His essay on Machiavelli is an eloquent portrait of a man who questioned this psychologically attractive doctrine in uncompromising fashion. As Berlin claims, "It is this rock, upon which Western beliefs and lives had been founded, that Machiavelli seems, in effect, to have split open."

In Berlin's view Machiavelli's central aim was to provide a set of therapeutic maxims designed to help the statesman in restoring Italy to a position of security and stability, vigor and magnificence, to create "a state conceived after the analogy of Periclean Athens, or Sparta, but above all the Roman Republic." To do so, the statesman must be realistic, "pagan": he must be prepared to use terrible measures to ensure the general good, be willing to kill the innocent to create a show of strength, to deceive and betray and falsify. Once he has embarked on the course of transforming a diseased society, he cannot be squeamish. As Berlin expresses Machiavelli's point,

> to be a physician is to be a professional, ready to burn, to cauterise, to amputate; if that is what the disease requires, then to stop half-way because of personal qualms, or some rule unrelated to your art or technique, is a sign of muddle and weakness, and will always give you the worst of both worlds.

The code of behavior the statesman must apply is not a game of skill unconnected with morality but a new ethic concerned exclusively with the good of all, with public, not personal, morality—and certainly not with the popular Christian personal morality of Machiavelli's time, which dictated humility, kindness, compassion, sanctity, and the quest for salvation in personal life.

Berlin finds much to criticize in Machiavelli's thought: "His human beings have so little inner life or capacity for cooperation or social solidarity that, as in the case of Hobbes's not dissimilar creatures it is difficult to see how they could develop enough reciprocal confidence to create a lasting social whole, even under the perpetual shadow of carefully regulated violence." But Machiavelli's "vision of the great prince playing upon human beings like an instrument" with the aid of a novel morality condoning murder, hypocrisy, and fraudulence raises a disturbing question, which Berlin regards as "the nodal point of Machiavelli's entire conception." Can these different moralities—the public "paganism" of the prince and the personal ethics of the Christian—be held by the same man at the same time?

Berlin believes that Machiavelli rightly held the two moralities to be not merely in practice but in principle incompatible. He thus posed a problem of choice: "One can save one's soul, or one can found or maintain, or serve a great and glorious state; but not always both at once." Two moralities, two sets of virtues, two ethical worlds—with no common ground—are in collision. Each is coherent and integral; we cannot have both. Machiavelli shocked his contemporaries (and many others since) by frankly renouncing Christian morality, but, Berlin claims, he did so "in favor of another system, another moral universe," "a society geared to ends just as ultimate as the Christian faith, a society in which men fight and are ready to die for (public) ends which they pursue for their own sakes."

Machiavelli's problem of choice, Berlin suggests, has outlasted the specific conflict to which it was addressed and lives with us still, not merely in its obvious applications to such questions as the propriety of the conduct of our statesmen, or indeed any officials authorized to protect the public good, but more pervasively, in a wide variety of cases in which he claims we must, like Machiavelli's men, choose between incompatible values.

Suppose, Berlin has asked on another occasion, we were placed in charge of a hospital's supply of kidney machines, costly machines vastly outnumbered by those who suffer from diseases from which they would provide relief: "If there is a great scientist who suffers from a kidney disease, should the only machine we have be reserved for him alone? Should we use the few machines we have only for gifted or important people who, in our view, confer a lot of benefit on society? If some child is dying whom the kidney machine might save, how do we decide between them?"[2] In deciding, should we think only of the happiness of mankind and therefore reserve the machine for the scientist, who is more likely to confer greater benefits on humanity than the child? But then doesn't this clash with the view that all human beings have certain fundamental rights, that we cannot grade lives in importance, that all have an equal claim to be saved? We must decide and yet what are we to do?

Berlin is careful to point out that this kind of conflict is not like the familiar ones we encounter in daily life; it is not like the business of adjusting the demands of work and leisure, or of choosing between a trip to the beach and remaining at home to watch a television program—a conflict that might be removed by a technological innovation (like a television set one could take to the beach). The kind of choice in question is radically unlike that in common speech and thought, where we choose among different courses of action—what school to attend, what stock to invest in—with the help of stable, previously held values and standards: living near our families, getting the best return on our money. Such values serve as a secure basis for determining the merits and demerits of the options.

In the dilemma posed by Machiavelli, we are dealing with a less familiar, more radical, kind of choice: There is no stable background of standards against which we can appraise the alternatives, no common criterion whereby a rational decision between them can be made. There are just the competing alternatives; we must somehow settle for one of them. As Berlin expresses it, such "choices must be made for no better reason than that each value is what it is, and we choose it for what it is, and not because it can be shown on some single scale to be higher than another." No alteration of our circumstances, no

[2]Bryan Magee, ed., *Men of Ideas* (New York: Viking, 1979), p. 31.

new technology or scientific knowledge can remove such conflicts. "Whom shall I save, the scientist or the child?" is not a *fact* to be discovered but requires a decision, a spiritual movement making one moral attitude to the problem *ours*—an "invention," as Berlin puts it, obedient to no preexisting rules. This radical kind of choice can be protracted and painful precisely because it concerns alternatives we care deeply about.

Machiavelli, says Berlin, "helped to cause men to become aware of the necessity of having to make agonizing choices between incompatible alternatives in public and private life (for the two could not, it became obvious, be genuinely kept distinct)." But, as this remark suggests, the "agony of choice" discovered by Machiavelli is double, not single: The moralities of the personal and public spheres of life are distinguishable; and they can collide. But a choice of the one affects the choice of the other. If we must have "dirty hands" in public life, we may find it impossible to remain Christians in personal life; if we are humble seekers of salvation in personal life, we may find it impossible to pursue the realization of the successful state. We are agonized in two ways: We must choose what we are to consider virtuous not merely in the personal sphere, but in the public sphere as well, and these choices may clash.

And of course the same problem of choice arises *within* these spheres in addition to arising between them. We could well be forced, for example, to make the sort of choice described by Machiavelli as a part of public morality—to choose, for example, between values like freedom or security. Is not the man who is troubled whether taxation is compatible with individual liberty concerned with a problem of this kind? As for personal life, do we not face Machiavelli's problem of choosing between incompatible values and ways of life when we ask ourselves whether we should become involved in social issues or "drop out"; whether we should devote our lives to active involvement in a consuming cause or to scholarly research; whether, like

Gauguin, we should dismiss our responsibilities to our family and flee to an undisturbed paradise in order to cultivate our genius?[3]

As Berlin sums up, Machiavelli discovered that "ends equally ultimate, equally sacred, may contradict each other, that entire systems of value may come into collision without possibility of rational arbitration, and that not merely in exceptional circumstances, as a result of abnormality or accident or error—the clash of Antigone and Creon or in the story of Tristan—but (this was surely new) as part of the normal human situation."

If what Machiavelli wrote is true, "the idea of the sole, true, objective, universal human ideal crumbles. The very search for it becomes not merely Utopian in practice, but conceptually incoherent." As Berlin interprets him, Machiavelli planted "a permanent question mark in the path of posterity" by his discovery of the diversity and incompatibility of human values—of "pluralism."

These themes arise again and again, not merely in these essays, but throughout Berlin's work. "If, as I believe," he writes,

> the ends of man are many and not all of them in principle compatible with each other, the possibility of conflict—and of tragedy—can never be wholly eliminated from human life, either personal or social. The necessity of choosing between absolute claims is then an inescapable characteristic of the human condition.[4]

[3]In his essay on Alexander Herzen, but more eloquently in intellectual portraits of Ivan Turgenev and Herzen in his *Russian Thinkers,* Berlin has explored the fascinating ramifications of value conflict in the personal sphere, in the dilemma of the Russian "superfluous men" of the mid-nineteenth century, who could not fit in their society, who lived continually in the shadow of a prodigious decision about what they were to do, to be, to become; or who, like Turgenev, could not "simplify" themselves, who "held everything in solution," remaining outside their cultural situation "in a state of watchful and ironical detachment."

[4]Isaiah Berlin, *Four Essays on Liberty* (Oxford: Oxford University Press, 1969), p. 169.

These contentions are of immense importance for that branch of philosophy called "moral theory," many of whose practitioners continue to seek ways to harmonize or systematically order our deepest values. Berlin nowhere, so far as we know, claims that all systems of this kind are necessarily false. Nor, on the other hand, does he merely assert that some such systems have been false. In agreement with the fundamental insight of Machiavelli, Berlin views conflict among values as a permanent feature of life, which no system or theory is likely to remove.

To reduce such conflict hastily and artificially by logical or theoretical means is for him a species of self-deception that could be dangerous; as he has written, the notion that "it is in principle possible to discover a harmonious pattern in which all values are reconciled . . . seems to me invalid, and at times to have led (and still to lead) to absurdities in theory and barbarous consequences in practice."[5]

II

If the "permanent question mark in the path of posterity" planted by Machiavelli is closely scrutinized, important consequences for our conception of human beings—of "human nature"—seem to follow from it. For example, if it is an "inescapable characteristic" of our lives that we make choices among absolute claims, choices that may have fruitful or ruinous consequences for human life, then must we not in some sense be unconstrained, undetermined, "free"? And if so, then doesn't this indicate an important fact about "human nature," about man and his actions, individual or collective, past or present? Berlin's essays on "The Counter-Enlightenment" and on Giambattista Vico explore the historical growth and consolidation of the "pluralist" insights he commends in Machiavelli as they were extended by other thinkers to address this question.

The eighteenth-century French Enlightenment philosophers —Voltaire, Diderot, Helvétius, Condorcet—further devel-

[5]Ibid.

oped, according to Berlin, the "ancient and almost universal" philosophical doctrine of the harmony of human values by combining it with a theory of human nature and by invoking the promise of new "sciences of man":

> The central doctrines of the progressive French thinkers, whatever their disagreements among themselves, rested on the belief, rooted in the ancient doctrine of natural law, that human nature was fundamentally the same in all times and places; that local and historical variations were unimportant compared with the constant central core in terms of which human beings could be defined as a species, like animals, or plants, or minerals. . . .
>
> It was further believed that methods similar to those of Newtonian physics, which had achieved such triumphs in the realm of inanimate nature, could be applied with equal success to the fields of ethics, politics and human relationships in general, in which little progress had been made; with the corollary that once this had been effected, it would sweep away irrational and oppressive legal systems and economic policies the replacement of which by the rule of reason would rescue men from political and moral injustice and misery and set them on the path of wisdom, happiness, and virtue.

In other words, on this view human nature is fixed and determined; underneath the apparent diversities of men lies an unchanging "nature," endowed with identical needs, motives, values. On this view, Machiavelli must have been in error; ultimate ends could not be in conflict; they are identical throughout the "species" of man, for is it not true that all men seek the satisfaction of hunger and thirst, the realization of security, justice, happiness? If Mongols, Hottentots, and Semites ostensibly differ from Parisians, the Enlightenment thinkers held, the new sciences of man will show this difference to be merely apparent. Human beings can be studied as ants or bees are; what can be applied with success to nature can be applied with equal success to human nature. Everything that exists on this view can be explained and possibly even predicted by general laws.

In opposition to this body of beliefs, a great stream of dis-

sident thought evolved in the late eighteenth and early nineteenth centuries, reaching its most eccentric, angry, and eloquent expression in the work of the German Romantics—
J. G. Hamann, his pupil J. G. Herder, F. H. Jacobi, the *Sturm
und Drang* poets, and their assorted idealist and irrationalist
successors. These men, who form the core of what Berlin calls
the "Counter-Enlightenment," protested the facile transfer of
scientific methods from the inanimate realm to the human:
Could Newton's methods for plotting the movements of the
planets, they asked, explain the efforts of an original artist?
Could mechanics or indeed any general scientific theory offer
understanding of a moral dilemma, the aspirations of those
touched by God, the radical choices performed by the free
and creative self—in short, the complex inner life of the spirit?
In the case of some of the Counter-Enlightenment thinkers,
like the strange Königsberg sage Hamann, the preoccupation
with the inner life led them to demand the total destruction of
Enlightenment values. In his essay on Hamann, Berlin vividly
describes how that thinker violently attacked not merely the
claim that science has something to say about human nature
but its claim to do anything useful at all.

According to Berlin, Hamann saw analysis, classification,
deduction, and system as "infantile" efforts to "confine the
unconfinable"; nature, he thought, could not be caught by the
simple nets laid out by the French and English scientists. Hamann held that only the man who feels and loves, the artist
and the poet, can fully understand nature; that faith in things
unseen was the foundation of true knowledge; art or religion
provide truth, not the "stuffed dummy" called "reason," which
creates foolish rules—"walls of sand built to hold back the
waves of an ocean"—and systems that ignore "the teeming
variety of the living world, the untidy and asymmetrical inner
lives of men, and crush them into conformity for the sake of
some ideological chimera."

Berlin writes, "No system, no elaborate construction of scientific generalities, will, in Hamann's view, enable a man to
understand what is conveyed by a gesture, a look, a style, or

to understand a line of poetry, a painting, a vision, a spiritual condition, an *état d'âme,* a form of life." Hamann's challenge in his fulminations against the Enlightenment was, in Berlin's words, "How dare these pathetic pedants impose on the vast world of continuous, fertile, unpredictable, divine creation their own narrow, desiccated categories?"

Hamann's celebration of natural variety and the free, rich, spontaneous patterns of the will and the inner life was shared by other German Counter-Enlightenment figures—Herder, and later Schelling, the Schlegels, Novalis, Fichte—and indeed artists and thinkers in other countries like Coleridge and Wordsworth, Blake, Chateaubriand, Stendhal and Emerson, Carlyle.

Berlin is sharply aware of the excesses of the Counter-Enlightenment thinkers—their haste, their gross errors of detail, their eccentric prescriptions, their wild mythologies—but he sees in their work sound intuitions, expressed perhaps most fully and coherently by Herder, but anticipated, with far greater force and depth, a half-century before him by the "obscure, poverty-ridden Neapolitan recluse" Giambattista Vico, a lonely professor of rhetoric "who might have had a decisive role in this countermovement if anyone outside his native country had read him."

According to Berlin, Vico was the most powerful of the Counter-Enlightenment thinkers, a man who in a single, complex vision discredited in advance the Enlightenment conceptions of human nature, the perfect society, the progress of humanity, the nature of history, a thinker who has a claim to be the founder of the history of ideas, of comparative cultural history, comparative anthropology, law, religion, aesthetics—indeed, of the modern "social sciences." Vico set in train the idea, as Berlin puts it, that

> history did not consist merely of things and events and their consequences and sequences (including those of human organisms viewed as natural objects) as the external world did; it was the story of human activities, of what men did and thought and suffered, of what they strove for, aimed at, accepted, rejected, conceived, imagined, of what their feelings were directed at.

Vico argued that history is neither a tissue of gossip and travelers' tales (as Descartes had argued a century earlier), nor "a collection of factual beads strung on a chronicler's string," nor (as his younger contemporary Voltaire thought) a disparate mass of instructive and entertaining truths retrieved from the past.

Closely linked to this view of history, Berlin claims, was Vico's bold idea that human nature is not unchanging—as the Enlightenment held, that human nature is not like a fan (or a peacock tail) that opens out over the centuries, showing now one, now another, color, with all its qualities and properties present (but hidden) at the beginning. In place of these views, Vico appealed to a radical new principle, that the "nature" of man is his history. Moreover, for Vico, man's history reveals that human beings have changed over time in vitally important respects: Men were once savage brutes; now they are democrats; but—in his famous "cyclical theory of history"—they will be brutes again.

In Vico's view, shared by Berlin, men have had different values at different times and in different circumstances. They have employed different concepts or categories of interpreting their experience; as these patterns have changed, so have men's reasons for acting, their ruling conceptions of good and evil, happiness and humor, their duties, their song, art, dance. The values men cherish have changed over time, in this view, as the interests, needs, desires in which these values are rooted change, as the ideas men formulate in response to the questions they ask of the world become obsolete.

History, then, for Vico and Berlin, is a process of man's self-creation, a transforming and correcting process; "a changing pattern," Berlin writes, "of great liberating ideas which inevitably turn into suffocating straitjackets, and so stimulate their own destruction by new, emancipating, and at the same time enslaving conceptions."[6] Each integral culture or age generates its own unique mode of expressing its response to the world,

---

[6]Isaiah Berlin, *Vico and Herder* (New York: Viking, 1976), p. 23.

which is intelligible only to those who understand its own internal rules and style. Historical change is a sequence of births and deaths of forms of life, with valuable modes of expression lost irretrievably along the way, with others cropping up continually, not necessarily more valuable than their predecessors: There is no sense, in this view, in speaking of "progress" in history. There is no need to compare and grade on some single scale of merit each cultural phase and its creations and forms of life and action; indeed, it is not possible to do so, for they are evidently "incommensurable."

These pluralist views were remarkably original, as Berlin persuasively argues by comparing them to those of the reigning arbiter of intellectual taste in Vico's time, Voltaire. But Vico also boldly challenged the claim that scientific method as it was conceived in his time could dominate the entire sphere of human knowledge, by asserting that it was not applicable to history and humane studies. As Berlin puts it, Vico thinks that

> to understand history is to understand what men made of the world in which they found themselves, what they demanded of it, what their felt needs, aims, ideals, were: he seeks to discover their vision of it, he asks what wants, what questions, what aspirations determined a society's view of reality; and he thinks that he has created a new method which will reveal to him the categories in terms of which men thought and acted and changed themselves and their worlds.

The "understanding" yielded by Vico's new method is entirely different from that offered by the natural sciences: The new method is not just a matter of raising hypotheses and testing them by simple observation or the use of refined experimental techniques, as geographers or microbiologists or mineralogists do. We have, Vico and Berlin claim, a special relation to the objects of our investigation in the humane studies—in history, literary criticism, political theory, in much of anthropology and sociology, and indeed in much of what passes under the name of "social science." We are, like our subject matter, human;

we can claim the understanding that participants in an activity possess, as observers cannot.

If we are to understand a text, an instance of behavior, a historical event (such as Xerxes' conduct at the Hellespont); if we wish to know why a financial panic took place, why bureaucracy diminishes productivity, why a people rebelled against their authorities; in short, if we wish to understand anything human, we need to do more than exercise our simple perceptions—discriminating differences of pitch and color; we need to do more than examine the physical states of our subjects—their weight, or blood pressure. As Berlin has written, we need also

> the capacity for conceiving more than one way of categorizing reality, like the ability to understand what it is to be an artist, a revolutionary, a traitor, to know what it is to be poor, to wield authority, to be a child, a prisoner, a barbarian.

This capacity, Berlin claims, is distinct from, and possibly more complex than, that exercised by a physicist in gathering observational evidence, or testing a theory, in registering points of light, or tracing the tracks of invisible particles. Unlike "simple" perception grasping empirical facts, this capacity is part imagination, part memory, part intuition, always governed by the conceptual patterns in which we think of other human beings, and never reducible to inductive or deductive rules of scientific research.

In the humane studies, Berlin claims, the understanding of subject matter (and possibly some ways of testing—as against discovering—of hypotheses concerning this subject matter) consists to a large degree in the exercise by investigators of distinctive, imaginative capacities of this kind, capacities—or, as Berlin sometimes calls them, "knacks"—which allow these investigators to enter into the lives and outlook of other human beings and cultures, past and present, to acquire the sense of what "fits" and what does not in an interconnected body of human activities, to acquire the sense of anachronism they employ when, upon reading a passage in Shakespeare, they know straight off that it could not have been composed by a Manchu or a Sumerian.

The investigator using this "new method" is able to obtain an "inner," direct grasp of events akin to self-knowledge because he, like his subjects, is a thinking, planning, acting being. The "knowledge" that results from his efforts

> is quite different from that in which I know that this tree is taller than that. . . . In other words, it is not a form of "knowing that." Nor is it like knowing how to ride a bicycle or to win a battle, or what to do in case of fire, or knowing a man's name, or a poem by heart. That is to say, it is not a form of "knowing how." It is more like the knowledge we claim of a friend, of his character, of his ways of thought and action, a species of its own, based on prior personal experience, memory, imagination, and communication with other human beings.

In *Against the Current* and in the more abstract writings collected in *Concepts and Categories* Berlin claims that the discovery by Vico of this special "mode of perception"—he admits that "knowledge" might be too strong a word for an activity "so obviously fallible" and in need of "empirical research to justify its findings"—marks the discovery of a central difference between the natural sciences (which need not employ it) and the humanities (which inescapably do), and confutes the possibility of a "scientific history."

Is this so? Berlin is, of course, entitled to claim that there may exist *particular* modes or capacities of cognition unique to the humanities. If the historian must understand what it is to be poor, the physicist is not concerned with what it is to be an electron. Still his account may be contested, and not only because he has not, as he acknowledges, explained exactly how people with radically different categories of thought "enter into" and "inwardly grasp" each other's views. (Nor did Vico.) It may be that Berlin is tacitly assuming too superficial a conception of the natural sciences when he draws a sharp distinction between scientific "experience" and that brought into play in humane studies. If recent researches in the philosophy of science by T. S. Kuhn, Karl Popper, and others are correct, even ordinary experimental interpretations in science are laden with preconceptions and categories that may undergo radical change in the course of scientific development. To understand different comprehensive scientific theories or deal with new data, natural scientists might also have to use "the capacity for conceiving more than one way of categorizing reality" and perform efforts of "resurrection" and reconstruction similar to those cited by Berlin as distinctive of humane studies.

If even natural scientists can, and indeed may have to, grasp radically different ways of interpreting the natural world, and if even their observations are "theory laden," the objectivity of science in some of the senses described by Berlin is open to question. Berlin himself in his earlier writings attacked the oversimplified accounts of historical knowledge as objective that were in vogue between the 1930s and the 1950s. It seems ironic that some philosophers would argue that this earlier account could in part be transposed to scientific knowledge as well and thereby challenge some of the distinctions Berlin draws between the natural sciences and the humanities.

The issues are far from settled and often not even clearly understood. Berlin might claim that whatever difficulties there may be in the understanding of new scientific theories they can, once understood, be objectively tested; not so for all theories and hypotheses in the social sciences and humanities. There is much current debate about the kinds of cognitive skills and commitments that are involved in the understanding, testing and accepting of scientific theories and hypotheses. The old empiricist claim that essentially the same methods can be used to test hypotheses in both the natural and social sciences is far from dead.

Whatever the outcome of these debates, it should be clear why the Counter-Enlightenment thinkers, taken together, are of such importance to Berlin. They, more than any other group of thinkers, saw how intellectual confusion can result from the deliberate or unconscious application of scientific (or pseudoscientific) methods and doctrines where they do not apply; and, despite their obvious shortcomings, they clearly saw that scientific methods could not adequately answer fundamental questions about human values. But perhaps even more important, they first set in motion ideas which provided the philosophical underpinning—the reasoned justification—for the facts Berlin claims were pointed out by Machiavelli: If men can choose, by their own lights, among incompatible alternatives, then their behavior could not be explained by appeal to a set of general laws—as some Enlightenment thinkers believed. They could not be the "mechanical" systems Condillac and perhaps in our own day B. F. Skinner take them to be; they could not be like computers or calculators. Their history must be an open process of self-creation, without a large strategy or inevitable trend.

This idea lies at the heart of Berlin's work, and he has often expressed it with eloquence—the idea, as he once put it, that man is

> incapable of self-completion, and therefore never wholly predictable: a fallible, a complex combination of opposites, some reconcilable, others incapable of being resolved or harmonized; unable to cease from his search for truth, happiness, novelty, freedom, but with no guarantee, theological or logical or scientific, of being able to attain them: a free, imperfect being, capable of determining his own destiny in circumstances favorable to the development of his reason and his gifts.[7]

But if human beings are, as the combined insights of Machiavelli and Vico suggest, free, spontaneous, choosing beings, with widely diverse values and cultural embodiments of these values, what political arrangements are best suited to their nature? How ought they to live in political association?

---

[7] *Four Essays on Liberty*, p. 205.

III

Berlin's views on pluralism, the necessity of radical choice, and on human nature interlock in his well-known writings in defense of liberalism, not merely in the essays on nationalism, on Georges Sorel, and on Alexander Herzen in *Against the Current*, but also, and more fully, in his *Four Essays on Liberty*, which is the main subject of *The Idea of Freedom*,[8] a collection of essays by distinguished scholars in honor of Sir Isaiah's seventieth birthday.

As Berlin noted long ago, political ideas always rest on a conception of what man is and can be; the philosophical ideas behind liberal doctrine and practice were, along with more arcane matters, a ground of battle between the Enlightenment and the Counter-Enlightenment. "European liberalism," he wrote, "wears the appearance of a single coherent movement, little altered during almost three centuries, founded upon relatively simple foundations, laid by Locke or Grotius or even Spinoza; stretching back to Erasmus and Montaigne, the Italian Renaissance, Seneca and the Greeks."[9] The demands for tolerance, freedom of speech and thought and assembly, for a minimum amount of liberty to be granted each individual, for the cultivation of choices available to men (as opposed to the coercion of choice), for the divorce of the content of justice from any specific doctrine of goodness—of the Right from the Good—these were the characteristic demands of liberals.

Liberals often also added theories about "natural rights" which were not obviously compatible with the "tentative empiricism," as Berlin puts it, that usually characterized their views. Rational morality, they thought, would secure universal truths and, when combined with acceptable economic theories, would encourage freedom, happiness, economic growth, and the decline of economic misery.

---

[8]Alan Ryan, ed., *The Idea of Freedom: Essays in Honour of Isaiah Berlin* (Oxford: Oxford University Press, 1979).

[9]*Four Essays on Liberty*, p. 8.

But, as Berlin continues this narrative, the nineteenth century saw disturbing developments which led thinkers as different as J. S. Mill and Nietzsche to rethink or modify or reject the simple philosophical underpinnings of liberalism inherited from Condorcet and Helvétius. Such developments included unbridled private enterprise, the rise of industrialization, the appearance of unexpected forms of concentrated political and economic power, the failure of education and legislation to ensure a just social order, the conformism and monotony of modern life. However, as Berlin adds, one antiliberal development "dominated much of the nineteenth century in Europe and was so pervasive, so familiar, that it is only by a conscious effort of the imagination that one can conceive a world in which it played no part." This movement is nationalism, and none of the aforementioned prophets—or their fellow futurologists Tocqueville, Weber, Jakob Burckhardt, Marx, Durkheim— "predicted for it a future in which it would play an even more dominant role."

The great German Counter-Enlightenment philosopher Herder, to whose ideas Berlin has devoted much attention, apparently coined the word "nationalism" and created the notion that "men, if they are to exercise their faculties fully, and so develop into all that they can be, need to belong to identifiable groups, each with its own outlook, style, traditions, historical memories, and language."[10] Like Vico (and, as Berlin's essay in *Against the Current* shows, like Vico's famous French contemporary Montesquieu, who dimly perceived the point), Herder argued against the Enlightenment belief in the unity of man. What Machiavelli had noticed about warring moralities, he said of cultures: They are "comparable but incommensurable," incapable of being arranged on a single scale of progress or retrogression, each having its own style of law, music, dance, gesture, handwriting. Men, he suggested, need to

---

[10] *Vico and Herder,* p. xxxii; for the origin of the word "Nationalismus," see p. 181.

belong to such a culture just as much as they need to eat or sleep. The groups Herder spoke of were not groups of men formed by focusing on attractive features of the world and then inviting others to join in preserving or contemplating them—like a film club or the hypothetical groups we find in some simple theories of social contract. They resembled more a family, or a clan or tribe: Jews, Kurds, Turkomans owe their very sense of identity, on this view, to their membership in their race or tribe; they do not choose to belong to them any more than they choose to love or identify with their parents. Their group values, according to Herder, are neither portable nor exchangable, but unique, historical, irreplaceable. This is why Herder thought imitation or transplantation of alien standards harmful and why he thought nothing more false than the idea—espoused by enlightened and zealous reformers of every age—that members of disparate groups, communities, and cultures could be transported *en masse* to a utopia on the outskirts of civilization, Oneida perhaps, or Red Bank, or Nauvoo, or Jonestown, there to create a politically perfect social mixture. As Berlin quotes him, "whom nature separated by language, customs, character, let no man artificially join together by chemistry."

Yet according to Berlin, Herder was not a "nationalist" in any dangerous sense; he valued, rather, the individuality and diversity of cultures (and thus his own, German, culture). His idea of "belonging" was posed as a social, not a political, idea. Moreover, Berlin claims, Herder believed that different nations or cultures can emerge alongside one another, respecting each other's activities, without engendering conflict; he held a

view of men and society which stressed vitality, movement, change, respects in which individuals or groups differed rather than resembled each other, the charm and value of diversity, uniqueness, individuality, a view which conceived of the world as a garden where each tree, each flower, grows in its own peculiar fashion and incorporates those aspirations which circumstances and its own individual nature have generated, and is not, therefore, to be judged by the patterns and goals of other organisms.

Although these ideas were not justifiable grounds for it, Berlin argues, they were developed into aggressive nationalism by German thinkers as a result of complex factors, among which was unquestionably the wounded collective pride experienced in Germany after the Napoleonic wars. They were distorted into not mere pride of ancestry but a consolidated movement of intolerant chauvinism, led by men in search of a base for power or "a focus for loyalty," and asserting the supremacy of their culture and sensibility. Such movements were to appear again, for example, among the Slavophils in Russia. Eventually they arose in Africa, the Balkans, the Middle East, and Southeast Asia.

Much as he deplores this development and is concerned to know why its rise was unforeseen or treated merely as a symptom of the craving for self-determination that would pass with time and social change, and how its more inflammable forms may be curbed or avoided, Berlin agrees with Herder that eliding or denying the need to be rooted in a particular group robs men of dignity and self-identity. He thinks this is confirmed in the case of Jews by the twisted self-perception of men like Disraeli and the "Jewish self-hatred" of Karl Marx—as his essay comparing "the search for identity" of these two deracinated Jews amply documents.

Berlin also hopes that Herder's idea may be confirmed in a different, more fruitful and tolerant way by the outcome of Zionism, which was virtually invented by another of his subjects, the nineteenth-century "communist rabbi," Moses Hess. In his youth this sensitive and truthful man had held the fashionable and "enlightened" belief that his fellow Jews, having served their historical mission, should "disperse and assimilate." He looked forward to a new, socialist world. As Berlin summarizes his view, "there was no room in the universal society of the future for sectional religions or interests. The Jews must scatter and vanish as a historical entity," suffer a "dignified dissolution." But by middle age, Hess regarded his earlier views as fallacious, arguing that the Jews had a historic task—to unite communism and nationality—and that they must find a homeland. As Berlin quotes him, "You may don a thousand masks, change your name and your religion and your mode of life, creep through the world incognito so that nobody notices you are a Jew," yet "neither reform nor baptism, neither education nor emancipation, will completely open before the Jews of Germany the doors of social life." Instead, the Jews must realize they are a separate nation and try to establish a home on the banks of the Jordan.

Berlin does not pretend to draw the line between beneficial and dangerous expressions of the idea of "belonging" but he sees this as an acutely pertinent question that must be faced for, as he writes, "no political movement today, at any rate outside the Western world, seems likely to succeed unless it allies itself to national sentiment." Nationalism is but one of the movements in the modern world that may endanger the existence or maintenance of liberal societies. To identify such movements, to understand their causes, and perhaps their justifiable ingredients (and to accommodate to these as best one can), to create means for protection from them: these are for Berlin prime responsibilities of the liberal. Indeed, Berlin's more theoretical work on liberalism is a sustained attempt to furnish a more truthful and effective philosophical defense of it. By making this attempt, he hopes the decay of liberal institutions may be stopped rather than unwittingly fostered.

IV

Berlin's most famous contribution to this end has been his effort to clarify or define the concept of liberty itself. Common sense and thought, he wrote in his "Two Concepts of Liberty,"[11] have no single meaning for the term, but there are two central senses of it, which have been distinguished and which he claimed are worthy of further analysis and classification— "negative" and "positive" liberty. "Negative" liberty he characterized very roughly as the absence of interference—by the

[11]Reprinted in *Four Essays on Liberty*.

state, a class, a corporation, or another individual—with what one wishes to do. As he wrote, "political liberty in this sense is simply the area within which a man can act unobstructed by others"; it is often understood as being left alone by others to act as you desire, so that the larger the range of your potential choice, the greater the extent of your "negative liberty." (He has also noted that this is not all that is involved in negative freedom, however. It cannot be *defined* as the lack of obstacles to the fulfillment of your present desires, for this would lead to the consequence that the person who has no desires at all is the freest.) "Positive liberty," on the other hand, is self-realization, bringing into active service our potentials and powers in order to pursue a goal we identify with; it is self-direction, the acquisition of a share in the authority ruling one:

> the "positive" sense of the word "liberty" derives from the wish on the part of the individual to be his own master. I wish my life and decisions to depend on myself, not on external forces of whatever kind. I wish to be the instrument of my own, not of other men's, acts of will. . . . I wish, above all, to be conscious of myself as a thinking, willing, acting being, bearing responsibility for my choices and able to explain them by references to my own ideas and purposes. I feel free to the degree that I believe this to be true, and enslaved to the degree that I am made to realize that it is not.

The distinction between positive and negative liberty is, for Berlin, of crucial importance for theory and practice, even though he writes that "the freedom which consists in being one's own master, and the freedom which consists in not being prevented from choosing as I do by other men, may, on the face of it, seem concepts at no great logical distance from each other—no more than negative and positive ways of saying much the same thing."

"Negative liberty," he thinks, is at least tolerably clear: Although there are of course subtle exceptions, we can tell with relative ease whether a man's actions are physically obstructed by another or by the state, and, perhaps less easily but in general accurately, whether he is being intimidated or threatened or otherwise prevented from doing something he wishes to do by these same agencies. The man may be an illiterate, a pauper, a victim of a crippling disease, a psychotic; he may lack the means, will, knowledge, confidence, to *use* his freedom—he may, in other words, lack what Berlin calls the "conditions of liberty"—but he is free in the "negative" sense if he is not interfered with or can legally regain his freedom if it is infringed. Defenders of negative liberty, he believes, should try to specify the conditions under which we are free to act. Specific desires and preferences should not be brought into the definition of negative liberty—rather, they are best regarded as presupposed by a claim that a person is in fact free; similarly for capacities or powers. This approach comports with common sense. Most of us, for example, are negatively free to walk on our ears or eat books; there is no law prohibiting us from doing these things; yet to be able to do them generally does not count as "freedom" precisely because most people do not have those desires or capacities, and accordingly it does not occur to us to speak of a corresponding freedom.

By contrast, the "positive" concept of liberty is opaque: Whether a man is free in this second sense depends on more than his having "negative liberty," on more than the absence of impediments to his action. But what more? One answer might be: having the right to participate in the sovereign authority. But there are others as well. It could be said that man does not possess "positive freedom" unless he possesses whatever means—money, success, friendship, luck, security—are necessary for him to realize his ambitions, just as it could be said that a man who has a low income, or who has never had a university education, or who has never been psychoanalyzed, is not "free."

Berlin suggests that this "positive" sense of freedom has repeatedly been debased, turned into a denial of present, negative liberty in the name of a "true" or "real" or "ultimate" freedom by specious argument. He agrees that we all wish to realize a variety of values—health, freedom from penury, leisure, wealth—and he shares these values; but he says that nothing good will come of confusing these with liberty. It is easy enough to gather all of these values together and call them "liberty," but we would still have to distinguish between them eventually, and failure to do so only encourages the illusion that they can somehow be combined into a single, coherent pattern.

Moreover, he thinks, we court dangerous consequences in theory and practice if we employ those interpretations of "positive liberty." To use an example of Berlin's, the German philosopher Fichte argued that even though men are in some sense rational, their rationality is often undeveloped; they are not self-directed because they fail to think, to discover their own real desires; they must be educated, as children are, for their own good; they will not recognize the reasons for such education now, but they will later. There are, of course, more recent examples of the same kind of fatal argument: True "freedom" has often been defended by authoritarian regimes both in advanced and developing nations.

Critics such as C. B. Macpherson and Charles Taylor in his essay in *The Idea of Freedom* argue that we do not desire merely freedom from external "obstructions to action." We wish liberty to pursue activities that are significant to us. We may not care much if we are prohibited from driving at 80 miles an hour, but we care deeply if deprived of religious liberty. Taylor also seems to argue that defenders of negative liberty are wrong to believe that people are uniquely privileged to know what is significant for them in ways that others cannot improve upon— in the way, for example, that they are in the best position to know whether they are in pain. If a person is neurotically unhappy or obsessed by emotions such as revenge or spite, his grasp of what is important for him may be so distorted that his freedom is thereby diminished.

We may imagine Berlin's response to such objections: First, it is not true that we desire liberty simply in order to realize ideals we currently have. We might develop new interests and new ideals, and we cherish liberty for allowing us to realize these possible values—which could include having some negative liberties for their own sake. Second, while agreeing that sheer lack of obstruction to our actions by the state is not all we desire, Berlin would add that liberty may very well be a prerequisite for the accomplishment of many of our desires, for example to communicate freely with others and to learn through them about ourselves. And he might argue that although some defenders of negative liberty held the views about self-knowledge that Taylor rightly attacks, he himself does not.[12]

In any case, the central question for the liberal throughout the history of liberalism has been one of how and where the frontiers are to be fixed between individual freedom and state interference. How does Berlin conceive the answer to this question? Is negative freedom (however it is to be precisely defined) for him an absolute value that is to be ensured before any other? Or is it a value among many that must be taken into account in the constitution of a state?

As might be expected from even a cursory knowledge of Berlin's complex conception of human values, one cannot find a simple answer in his work. On the one hand, he sometimes writes as if negative liberty is just one among the many "ultimate" values human beings possess; "positive liberty" is another; none is "absolute" or to be favored over the others; each is an ingredient (and only that) in the pattern of life we desire. This is the pluralism we have seen Berlin praise Machiavelli for discovering: freedom is not the only value human beings have; it is not "superior" to, or more "true" than, other values, such as happiness or loyalty or economic security. "The issue," Berlin writes,

> is more complex and painful. One freedom may abort another;
> one freedom may obstruct or fail to create conditions which make

[12]Other problems about Berlin's distinction between positive and negative liberty have been raised by John Rawls, Ronald Dworkin, and G. MacCallum. Taylor's essay in *The Idea of Freedom* contains useful discussion of various other issues raised by Berlin's distinction.

other freedoms, or a larger degree of freedom, or freedom of more
persons possible; positive and negative freedom may collide. . . .
But beyond all these there is an acuter issue: the paramount need
to satisfy the claims of other, no less ultimate values: justice, happiness, love, the realization of capacities to create new things and
experiences and ideas, the discovery of the truth.[13]

On this view, then, the distribution of these many, competing
values is a matter of balance, of intelligent adjustment, case
by case, as each situation demands, with no guarantee that
each value will be satisfied to the same degree as the others.
This is presumably the reason why Berlin could write that the
New Deal was "the most constructive compromise between
individual liberty and economic security which our time has
witnessed."[14] Even if negative liberty—freedom from interference by others—was lost to some degree under the New Deal
by the rich and by businessmen, the situation as a whole realized
a blend of values which was preferable as a total pattern to
that offered by other blends, such as one which would preserve
existing negative liberties and contain uncontrolled private enterprise and mass unemployment.

On the other hand, Berlin also seems to sympathize with the
position that freedom should be ensured before other social values are. Freedom, he writes, is valuable because, as we saw earlier, "the necessity of choosing between absolute claims is an
inescapable characteristic of the human condition" and is therefore not just a means but an end in itself: "to be free to choose
and not to be chosen for, is an inalienable ingredient in what
makes human beings human"; this fact "underlies both the positive demand to have a voice in the laws and practices of the
society in which one lives, and to be accorded an area, artificially carved out if need be, in which one is one's own master."

If one has less than this amount of freedom from interference
one is "dehumanized": This is a fact, Berlin claims, not perhaps
like a fact that can be verified by observation, but a truth about

[13]*Four Essays on Liberty*, p. vi.
[14]*Four Essays on Liberty*, p. 39.

the concepts and categories we use to interpret the world. Sheer indifference to freedom is not compatible with being human. This conception has not always prevailed—Vico has shown that our concepts and categories of interpretation have changed over time—but it is a fact about how we now happen to conceive the world.[15]

[15]The appreciation of this fact (if it be one) is what lends poignancy to Berlin's more abstract essays on freedom and knowledge, his " 'From Hope and Fear Set Free' " in *Concepts and Categories* (New York: Viking, 1979), and his earlier "Historical Inevitability" (reprinted in *Four Essays on Liberty*). It may be, he says in these works, that our current mode of interpreting the "facts," other persons, the world, is one according to which men are "free"—in some sense of this ambiguous term, he never makes clear exactly which sense—free to form new ideas, to take new paths in life, to make choices among values and forms of life. But, he asks, might not the growth of knowledge change all this?

> If a great advance were made in psycho-physiology, if, let us suppose, a scientific expert were to hand me a sealed envelope, and ask me to note all my experiences—both introspective and others—for a limited period—say half-an-hour—and write them down as accurately as I could; and if I then did this to the best of my ability, and after this opened the envelope and read the account, which turned out to tally to a striking degree with my log-book of my experiences during the last half-hour . . . we should then have to admit, with or without pleasure, that aspects of human behavior which had been believed to be within the area of the agent's free choice turned out to be subject to discovered causal laws.

Indeed, haven't psychology and other social sciences shown us repeatedly that many of the actions we commonly assume to be under our control (or that of our parents, or our statesmen, or other authorities) are in fact owing to heredity or have biological or psychological causes, or are owing to our educational history, or our social and environmental background—at least to a larger degree than we had previously thought? And might it not be that the growth of such knowledge will increase rapidly over time, increase the range of explainable and predictable events taking place in a human being and eventually snuff out entirely our ordinary concept of a "free" agent? Further, Berlin asks, would such discoveries not radically alter our way of approaching the world? Would it not shake our estimation of the worth of political liberty? Or would we trade rational analysis and science for our established convictions and repudiate such knowledge, cease the research that generated it, and reaffirm what is now "common sense"? These are brave and absorbing questions that deserve fuller treatment by contemporary thinkers.

When Berlin speaks in this way, as he does often, it seems he is claiming that freedom is *not* on a par with other values we treasure. On this view, freedom is of prior importance, a more fundamental aspect of humanity; values other than freedom may override freedom only in order to secure greater freedom; the realization of values like happiness, mercy, efficiency could not compensate for the loss of liberty.

In other words, Berlin does not claim that negative liberty in general must be preserved at any cost. His answer to the question of the place of negative liberty in a desirable society seems to be, rather, that at any time *some* negative liberties must be preserved—an example might be the freedom from arbitrary arrest—but that some of these may be overridden for the sake of other, more pressing values. There is no general answer available to the question of which negative liberties should be present at any given time. For example, developing countries that lack productive resources might understandably claim that the negative liberties granted by them to entrepreneurs should differ from those in an advanced country like the United States.

Berlin's view expresses a distrust of general formulas and principles which pretend to offer universal—as opposed to concrete and specific—and final or permanent—as contrasted with temporary and tentative—claims or solutions. None of this implies, however, as some of his critics have urged, that Berlin is an indecisive liberal who distrusts efforts to solve political problems. Berlin is claiming, instead, that different, unpredictable problems arise in different circumstances and at different times and that they demand solutions that are appropriate to their situation; solutions that purport to be permanent and general, he thinks, are rarely "solutions." Each situation, he thinks, calls for its own policy, not the automatic application of abstract "keys" or theoretical principles that are supposed to be "guaranteed" to solve all political problems wherever they arise. Nor does his view entail that no radical or fundamental changes should be undertaken in society. It is of course not clear what the radical's call for "fundamental changes" means; nor does Berlin analyze in detail what he means by a "solution" to a deep human problem. But if Berlin's claim about social and political problems does not exclude the attempt to introduce broad changes in social arrangements, then the issue turns on what concrete information we possess about the political situation under discussion. As such, Berlin's point about the complexity of social problems might be helpfully applied both to the arguments of those who seek "radical" change and of those who seek social reform, and might act as a corrective or an encouragement to both.

V

Still, there are important questions that remain to be answered within the liberal tradition advocated by Berlin. The complex social arrangements of the modern liberal society have often compelled its members to lead unimaginative and mechanical lives, filled with drudgery and monotony. Doesn't such a state of affairs mock liberal ideals? In *Against the Current,* the essay on Georges Sorel discusses a recent thinker—he died in 1922—who closely examined this problem. According to Berlin, Sorel realized that the eighteenth-century confidence in "scientific," rational politics—once a progressive faith used to attack conservatism—had, in his day, itself become the orthodoxy, expressed in the triumph of the technocratic society, with its experts and specialists, in Berlin's phrase its "bureaucratic organization of human lives."

Sorel deplored this development: As Berlin describes him, he loathed the bourgeoisie, the flatness of their lives, their materialism and hedonism; for him they were "squalid earthworms," "sunk in vulgarity and boredom in the midst of mounting affluence." He hated the technological disciplines that were beginning to dominate business and politics in his day, run by narrow specialists and dedicated to adjusting men to the new social order; he felt that humanitarian democracy robbed men of their most distinctive characteristics, their need to express themselves, to rise above the norm, to find dignity in fulfilling work.

The desire to satisfy this need is what Berlin claims underlay Sorel's continuous search for a group, or a class, which would "redeem humanity, or at least France, from mediocrity and decay"—what Berlin points out is now called a "counterculture." The desire drove him, with "the moral fury of perpetual youth," from one extreme to another in the service of this cause. He was successively a Marxist, a Dreyfusard, a royalist, an anti-Dreyfusard, a Bolshevik, and an admirer of Mussolini. He eventually discovered that the proletariat was the only truly creative class of society and thenceforth struggled to formulate the energizing social myth of a general strike that would

> call for the total overthrow of the entire abominable world of calculation, profit and loss, the treatment of human beings and their powers as commodities, as material for bureaucratic manipulation, the world of illusory consensus and social harmony, or economic or sociological experts no matter what master they serve, who treat men as subjects of statistical calculations, malleable "human material, forgetting that behind such statistics there are living human beings."

Although Sorel was largely ignored by the workers, he spoke to them above all of defiance, resistance against devitalizing forces of mechanization and technology, against "those who turned every vital impulse into abstract formulas, Utopian blueprints, learned dust."

Berlin's essay skillfully retrieves Sorel from his reputation as an eccentric, a fanatic, an intellectual misfit; it establishes that Sorel's ideas anticipated those of later men like Franz Fanon and Che Guevara, as well as the disaffected "grimmer dynamiters of the present," that "his words still have power to upset." Berlin has written elsewhere of his own reaction to the social developments denounced by Sorel, which he believes have intensified in the vast totalitarian regimes of our time, as well as in some of the new sovereign states of Africa and Asia, governments that hold that individuals are incapable of making choices, of raising upsetting questions, governments that employ "the calm moral arithmetic of cost effectiveness which liberates decent men from qualms,"[16] and that treat the solitary questioner as "a patient to be cured."[17]

To be sure, Berlin does not condone Sorel's remedy: He is aware that violent means or the loss of existing liberties, or of habits of courtesy and decency, can spoil laudable ends. He is aware that, as he once expressed it,

> a humane cause promoted by means that are too ruthless is in danger of turning into its opposite, liberty into oppression in the name of liberty, equality into a new, self-perpetuating oligarchy to defend equality, justice into crushing of all forms of nonconformity, love of men into hatred of those who oppose brutal methods of achieving it.[18]

We must not, he says, be magnetized to security or to happiness at the expense of existing liberties; we must be tolerant of idiosyncrasy, even inefficiency; we must live with "logically untidy, flexible, and even ambiguous" political adjustments: These will, he says, "always be worth more than the neatest and most delicately fashioned imposed pattern."[19]

Berlin seems to sympathize with the social perceptions of thinkers like Sorel (and Bakunin) who make a devastating case against the miserable lives people are often forced to lead—in spite of their possession of liberty. It is commonly argued that the remedy for such developments lies with government, that private associations will fail to provide solutions. But here Berlin might balk. He deeply fears the mentality that looks to government to solve human problems, and indeed much of his political writing is addressed to the classical question of the individual's rights against the state. The emphasis in the writings of anarchists on achieving desirable social results through cooperation and voluntary means seems more congenial to him

[16]Isaiah Berlin, *Russian Thinkers* (New York: Viking, 1978), p. 300.
[17]See "Political Ideas in the Twentieth Century," in *Four Essays on Liberty*.
[18]*Russian Thinkers*, p. 297.
[19]*Four Essays on Liberty*, p. 40.

than the insights of some socialists and "planners," provided that individual liberties are secure. More generally, greater respect for charity, openness, decency—as against a tradition that views society as "a trading company held together solely by contractual obligations"—might permit, he thinks, the liberal society to remold its institutions so that the continual agony of balance and compromise is lessened. But these will not disappear altogether. We must therefore be prepared to endure the agony of political choice, which, he thinks, is just a special instance of the lesson, sprung upon the Western intellect most vividly by Machiavelli, that in both our personal and social lives, beneath the surface of an apparently clear pattern of moral values lie contradiction, collision, conflict.

This conclusion, as Berlin's essay in *Against the Current* shows, is strikingly like the ideas of that nineteenth-century radical Alexander Herzen, the "Russian Voltaire" as Berlin calls him, the great populist who, twice imprisoned by tsarist authorities, fled Russia in 1847 and spent the rest of his life wandering about Germany, Italy, France, and England, composing sharp analyses of European political affairs in the turbulent years following the revolution of 1848, in journals he founded and subsidized.

As Berlin describes him, Herzen was equipped with unusual independence of mind and an exceptionally keen and self-critical awareness of the twin agonies of choice analyzed by Berlin: He occupied throughout his life a thankless, middle ground of moderation amid the political convulsions surrounding him, and was morally offended by both the callous men to his right and the boorish and hysterical young revolutionaries to his left. He fought all of his life for freedom and yet he permitted himself to wonder whether men, after all, really did want freedom, or whether the men who did were not, in contradiction to his deepest convictions, exceptions in their species, like fish that fly.

His ideas were constantly tested and refined by self-questioning and by events themselves. He consistently believed, as Berlin quotes him, that "art, and the summer lightning of individual happiness" are the "only real goods we have." It is indeed irresistible to compare Herzen and Berlin in a less superficial manner. Both are sharp, urbane, multiply talented writers, "talking" writers resistant to academic classification. Both are highly self-critical, skeptical of their skepticism, combining deep respect for learning and a sense of the great importance of ideas in our lives, with a concern for dignity and decency. Both are thinkers who rest their views on common sense and experience and who are willing to accept the metaphysician's taunt that they are abdicating their responsibilities in favor of "brute facts."

Both fear "the despotism of formulas" and continuously stress the diversity and incompatibility of human values and the inescapable predicament of choosing between them. Both are moralists who openly respect the free play of individual temperament, exuberance, variety, independence, distinction. Both recognize that, as Herzen wrote, "one must open men's eyes, not tear them out," and ask that men be content with piecemeal, fallible, gradual solutions to their most pressing problems and not be fooled by metaphysical nostrums that require brutal methods of social reform.

Indeed, seen in this light, their works—ostensibly those of "foxes" (to use the terminology of Berlin's famous essay on Tolstoy), of marvelously scattered intellects dispensing interesting and informed judgments on unconnected topics—have a striking affinity. An ironist would remark that they are indeed not foxes (who "know many little things") but hedgehogs (who "know one big thing") and the one thing they say again and again is that questions such as "What is *the* goal of life?" or "What is *the* meaning of history?" or "What is *the* best way to live?" can receive no general answer—that is, that there is not, or should not be, any hedgehog's thesis about human affairs to expound.[20]

---

[20]"The Hedgehog and the Fox," in *Russian Thinkers*. For further discussion of the history and meaning of the distinction between hedgehogs and foxes, see our exchange with John S. Bowman, *New York Review of Books,* September 25, 1980, and a letter from Isaiah Berlin, *New York Review of Books,* October 9, 1980.

VI

We have already noted some of Berlin's central points that require further elucidation. In addition, several of his analyses of the freedom and unpredictability of human choice appear to undermine psychological determinism—the view that all our actions can be explained by general laws and information about our desires, preferences, and beliefs. He does not (nor does he intend to) disprove or conclusively refute psychological determinism. But this point is in need of refinement. We may be able to explain one aspect of a person's choice but not another. To take a common example, a young friend may be torn whether to become a poet or a mathematician. We may not be able to explain why our friend chose to become a poet rather than a mathematician, but we can explain why he did not become a clown or a pilot. In view of his background, certain choices were not plausible for him. In his writings Berlin emphasizes freedom, but his view of the interplay between freedom and the conditions that restrain freedom deserves further development.

Another element in his thought that needs clarification concerns the nature of history. Berlin rarely fails to denounce interpretations of history as conforming to laws or rules or inexorable trends; this, he says, would run counter to our view of man as free, creative, and responsible for his actions. Yet when he comments sympathetically on the work of Vico, Berlin himself agrees that history is an account of gradual changes in ideas, ideals, forms of life, and cultures, along with the self-transformation of humanity. History can be understood, he seems to say, as a process of self-correction, for men seek ideas and patterns of life that are adequate to their needs and their dominant questions; when these outlooks begin to collapse, men discard them in favor of better ones. This, he adds, is a fact we can discover with the help of imaginative reconstruction and empathy. How do we reconcile these views? It seems Berlin is not offering us a general theory of history in the sense that Newton offered us a general theory of matter; he is, rather, giving us a picture or general approach to history. The issue of when general pictures (as against theories) of history are acceptable, tenable, or indeed indispensable needs clarifying.

A final issue in Berlin's thought that might be usefully amplified also derives from his discussion of Vico. Berlin agrees with Vico that we can grasp the values of alien cultures with the help of sympathetic imagination. He can be interpreted as suggesting that once we do this, we realize that these values are not random preferences; they are rooted in deep human interests and needs, and expressed in different cultural settings. A theory of ethics based on shifting and often conflicting human interests seems implicit in Berlin's work and might be developed further as an alternative to theories grounded on a fixed or eternal "human nature."

However this may be, we must be grateful to Isaiah Berlin: as a philosopher, for puncturing shallow theories of man that ignore our freedom; as a historian of ideas, for exploring, with resilience, sympathy, and lack of dogmatism, neglected ideas about man, and thereby reanimating misunderstood intellectual undercurrents of the past. In his recent as in his earlier work, Berlin presses home a conception of life that is at once morally invigorating and hopefully true, a view he himself admirably summarized when he once wrote that

> the principal obligation of human beings seems to me to consist in living their lives according to their own lights, and in developing whatever faculties they possess without hurting their neighbors, in realizing themselves in as many directions as freely, variously, and richly as they can, without worrying overmuch whether they are measuring up to the peaks in their own past history, without casting anxious looks to see whether their achievements reach the highest points reached by the genius of their neighbors, nor yet looking at other nations, or wondering whether they are developing precisely as they expect them to develop.[21]

[21]"The Origins of Israel," in Walter Z. Laqueur, ed., *The Middle East in Transition* (London: Routledge & Kegan Paul, 1958).

Karl Popper:
Romantic Rationalist

I

Karl Popper is the author of a striking treatise on scientific method, *The Logic of Scientific Discovery*,[1] as well as the celebrated wartime tract against totalitarianism notorious for its irreverent denunciations of Plato and Hegel, *The Open Society and Its Enemies*. He is an independent, versatile, lucid, and eloquent philosopher, among the most distinguished of contemporary thinkers who have undertaken the task—once a commonplace aspiration among philosophers but currently regarded by most of them as unduly ambitious—of constructing a rational critical system that would illuminate the entire range of human experience—science, art, morality, politics.

Though he has been much honored, his reputation has always

[1]Karl R. Popper, *The Logic of Scientific Discovery* (New York: Basic Books, 1959). A long postscript to this book, written over the past twenty-five years, was published in three volumes in 1982: Karl R. Popper, *Postscript to the Logic of Scientific Discovery*, W. W. Bartley, ed. (London: Rowman and Littlefield, 1982); Vol. I, *Realism and the Aim of Science*; Vol. II, *The Open Universe: An Argument for Indeterminism*; Vol. III, *Quantum Theory and the Schism in Physics*.

been uncertain. Some—and not only philosophers, but scientists, politicians, artists—have professed to find unsurpassed wisdom in his works, while others, no less acute, regard the work as too blunt, oversimplified, audacious, disfigured by blunders, by poor scholarship, and by ungenerous presentations of opponents' positions. For many, Popper's work is the last expression of the neo-Kantian critical rationalism that flourished over a century ago, before skeptical intellects rendered it obsolete.

Popper has been for many years engaged to show through argument and illustration that a pervasive way of thinking about human knowledge should be replaced by what he regards as a more rational and coherent one. What in fact goes on when we come to know a mathematical proof or the chemical composition of a substance or the name of a neighbor? What procedures do we follow, if any? And what, after all, is human knowledge? These questions have led Popper, like so many other philosophers, to the somewhat abstract concerns of the "theory of knowledge" and particularly to the analysis of the methods and aims of science and scientific knowledge, the most successful and reliable knowledge we possess.

A prominent tradition in modern philosophy has held that all of human knowledge is founded or "based" on "experience." As Popper describes one version of this view, the mind at birth is like an empty box. The box has windows or openings—the senses—through which information passes in the form of "ideas," "atomic data," "molecular experiences." These items are pure, and "directly" perceived by us; they form the building blocks or "foundations" of all our knowledge. They "associate" with one another, giving rise to concepts ("swan," "whiteness") and to expectations ("All swans are white"), which are strengthened by repetition of confirming instances; even the most complex, abstract theories of modern physics could be shown by a patient genetic analysis to be "built up" from these humble beginnings.

It is no longer widely held that we *arrive* at hypotheses like "All swans are white" by "abstracting" them from elementary experiences, but nearly every modern philosophy of science has agreed with the box theory that repetition of certain instances somehow supports or *confirms* our hypotheses and raises the degree of rational confidence we may have for claiming them to be true.

This entire view of science, according to Popper, is misconceived. To him it suggests that scientists are engaged in an impossible "quest for certainty." For one thing, it relies on a primitive psychology that supposes that there could be an infallible foundation in experience for human knowledge. Like the pragmatist John Dewey and his own teacher, the psychologist and educational theorist Karl Bühler, Popper believes that in our quest for knowledge there simply are no "secure" starting points that do not have presuppositions; such starting points can be found neither in a priori dogma nor in sense experience: We are, he says, never in a situation prior to all theorizing. Whenever we see or smell or listen, or indeed think at all, we are in a determinate situation comprising prior interests, theories, needs, aims, expectations; the "pure" elementary data of the box theory are figments plucked out of thin air.

Second, Popper thinks that induction is mythical. No one has encountered or inspected all possible polar bears, but judging from the sample we have come across, can't we rationally claim by induction that most polar bears are white? And can't this claim—while of course it cannot ever amount to a proof—be strengthened by seeing more white polar bears? Do we not know generalizations (such as "Most polar bears are white") based on observed instances that are extrapolated to cover unobserved instances in the past and future? And is it not perverse to deny that we rely constantly, in science and in daily life, upon propositions for which the available evidence is not logically conclusive? And is it not perverse to deny that such nondemonstrative evidence can be graded for its probative force? Indeed, don't men's lives depend upon such discrimination in the law?

We have already seen that Popper denies that we generalize from "sensations" or pure "elementary experiences" to the truth of hypotheses like "All swans are white." If by "induction" he meant merely this, most contemporary philosophers would agree with him; for there are no "pure" sensations, and even if there were, they couldn't entail the truth or falsity of a hypothesis. But Popper rejects "induction" in a second sense as well: He denies that we can rationally generalize from any number of *statements* such as "This is a white swan" to claims about the truth or probability of hypotheses such as "All swans are white." Like David Hume, Popper argues that induction (in this latter sense) is not a logical reputable inference: A hundred or a million observed white polar bears provide no decisive reasons for thinking that all polar bears are white; good reasons could only be found by inspecting all polar bears that have existed, exist, or will exist and concluding that each of them is white. There is no "justification" of induction, for all attempted ones end up in an infinite regress or in some a priori dogma. We cannot be sure the future will resemble the past. No matter how many times you have witnessed the rising of the sun, you are not entitled to assume rationally that it will, or even probably will, rise tomorrow; it might explode tonight, or melt, or, for that matter, burst into song. This much can be found in Hume; but unlike Hume, Popper does not claim that induction must therefore be a nonrational habit or custom. He argues the startling and provocative position that induction does not exist and has never been used. We do follow something like a "method" in acquiring knowledge, he says, but it is quite different from induction.

Popper is especially concerned to point out the flaws of the box theory and the belief in induction in the case of science. No scientific theory, he claims, not even the greatest of them, Newton's universal mechanics, has ever been "established" or "verified": After all, if Newton's theory was certain or "inductively proved," how could it have ever been overthrown and superseded by Einstein's theory of relativity? The simple fact, says Popper, is that we cannot "justify" a claim to the truth of *any* empirical hypothesis. Even trite statements like "This is a glass of water" or "This is a polar bear" are unverifiable; indeed, according to Popper, *no positive reasons* can be given for their truth.

Why is this so? The reason is that the words that appear in them, such as "glass" or "water," are in Popper's view "universals"—they depend on definitions that apply to all glasses and all water—and "cannot be correlated with any specific sense-experience. (An 'immediate experience' is *only once* 'immediately given'; it is unique.)"[2] Moreover, these universal items denote "law-like behavior" on the part of the objects they describe, and so "transcend experience": To call something a bear, for example, implies many things that go far beyond what we actually observe, e.g., that it will die, that it will not grow wings, that it was created through sexual reproduction. For this reason, ordinary "observation" statements like "This is a bear" are "soaked in theory" and possess no privileged status as "final" or "ultimate" or as "more certain" than other statements.

Indeed, according to Popper, their epistemic status is no different from that of universal statements like "All polar bears are white," although they are logically simpler. Nevertheless, even though the problem of showing *one* single object to be a polar bear is logically as difficult as showing that all are, Popper asserts that the simpler statements of observation are "easier to test" and might be more likely to be agreed on than other statements. But this is not because experience *proves* them; as he frankly acknowledges, experience can cause or "motivate," us to "accept" or "reject" such statements, but this "acceptance" or "rejection" is logically a "free decision" or "convention." Nothing in life or logic compels us to accept it. So, in effect, according to Popper's view, *all* empirical hypotheses—whether that copper conducts electricity or that this is a pencil—are "conjectural" in the radical sense that we shall never be able to have rational confidence that they are true, let alone "know" them for certain or with probability. Whatever knowledge we have is *permanently* "fallible" and "conjectural," al-

[2]*The Logic of Scientific Discovery*, p. 95.

though most of us would agree to accept some conjectures as more credible than others.

But if this is so, how can we go about trying to secure human knowledge? Popper thinks he has a more rational and coherent answer than "inductivism." We cannot justify a claim that a hypothesis is true, but we can retain both rationality and the empiricist's demand that our knowledge be supported by observation. For while no number of white polar bears could establish or verify the claim that all are white, nevertheless a single polar bear that is *not* white can *falsify* the hypothesis. This inference, he says, is rational (unlike induction) and, moreover, is "based" upon observation—for people might come to "agree" that a particular black polar bear exists.

Popper's description of the "logic" of the natural and social sciences rests upon this logical insight. We need not be disturbed by the loss of induction and the foundations of the box theory, he says: If we wish to seek the truth, then the only rational way of doing so is to do it indirectly. We cannot give any positive reasons for holding our theories to be true or probable. But we can replace justification—the practice of producing valid reasons in favor of the truth of our theories—by rational criticism—the practice of producing valid reasons against them. In science, instead of trying to show how right we are, we should forget about starting points and try to *improve* our current hypotheses, whatever their source. First of all, we should make our ideas logically falsifiable or capable of being criticized. This is something like an intellectual duty of the scientist—a duty, Popper claims, that was not fulfilled by those thinkers like Freud and some followers of Marx who claimed to be "scientific" and yet failed to lay down in advance the conditions under which they would give up such theories as that all dreams are "wish-fulfillments" or that the collapse of capitalism will occur. Second, we should systematically *search for errors* in our theories. We should jump to bold conclusions and then ruthlessly try to overthrow them by tests; this is the rational way by which we might, with luck, learn from our mistakes and draw nearer to the truth.

We will, of course, on this view, never be able to be sure we have *found* the truth. All that we will be able to do is to claim that our theories have *so far* not been falsified by severe tests, that they have withstood our efforts to overthrow them. In other words, the best we can hope for is that we find not positive but "critical" reasons for thinking that our ideas are not true but "preferable" to other theories in the *search* for truth. Popper believes that it is on the basis of such critical reasons that we are convinced, for example, that the Copernican model of the solar system has more truth to it than, say, Aristotle's: our reasons for this conviction, he writes in his *Postscript to the Logic of Scientific Discovery*,

> consist in *the story of the critical discussion,* including the critical evaluation of observations, of all the theories of the solar system since Anaximander, not overlooking Heraclitus' hypotheses that a new sun was born every day, or the cosmologies of Democritus, Plato, Aristotle, Aristarchus, and Ptolemy. It was not so much the accumulation of observations by Tycho as the critical rejection of many conjectures by Kepler, Descartes, and others, culminating in Newton's mechanics and its subsequent critical examination, which ultimately persuaded everybody that a great step had been made towards the truth. This persuasion, this belief, this preference, is reasonable because it is based upon the result of the present state of critical discussion; and a preference for a theory may be called "reasonable" if it is arguable, and if it withstands *searching critical argument*—ingenious attempts to show it is not true, or not nearer to the truth than its competitors.[3]

II

This picture of science as a matter of conjectures and refutations has not been without critics of its own. Falsification as a logical technique among others in science was known to some medieval writers and was stressed at the beginning of our century by the American pragmatist C. S. Peirce. But critics com-

[3]*Realism and the Aim of Science*, p. 59.

plain that Popper not only places too stringent demands on scientists in making their hypotheses falsifiable, but vastly exaggerates the role of falsification in scientific inquiry. He requires that scientists formulate their ideas so that potentially refuting instances be specified *in advance* of testing them; and further, that should the theory be contradicted by results of tests, it should not be rescued by ad hoc hypotheses that do nothing more than account for discrepancies and make no new predictions.

But critics of Popper, such as Anthony O'Hear[4] and T. S. Kuhn, have suggested that many great theories in science, such as Newton's theory of universal gravitation, were not falsifiable in this sense. For one thing, the interpreters of these theories frequently referred to such "ideal" or "limiting" conceptions as "frictionless surfaces," and "perfectly rigid bodies," which are only joined to the materials of actual experiments through long chains of reasoning and subsidiary hypotheses, so that the status of experimental evidence as confirming or refuting such theories is inherently vague. The adverse outcome of tests need not be taken as falsifying them, but rather as clarifying their scope of application.

Second, most important scientific theories are flexible systems of assumptions compatible with a variety of specific formulations: Newton's theory, for example, does not predict observational results unless it is joined with a large number of other assumptions, themselves modifiable; we cannot therefore regard a false prediction as decisively overthrowing the *theory*—as opposed to one of these auxiliary assumptions. If the planet Jupiter were tomorrow to assume a square orbit, we most likely would not condemn Newtonian theory before postulating that some unusual interfering force created the deviation from Jupiter's predicted orbit.

Finally, critics say that the historical behavior of scientists has rarely conformed to Popper's prescribed method; when

[4]Anthony O'Hear, *Karl Popper* (London: Routledge and Kegan Paul, 1980).

theories have gotten into trouble—as Newton's "celestial mechanics" did on more than one occasion—scientists have often invoked ad hoc hypotheses to rescue them. And O'Hear notes, the physicist Pauli "postulated the existence of the neutrino simply to preserve energy conservation in the theory of radioactive nuclear disintegration long before any test was envisaged or there was any theoretical basis for it."

Was it necessarily "wrong" or "irrational" for scientists to behave this way? Such thinkers as Kuhn and Popper's close colleague, the late Imre Lakatos, have claimed it was not: In their view, Popper incorrectly focuses upon the testing of individual theories, whereas in fact what is critical in science is the development of some fundamental insight or "paradigm"— that all things are composed of atoms, that light is a wave phenomenon. According to some of them, the improved expression of such an insight in a *series* of theories is what constitutes most scientific research. Such theories are rarely thought by scientists to be the whole truth in any case—they are called "promising" or "worthy of attention"—so that to try to refute them may be gratuitous.[5]

What testing accomplishes, these writers claim, is to assist us in locating the shortcomings of our ideas and to help us to improve them, so that it may be perfectly "rational" for scientists occasionally to dogmatically set aside apparent falsifications as "anomalies." If they did, the merits of their ideas might never be discovered. Popper's exclusive stress on negative arguments, "counterexamples," and destructive criticism would eliminate, in practice, both the leniency and the useful dogmatism that characterize science.

[5]See, for example, the papers of Kuhn and Lakatos in *Criticism and the Growth of Knowledge,* edited by Lakatos and Alan Musgrave (Cambridge: Cambridge University Press, 1970).

III

Popper's most ferocious critic, his one-time disciple Paul K. Feyerabend, goes much further. He not only argues that most celebrated scientific theories have never been "falsifiable" or "falsified" in the sense Popper prescribes, but also insists that his "criterion" of falsifiability demarcating science from non-science is just a logical toy, one more instance of the depressing attempt on the part of so-called philosophers of science to squeeze and warp the teeming variety of scientific attitudes and inquiries—for example, the different ways in which they appraise evidence—into pointlessly severe logical calculi and formal rules.[6]

According to Feyerabend, a science neither is nor ought to be conducted in accordance with a constitutive method, and scientists and philosophers should adopt a position he entitles "epistemological anarchism." The latter position, he tells us, is superior to any method, with respect to whatever aims scientists may choose.

No methodological rules or standards ought to be adopted by scientists, on Feyerabend's view, for "rules of method" are rarely observed by the best scientists, are frequently not applicable, and, if used, would probably retard the progress of science. This inverts the traditional view that the nature of science can be clarified only by postulating the existence of a method distinctive to it. It is frequently argued that science cannot be understood by its results, since these are frequently revised, and are at any rate impossible to identify as "scientific" without appeal to considerations of how they are accredited by scientists. If we wish to have a clear conception of science at all, it is said by many philosophers of science, we must shift attention from specific provisional results to some more con-

[6]Paul K. Feyerabend, *Against Method* (New York: New Left Books/ Schocken, 1978), from which all the quoted passages in this section of my essay are drawn. See also his *Realism, Rationalism, and Scientific Method* (Philosophical Papers, vol. 1) and *Problems of Empiricism* (Philosophical Papers, vol. 2) (Cambridge: Cambridge University Press, 1981).

stant feature of scientific inquiry. A constitutive method, which is not itself challenged by particular claims but is instead responsible for appraising them, helps us to make sense of the success of science in providing systematic knowledge. Moreover, without a methodological magnet to objectively control the materials of science, it is said, they would fall apart in an incomprehensible disorder.

The important issue, for Feyerabend, is not whether there are or ought to be "rules" governing scientific practices such as performing accurate measurements, staining cells, or calculating trigonometric functions. Rather, what Feyerabend is concerned to repudiate are all attempts to provide a "scientific method" in the minimal sense of a well-defined set of general standards intended to govern the critical *evaluation* of hypotheses as they arise in scientific research. The alleged reasonableness of *any* proposed methodological rule can be defused, he thinks, by demonstrating the rationality of its counterversion—a new rule that recommends a course of action contrary to that proposed by the rule.

We are also told by Feyerabend that great scientists have never felt *constrained* by "rules of method." Fully a fourth of his book *Against Method* is devoted to illustrating how Galileo's defense of the Copernican hypothesis of terrestrial motion "runs counter to almost every methodological rule one might care to think of today." Aristotelians claimed that, if the earth were indeed in motion, a stone dropped from a tower would fall not to its base, which would be carried along with the rest of the earth, but some substantial distance away; since this phenomenon simply does not occur, we may deductively infer that the earth is not whirling in space. Galileo responded, according to Feyerabend, not with effective arguments, but with "tricks, jokes, and *non-sequiturs*"; he "let refuted theories support each other . . . built in this way a new world-view which was only loosely (if at all!) connected with the preceding cosmology (everyday experience included) . . . established fake connections with the perceptual elements of this cosmology . . . replaced old facts by a new type of experience which he

simply *invented* for the purpose of supporting Copernicus."
Indeed, according to Feyerabend, the entire historical transition to the acceptance of the Copernican world picture pro-
ceeded by elaborating an initially absurd idea until it was "rich
enough to provide independent arguments for any particular
part of it."

The "essence of empiricism," Feyerabend says, consists in
the rule that experience must measure the adequacy of proposed theories, and thus conflict with observed "facts" must
be regarded as impugning them. But, Feyerabend claims, this
rule would be reasonable only if our "facts" were unprob-
lematic. Indeed, respect for such "facts" may be utterly
misguided if they are only the calcified residue of older "ideologies": Even our observations may be impregnated by hidden
or forgotten prejudices. The only way we can examine the
assumptions that may poison our evidence is by contrast: "We
need an *external* standard of criticism . . . an entire alternative
world, *we need a dream-world in order to discover the features
of the real world.*" A consistent or "true" empiricism, he concludes, must be pluralistic: The empiricist must "compare ideas
with other ideas rather than with 'experience,' and he must try
to improve rather than discard the views which have failed in
the competition." He must attend closely to views like Voodoo
"which the conceit of ignorance" has already put into "the
dustbin of history," for if "developed," such views might yield
relevant "facts" decisive in refuting other theories. An enlightened empiricism issues in an *"ocean of mutually incompatible
(and perhaps even incommensurable) alternatives,* each single
theory, each fairy tale, each myth that is part of the collection
forcing the others into greater articulation and all of them
contributing, via this process of competition, to the development of our consciousness. Nothing is ever settled."

What are we to make of this? We can admit the restricted
points that *some* "facts" are indeed "soaked" in theory and
that *some* choices of theory have in fact depended upon "cosmological" predilections. But a responsible empiricist will note
that Feyerabend's claim that the violation of even the most

obvious methodological rule is *"absolutely necessary* for the growth of knowledge" is not supported by amassing a few cases where, as a matter of fact, such rules were transgressed *and* progress made; more is required to show that "progress" occurred in these cases, or generally occurs, *only* on the condition that these rules are violated. Moreover, some historians of science do not assent to the historical exegeses that Feyerabend employs to support various "counterrules."[7]

Finally, in discussing "empiricist rules" Feyerabend tends to treat tentative formulations or sketches of rules as unmodifiable pronouncements, collects together philosophical assumptions, principles, and maxims under the rubric "rule," regards faulty applications of a rule as sufficient grounds for rejecting it, and generally fails to observe the distinction between the content of a rule and a specification of the conditions for its intelligent application. To illustrate the last-mentioned point, consider that because "methodologists may point to the importance of falsifications—but they blithely use falsified theories," the empiricist demand that theories be judged by experience is "useless." But the cited consideration does not dispose of the demand. There are a variety of *purposes* (e.g., computational or technological) for which scientists "use" or "accept" theories, and judgments of "irrationality" are likely to misfire unless accompanied by a study of the reasons offered for retaining a theory that has been deemed false at some prior time. Neither does the empiricist demand in question require "instant assessment" of a new theory or specify that *only* "experience" is pertinent to such an assessment. Feyerabend's dismissal of "rigid" methodological rules is neatly balanced by his own rigid conception of the attitudes the scientist brings to bear upon his hypotheses.

[7]Cf. E. McMullin, "A Taxonomy of the Relations between History and Philosophy of Science," in Roger H. Stuewer, ed., *Historical and Philosophical Perspectives of Science*, vol. 5 of Minnesota Studies in the Philosophy of Science (Minneapolis: University of Minnesota Press, 1970). It deserves to be noted, however, that Feyerabend responds to McMullin on special points in the same volume (pp. 85n, 126–27n).

The empiricist will argue that he seeks the *truth*, as embodied in explanatory laws of nature, whereas Feyerabend's pluralism, though it pretends to be an improved empiricism, voids this very aim. If it is indeed true that our observational data are permeated by unknown hypotheses which can be assessed only by constructing a "dream-world" to serve as a "yardstick of criticism," *actual* criticism appealing to this alternative cosmology will possess no force whatsoever unless the alternative has some claim to our belief. But whether this is so can be ascertained only by erecting an alternative to *it,* and so on, ad infinitum. As it stands, our initial cosmology is symmetrically a critical yardstick for the "dream-world," and, however much "self-consciousness" we may develop while engaged in the process of examining it, we should come no closer to progress or truth than if we had adopted it in the first place.

What of Feyerabend's positive view—his "epistemological anarchism"? It rejects, we may recall, *all* methodological constraints upon the activity of the scientist and all "universal standards, universal laws, universal ideas." It does not replace one set of standards by another, but holds that "all methodologies have their limitations and the only 'rule' that survives is 'anything goes.' " Anarchism is neither skepticism nor pluralism, not incompatible with temporary submission to even the most stringent rules. What is distinctive of the anarchist is that he does not *espouse* "rules of method," but respects his own idiosyncrasies and lets his "inclinations go against reason *in any circumstances.*"

Feyerabend argues not only that rules of method are not in fact used by scientists, and that it is a "fact of history" that their violation is necessary for progressive scientific change, but also that "every methodological rule is associated with cosmological assumptions"—assumptions about the world and about human observers of it—"so that using the rule we take it for granted that the assumptions are correct." As these assumptions are typically unknown or resist noncircular test by their associated methods, we cannot be sure that the adoption of a given method is preferable to that of another or to none at all. Accordingly, if we refrain from adopting rules of method we "keep our options open."

Are these acceptable arguments? Feyerabend is right to say that the *use* of a method is bound to some assumptions that are "cosmological" in his sense, and that no one can *guarantee* that any given method is intrinsically superior to another. By avoiding all methods whatsoever and not restricting ourselves in advance, we *might,* as an abstract possibility, be likely to obtain more progress toward a chosen aim than we should by adhering to some given set of rules. If this conclusion is all that is meant by the anarchist thesis, then it is a banal logical possibility. The thesis is meant, however, to assert that "nonmethod" is, *in fact,* more likely to lead to progress than is any "method." But Feyerabend has not "shown" that the transgression of even the most obvious rules of method is "absolutely necessary for the growth of knowledge" nor is his thesis that all methodological rules have *limitations* (insofar as circumstances can be devised in which it might appear reasonable to violate or suspend them) likely to surprise anyone except Feyerabend's largely imaginary "Methodologist" who conceives of rules as immutably formulated, "absolutely binding," and inflexibly enforced. But there is an additional difficulty with Feyerabend's historical evidence if it is employed to supply factual grounds for accepting the anarchist thesis: Why should we be in the least inclined to take this historical material seriously unless we presuppose the falsity of the very thesis in question? For are we not prepared to regard this material (including such commonplaces as the claim that a man called "Galileo" existed) as capable, in principle, of furnishing factual *support* for the anarchist thesis only if the material is not just a jumble of fables but can be shown to meet independent criteria of assessment involving the use of natural laws, testimony, and documentations? And if we all *do* admit this, as I suspect, then we must equally acknowledge our tacit conviction that discovering the truth about past events is *not,* in fact, best conducted by rejecting all rules and standards of evaluation.

Feyerabend's argument is really a form of skepticism. But

to say, as he does, that since all rules are impregnated with cosmological assumptions that *may* be false, we should therefore avoid them altogether, is as sensible as arguing that, because the human preparation of food *can* expose us to noxious germs, we therefore ought never to eat in restaurants. No doubt Feyerabend is right to say that the use of rules takes place against a backdrop of assumptions and that the adoption of some of these rules may inhibit scientific progress. But it is an error to argue that since all rules are subject in principle to revision and none certifiable in advance, we ought to "follow our inclinations" and at no time *espouse* such rules, however much we are permitted to feign or mimic such espousal. One might also point out that human *inclinations* are as theory-soaked as rules of method, and that we should therefore pay no attention to them either. It is also worth remarking that few, if any, scientists believe their results to be secured by vote or, for that matter, by hypnosis, murder, and other possible manifestations of "following one's inclinations." Their generally censorious reaction to those of their colleagues who deliberately falsify or manufacture evidence confirms this. Is it really possible that they all fail to understand the "true" nature of science?

None of Feyerabend's arguments establishes the anarchist thesis, which should not surprise us, insofar as the outstanding obstacle in the way of our endorsing it is that, if it were acceptable on the basis of cogent argumentation, we would possess no means of certifying that it is. For how could we estimate the success or failure of arguments for a conclusion that uproots the very means we could have for making this estimate?

IV

Popper has not spent a great deal of time in rebutting Feyerabend and other critics. He has altered few of the philosophical tenets he first formulated in his twenties and thirties, and has instead vigorously redefended his position and prodigiously extended and generalized his views in a metaphysical world picture unexpected from a philosopher widely thought to confine himself to the narrow ambit of epistemology and the logic of science.

A common misunderstanding of Popper's work should be clarified. His preoccupation with the logic of scientific method and his early association with some members of the Vienna Circle have frequently led readers to link him with logical positivism and a contempt for metaphysics. But in fact Popper has devoted a number of years to outlining a metaphysics of his own, one drawing on evolutionary theory, that depicts the continuity of method between men and other organisms and more generally articulating the place of man and his intellectual products in nature. This vision, he reminds us, is not a scientific theory itself: It is not falsifiable. Popper regards his own "metaphysical" theory and his evolutionary epistemology as "conjectural" in character; while such conjectures are not empirically testable, he claims, they may, like other nontestable and nondemonstrable theories, such as realism and idealism, be helpful to us. Furthermore, they might be arguable.

What is this "vision"? Popper conjectures that "what is true in logic is true in psychology." Induction is logically invalid, does not "exist" in logic and so no one (and no animal) has ever performed one. All organisms, according to Popper's phrase, "from the amoeba to Einstein," are problem solvers who use the method of trial and error. In nature, as Darwin taught, the plural forms of life evolve from a small number of simple forms by virtue of the mechanisms of heredity, variation through mutation, and natural selection. Of course, the lower organisms lack language and cannot formulate their hypotheses and guesses, but even they do something similar to what we do: They carry out "trial" solutions to problems of adaptation and adjustment, and the "errors" in these trials are eliminated by natural selection. As we solve problems of bridge building or scientific explanation, then, so spiders "solve" problems of where to build their webs and bacteria "solve" problems of overcoming antibiotics. Most organisms other than man *incorporate* the "solutions" to the problems confronted by their predecessors in their very anatomical design; they die off when these solutions are no longer successful.

With man, according to Popper's "metaphysical" conjecture, things are different. Our invention and use of language create a new "world," an "ontologically distinct" realm, which he calls "World 3" or the "third world." He thinks that it exists alongside the "first" world of material objects like glasses and polar bears—objects for whose existence, as we have seen, he cannot advance any decisive *empirical* reasons, only a "metaphysical" faith—and the "second" world of purely mental states, feelings, emotions, dispositions to act. The third world is the world of documented theories, problems, errors, standards, rules, values, the world of "objective knowledge"—knowledge that is an *object,* not (as the old "subjectivist" theory held) something that is "in" you or me, or "held" by you or me, or an expression of some mental state like certainty or "justified true belief."

This third world is composed of abstract entities—the discoveries of William Harvey, of Hilbert and Planck and Carnot, the imaginative worlds created by Pope and Swift and Flaubert; it contains the things we argue *about* when we discuss the truth of a prediction about money markets or the future or a political party. It contains the *content,* for example, of the passage in John 6 that Luther and Zwingli argued over, a content that was not identical with either the spoken or the written words used by these men or with their subjective states, a content that is not "subjective knowledge" but a public object. The third world is historical, for the ideas of men have arisen in time; it is also to a considerable degree autonomous, for it contains not only the ideas that men have proposed, but also their interrelationships and unintended consequences. For example, the existence of prime numbers was surely not intended by whoever invented the natural numbers. Indeed, the third world even contains logical truths *about* these unintended products, truths, as Popper says, we can do nothing about, such as the nonexistence of a greatest prime number.

The third world is deeply implicated in the themes of Popper's mature philosophy: For example, he tries to use it to show that violence is not necessary. Unlike animals, he says, we need not die if our theories are refuted, for theories are in the third world, not in our organisms or genetic system. In the democratic and pluralistic "open society" Popper cherishes, criticism of policies and institutions (which are World 3 objects) must therefore be protected and encouraged, and governments can be revised or replaced through critical discussion and without bloodshed, rather as hypotheses are replaced in science. This political system—as contrasted with systems that rely upon uncritical "nonfalsifiable," utopian, revolutionary, "total" blueprints for maintenance or change of the political order—is for Popper the embodiment of critical reason in human affairs.

The third world is even invoked in Popper's embryonic philosophy of art. Just as we must give up the "subjectivist" view that human knowledge is an expression of some interior state, we must resist the theory that art is "self-expression," an overflowing of the contents of the mind onto a medium, paper or canvas or marble, and the language of aesthetic criticism—of "authenticity," "integrity," "sincerity"—that goes with it. All great art, Popper says, is anchored in the third world, in inherited problems and stylistic traditions. "Subjective" artists like Beethoven or Wagner did not regard their art as a means of self-transcendence but as the expression of something "inner" or "private": The attitude of "objective" artists like Bach, on the other hand, conforms to the principle that "the best work in science or in the arts or humanities is done when we forget about ourselves, and concentrate on World 3 issues as much as we possibly can."[8]

But more than this, the third world is connected with Popper's view of the self and human freedom: He believes that our very minds and selves have come into existence in the evolutionary process because of the invention of language. We

---

[8]Fons Elders, ed., *Reflexive Water: The Basic Concerns of Mankind* (London: Souvenir Press, 1974), pp. 103–104 (debate between Sir Karl Popper and Sir John Eccles).

are self-conscious because we have learned language, and our minds are the evolutionary products or vehicles that enable us to grasp the abstract World 3. The *Postscript to the Logic of Scientific Discovery* contains Popper's most ambitious statement of a metaphysics of the universe.[9] Like his theory of the three worlds, which it deepens and refines, this cosmological work defends metaphysical realism against idealism and subjectivism. One long volume of it argues against the intrusion of subjectivism in quantum mechanics. Many paradoxes in the theory of quantum mechanics derive, according to Popper, from the so-called "Copenhagen" interpretation of it promoted by Niels Bohr and his followers. This view holds that Heisenberg's celebrated "uncertainty relations," which follow from the theory, actually set "limits" to our knowledge in the realm of atomic physics because they imply that measurements of an elementary particle (such as an electron) "disturb" it, or "interfere" with it, thus making the measurement "dependent" on the "observer," and rendering objective knowledge of matter impossible.

Popper rejects this view as a species of "subjectivism" and argues that it is based not only on an arrogant suggestion that quantum theory is the last word in atomic theory, but also on a misunderstanding of the essentially statistical character of the theory. According to him, quantum theory is just like any other statistical (but objective) theory in physics: The "uncertainty relations" have nothing more to do with "uncertainty" or "limits of our knowledge" than any other statistical predictions. They show, if anything, the limitations of a probabilistic theory like quantum theory.

But Popper does not contest the "Copenhagen" view of quantum theory as implying that nature is "indeterministic." Indeed, he criticizes several forms of "scientific" determinism—the idea that if we know the present state of the world, all physical events, whether in the past or in the future, can be predicted (or retrodicted) with any desired degree of precision,

---

[9]See note 1, regarding the *Postscript*.

including all the movements of human beings. He advances an array of logical arguments, some of them rather crude but others ingenious, against this famous principle. But his most passionately argued attack on it is based on considerations of human creativity and freedom. It is absurd, he writes, to suppose that "billions of years ago, the elementary particles of World 1 contained the poetry of Homer, the philosophy of Plato, and the symphonies of Beethoven as a seed contains a plant," or that a physicist, by studying the bodies of Mozart and Brahms with meticulous care, could write scores which were not actually written by them, but which would have been had, say, their diet been different.

In Popper's own metaphysical view the universe is "open": It has "pockets" of causality—ranges of events that are fully determined—but also realms that are unpredictable. One important reason for this conclusion, he says, is that human beings have introduced, through World 3, completely novel ideas into the universe, ideas which through human action have made a genuine difference to the course of events. He asks us, however, to distinguish carefully: It is one thing to say that determinism in one or another version is false; it is another to ensure the possibility of human freedom. The denial of determinism is not sufficient to make room for human freedom or creativity, he says, for what "we want to understand is not only how we may act *unpredictably and in a chancelike fashion,* but how can we act *deliberately and rationally,*" how things like plans, purposes, arguments, and decisions can actually bring about modifications in the world. To do so, he continues, we need the extra notion that the world of particles and other material objects is *incomplete,* that it can be influenced by Worlds 2 and 3 and interact with them.

Popper's reflections on quantum theory and indeterminism are woven together in a remarkable "Metaphysical Epilogue," which adumbrates what he calls a "new and promising way of looking at the physical cosmos," a piece of "speculative physics," which, like other research programs in the history of science—like atomism or the unified field theory—is not itself empirically testable, but which might assist scientists in coming up with fruitful ideas. As he explains his "dream program," it is intended to preserve elements of the two views that created a schism in twentieth-century physics: the indeterminism of quantum theory on the one hand, and on the other the aspiration of Einstein and the rest to construct a "unified field theory" in which the opposition between matter and "field" (of force, say, or energy) could be superseded and particles explained as "produced" by properties of fields or interactions between them.

In one interpretation of Einstein's view, matter was a "form" of electrical energy. Popper also seeks a unified field theory, but of a more ambitious variety. For him, the properties of matter—as well as its creation or destruction—might be explained as arising from fields of what he calls "propensities." But whereas earlier theories sought to explain no more than the disposition or propensity of particles to *behave* this way or that, Popper thinks that *all* physical properties of the world— shapes, colors, magnitudes like length or height—are propensities. Particles are just propensities to "realize" this or that behavior. But at the same time they are the result, or "actualization," of *other* propensities that make up the physical world. These propensities or possibilities, moreover, are real, as real as the gravitational forces that lock the planets of the solar system in their orbits, although some of them are unpredictable, "open." Popper only sketches his program, but he claims, or hopes, that if taken up by others, it will help resolve many problems: not only the metaphysical problems of matter and change and space and causation, but also the major difficulties that have been bedeviling quantum mechanics since its inception.

If nothing else, these views will remind readers that Popper differs radically from those logical positivists with whom he is still sometimes identified, who held that nontestable cosmological speculation of this kind is a form of superstition or chicanery, if not simply nonsensical, or who denied that the formulation and preparation of aperçus and insights for testing

is as much a part of science as "testing" them. The emphasis
placed by Popper on human creativity and the constant interaction of the three worlds should also highlight the oddity of
Anthony O'Hear's criticism, suitably accompanied by quotations from Lukăcs, that Popper's third world is an untenable
"reification" of language and criticism and has an "alienating
quality," encouraging in us the idea that human institutions
and human knowledge are governed by "inhuman laws."[10]

V

It is difficult to convey the generosity and sweep of Popper's
ideas—ideas which must have appealed powerfully to the young
English philosophers he encountered when, returning to Europe from New Zealand (where he spent the war years), he
first taught at the London School of Economics students who
had been starved on a diet of logical analysis and problems of
sense perception. A dry catalogue of the errors in Popper cannot communicate the heat of the vision that turned a good
number of these students into disciples and evangelists, into
members of a "Popperian" school, bound to their master by
undeviating loyalty (and subject to expulsion if remiss in this
respect), convinced that he had struck a serious alternative to

[10]It should lead us as well to re-examine the related criticisms, found in
the dark pages of the Frankfurt school, in Adorno and Habermas among
others, that Popper is a "positivist," not perhaps a logical positivist, but
someone who is hostile to theory and speculation, who believes in the "cognitive monopoly" of science and its supreme authority in matters of fact, or
that rationality and knowledge are to be identified with scientific rationality
and scientific knowledge, that all cognitively respectable investigations, whether
in the social or the natural realm, should follow a specific "scientific methodology," and that technological control is the key to scientific success. In
fact, Popper is committed to none of these views. On the question of the
authority, exactitude, and reliability of science, compare Popper's remarks
in his *Realism and the Aim of Science:* "I see science very differently. As to
its authority, or confirmation, or probability, I believe that it is nil; it is all
guesswork." Or: "I hold that science has no certainty, no rational reliability,
no validity, no authority."

certain fundamental beliefs (like induction) woven into the texture of human thought.

Still, there is truth in the widespread impression that something is deeply amiss in Popper's philosophy of science. According to some critics of Popper, what is wrong is that he fails to appreciate how firmly entrenched induction is in our ways of thinking and acting; scientists "need" induction in order to perform actions—such as choosing between competing scientific theories—that arise in ordinary scientific research. And in any case, they say, Popper himself cannot do without induction. For if we take him at his word, he is left with no resources for establishing reasons for rational choices between theories in science—indeed, with no good reasons for our "embarking on the scientific adventure," as he defines it. Such reasons could only arise from the admission of some determinate link between failed refutations, or "corroboration," on the one hand and truth on the other. When the full implications of Popper's rejection of induction are digested, we see that he is in fact committed to an unacceptable skepticism—a skepticism that Popper tries again and again to escape, sometimes by coming perilously close to admitting to the existence of induction after all.

This is true as far as it goes, but it does not go far enough. It does not really take Popper seriously enough. He is, as he writes, not interested in doing justice to "inductive intuitions"; he states again and again that induction is a myth; he is trying to *replace* our "inductive intuitions" with a different view of human knowledge and scientific method that dispenses with induction entirely. The problem is not just that Popper's alternative way may offend common sense and the requirements of action, and that his argument would be better off if an element of induction were admitted into it. It is that he has not offered a coherent alternative at all. For as he describes science, it is self-defeating to engage in it: If you adopt his description of the aim of science as the truth, it is pointless to pursue his method of conjectures and refutations, for he denies they can arrive at any rational claim to the truth; on the other hand, if you endorse his method, the aim of science, astonishingly enough, has no legitimate connection with scientific research. This is not, perhaps, a logical inconsistency in his thought, but it amounts to something like a practical one.

One way of illustrating this difficulty focuses upon the role of testing in Popper's scientific method. For him, arriving at hypotheses—whether about the symptoms of a disease or voting patterns or astronomy—is a matter that is not susceptible to logical analysis; hypotheses are "free creations," and indeed it does not matter much where they come from. What matters is the "severe" critical controls that are applied to them in the stage of testing. It is these sober efforts that make science rational and distinguish it from pure speculation. They explain, for example, why we in some sense "know" that iron is heavier than water or that air has pressure, and why, on the other hand, we no longer take seriously the views that music has magnetic effects or that disease is a function of a person's "humoral economy." Scientists want to contribute to the "growth of knowledge," by which Popper means not just an aimless proliferation of hypotheses, but the critically controlled transformation of what we currently hold or take for granted—what he calls "background knowledge"—into a new body of conjectures which we hope might be nearer to the truth. Choice on the part of scientists in selecting theories to add to, or subtract from, "background knowledge" is therefore at the heart of Popper's concerns; presumably, these choices can be rational because they are informed by the results of testing and criticism. As he has written, "It is the *growth* of our knowledge, our way of choosing between theories, in a certain problem situation, which makes science rational."[11]

But what exactly do the critical controls amount to, according

[11]Karl Popper, *Conjectures and Refutations: The Growth of Scientific Knowledge* (New York: Harper & Row, 1963), p. 248.

to Popper's noninductive view? If we acknowledge, as he insists we should, that there is no *proof* that we will find the truth, how can they even assist us in searching for the truth? The answer is that they could not amount to very much, since Popper has, in effect, pulled the rug from under our feet. Our tests, he says, can provide no positive reasons for the truth of any of our empirical hypotheses. But neither can they give us worthwhile negative or "critical" reasons: They are simply a report of failed attempts to falsify our ideas and make no reference to how these theories might fare in the future. In neither case can testing—the "rational" element in science—bear upon considerations pertaining to our aim of truth or even something like the truth.

Why, then, should scientists bother to test their hypotheses at all? Why should they, if such tests could never *in principle* provide them with any good reasons for thinking their hypotheses true? Would it not in fact follow that any hypotheses would be *as conjectural after any amount of testing is over* as it was before testing began? And if this is so, what critical controls could govern the so-called "growth of knowledge"— the alteration of the existing or "background" knowledge we currently accept in the search for truth? What considerations could possibly control this alteration? Since background knowledge is "taken for granted" and used to direct and guide future scientific inquiry, how could we ever find good reasons for introducing new hypotheses into background knowledge, and then taking them "for granted"? And if there is no answer to this question, what significant reasons could there possibly be for ever assuming that we have altered background knowledge in a manner favorable to the search for truth? It is amusing to read Popper remark that in his own view the success he happens to believe science has enjoyed in the past is "miraculously improbable, and therefore inexplicable."[12]

---

[12]Karl Popper, *Objective Knowledge: An Evolutionary Approach* (New York: Oxford University Press, 1972), p. 28.

It might be said, however, that Popper does provide something like critical checks in science insofar as our tests, while they cannot help us in detecting the truth, might yet decisively knock out or falsify many of our hypotheses. After all, finding a black polar bear *does* refute "All polar bears are white."

But even this modest claim is undermined by Popper's own view, for the same difficulty about testing we just examined breaks out when we consider the statements that falsify theories. It is formally correct to say that the statement "This is a black polar bear" falsifies "All polar bears are white." But then the latter statement also falsifies the former; logically, all we know is that the two clash. The issue turns on the claim that we have *found* a black polar bear. After seeing such a bear, most of us would no doubt say that our experiences have given us some reason for making such a claim.

But as I explained earlier, Popper does not hold this view. For him, "This is a black polar bear" is impossible to justify; it implies a vast number of testable consequences that "transcend" all observational experience. The word "bear" is a construction intended to apply to all bears; it is not derived from direct experience. While the "acceptance" of its use might be caused or "motivated" by experience, it cannot be justified by it—"no more than by thumping the table."[13] According to Popper, all we can do with any such statement is to "decide" whether to "agree" to accept it: "From a logical point of view, the testing of a theory depends upon basic statements whose acceptance or rejection, in its turn, depends upon our *decisions*. Thus it is *decisions* which settle the fate of theories."[14] And these decisions are "free," ungrounded, and ungroundable in any decisive positive or negative reasons. "The acceptance of a refutation is nearly as risky as the tentative adoption of a hypothesis: it is the acceptance of a conjecture."[15]

[13] *The Logic of Scientific Discovery*, p. 105.
[14] Ibid., p. 108.
[15] Karl Popper, *Unended Quest: An Intellectual Autobiography* (La Salle, Ill.: Open Court, 1976), p. 99.

But we are once more in a bind: If what Popper says is true, if even banal elementary statements of observation like "This is a glass" are unjustifiable, so that experience provides *no good reasons* for claiming them to be true, why should scientists make observations at all? Especially if they are interested in the *truths* that falsify hypotheses? How *could* rejection of theories as "falsified" be critically controlled on the basis of these "free decisions"?

It would seem, then, that the rational element in science—its critical controls and "our way of choosing between theories"—is for Popper entirely detached from the aim of finding the truth about the universe. This is the result of a conflict of doctrines within Popper's own view. If you seek the truth, the ban on induction prevents testing from making any determinate impact on your decisions to alter your "background knowledge" in the search for truth. From the point of view of seeking truth, you might as well just make guesses, since testing can in principle give you no good reasons for thinking you are making progress. On the other hand, if you adopt the *method* prescribed by Popper, you might as well give up the search for truth. If you adopt both Popper's aim and his method, then in practice not only are the "trials" or hypotheses in science "free creations" but so also are the guesses that "weed out errors"—so that all of science consists in "trials." But if this is so, then what of the "critical discussion" of science from Heraclitus to Einstein that Popper claims persuaded people that a "great step had been taken toward the truth"? Is this critical discussion distinguishable from a pointless multiplication or proliferation of guesses, a self-defeating enterprise checked only by the one thing we can be sure of, the inspection of logical relationships between statements?

While Popper can be admired for his stress on the critical nature of tests in science, and for his rejection of crude empiricist psychologies and the search for secure foundations of human knowledge, he has not succeeded in returning satisfactory answers to these simple questions.[16] Insofar as he has addressed them at all,[17] his response is this: Testing is an important critical control on our search for truth because while it is true that failed refutation, or "corroboration," is not a measure or indicator of truth it does indicate how the truth *appears* to us in light of the present discussion; moreover, corroboration—whether of a theory like Newton's or of a statement like "This is a glass of water"—does provide good reasons not for the truth of these hypotheses, but for a *preference* for one of them in the *search* for truth. It provides "logically inconclusive reasons," that is to say, "for *conjecturing* that it is the most truthlike of the hypotheses competing at the time."[18] And this "conjecture" or "preference" is a "guess" of a higher order or level, a "metaconjecture" that the hypothesis is truthlike or that "further tests will not lead to any deviating results."[19]

But this solves precisely nothing. To say that we "prefer" "All polar bears are white" in the search for truth to "Some polar bears are white and some are black" in light of the present discussion just repeats what we already know, that we have not yet "decided" that we have found any black polar bears,

[16]Nor has his most scrupulous and diligent foot soldier; *In Pursuit of Truth,* a collection of essays in honor of Popper's eightieth birthday, contains, together with many sugary and obsequious expressions of praise from far-flung sources (including Isaac Asimov and Helmut Schmidt), a contribution by Professor David Miller which purports to "refute" the major "falsifications of falsificationism." But, as he admits, the essay contains little that is not found in Popper. For the most part, it masterfully disposes (as does Popper) of relatively unimportant objections to falsificationism, and sidesteps the fundamental issues of why, on Popper's paradoxical view of science and its aims, we should bother to start, or stop, testing our hypotheses. Miller triumphantly ends his essay with the standard Popperian "challenge" to critics who do not "see" what he is trying to do, or "understand" him, to try to be more careful and to formulate their criticisms more clearly.

[17]*Objective Knowledge,* Appendix 2.

[18]Ibid., p. 84.

[19]P. A. Schilpp, ed., *The Philosophy of Karl Popper* (La Salle, Ill.: Open Court, 1974), p. 1,114.

and contrary to Popper, does not provide any good reasons even for guessing that it is "the most truthlike of the hypotheses competing" at the present time.

But more disturbing than this, if induction really does not exist—if we cannot rationally rely on inconclusive evidence for our beliefs—*how could* the results of testing provide any good reasons for a "higher-order conjecture"? How could testing provide good reasons for the conjecture that *testing* the proposition "All polar bears are white" will not lead to its falsification in the future? The truth or falsity of this conjecture is given no rational warrant by any of the tests we have performed so far, so why couldn't we have simply made this higher-order guess prior to testing? Why should we test a guess just in order to advance it as a guess all over again? Popper suggests, moreover, that it is rational to act on a well-tested hypothesis or conjecture—to use it—not because there are no reasons for thinking it true but because there are no responses for supposing it is not true. But this is a desperate move. There are, on Popper's skeptical premises, all kinds of reasons for doubting any hypothesis. Why should we accept the higher-order conjecture? Why should we not test *it* in turn?

Popper, in short, claims that there are no good reasons for thinking a theory is true, but that there are nevertheless good "critical" reasons for conjecturing it to be true; but these critical reasons are of no account unless we have some reason for believing that we are thereby getting closer to the truth, and Popper fails to supply us with a good reason for doing so.[20]

[20]Professor David Miller subsequently complained in a letter to the *New York Review of Books* (April 28, 1983) that I was asking "falsificationism" to "justify its own success," a goal that is, in the words of his essay, "utterly pointless." But this was not my intention: No more than Mr. Miller did I demand that Popper's method certify itself, although I also claimed that asking for reasons (not proof) for espousing a method is not "utterly pointless" and that these reasons are not always formal. Indeed, the history of science suggests that our appraisal of methods depends on the extent to which they aid us in our inquiries; as such, our assessment of methods is in part an empirical question. At any rate such an assessment cannot be founded ex-

His "preference" theory covers up with a cloud of words the problem of how testing serves any determinate and rational purpose in his scientific method. The problem is unaffected. That it remains so hints at difficulties relevant not only to his philosophy of science but more generally to his theory of knowledge as a whole, and even to some of his justifications of the open society as a social order designed to promote unfettered criticism, criticism that will encourage in its turn the growth of knowledge and better, more informed decisions concerning the "piecemeal social engineering" that is intended to improve the lot of the citizenry. Why should there be unlimited criticism of this kind if the results are as pointless as we have suggested? At the very least, it is impossible to accept Popper's grotesquely immodest claim to have completed the solution of the philo-

clusively (as Popper's seems to be, despite his celebrated "anti-essentialism") on conformity to principles that are presumed to definitively characterize rationality in all circumstances.

I do not ask that Popper's method be judged against a standard of proof foreign to it, as Miller charges. I claimed that it is internally flawed. Popper attempts to provide a noninductive account of scientific method, which regards the aim of science as the truth. We try to falsify our theories and so get closer to the truth. It makes no sense to engage in it, however, for Popper primarily (though not exclusively) identifies the "critical control" of science— what distinguishes it from myth or magic—as severe and rigorous testing. Yet he also implies that any hypothesis would be as conjectural *after* any amount of testing is completed as it was before such testing began. It is indeed a sobering thought to imagine Mr. Miller addressing the following advice to a scientist: "You have created a hypothesis designed to solve a significant scientific problem. You must now test your idea by trying to falsify it. Induction is nonexistent, and this is the only 'rational' way of trying to get closer to the truth. But you must also be aware that your testing, however prolonged, will never provide you with a scintilla of rational evidence for thinking you are advancing toward, or receding from, the truth, the goal of your inquiry. It cannot even do so for the claim that you have found out your hypothesis is empirically false. Nevertheless you must continue testing. And when you stop testing, remember that your tests will have given you no help in rationally deciding whether your hypothesis is true or not; you must simply guess that it is true, or discard it, because it contradicts some other hypothesis which you have decided is true, once more without rational grounds."

sophical problem "whose more fundamental half was already solved by Hume," a problem he describes "with a little generosity" as "the problem of human knowledge."[21]

Popper's philosophy of science is profoundly ambiguous: It is, he says, "empirical," but it is left unclear why scientists should consult experience. It is called "fallibilism," in which we "learn from our mistakes," but it is really an ill-concealed form of skepticism. It claims to surrender the quest for certainty, but it is precisely the standards of this quest—that if one is not *certain* of a proposition, one can never be rationally justified in claiming it to be true—that underlie Popper's rejection of induction (and the numerous doctrines that stem from this rejection). He asks scientists to search for new facts, new theories, new truths—but then adds that no matter how hard they search, all they will ever be able to know will be as risky when they are finished investigating it as it was when they began, and that the only things that can be other than "daring" guesses[22] are empty logical truths. This is not abandoning the straitjacket of the quest for certainty but turning it inside out.

By a queer transition, Popper calls his skeptical view "critical rationalism" and "objectivism." But it is small wonder that the most consistent of all "Popperians" have been precisely those lapsed disciples of his, "anarchists" and "subjectivists" like Feyerabend, who have persuaded themselves that psychological compulsions, habits, and whims are the actual, if universally unacknowledged, motors of scientific change—an irrationalism similar to that which Popper deplored in Hume— and that science neither follows bodiless formulas nor yields genuine knowledge. *Les extrèmes se touchent:* As happens so often in the history of ideas, a formal "arch-objectivist" view offering precious little guidance to actual activities but trumpeting abstract formal principles leads through superficially persuasive steps of reasoning to a doctrine of "anything goes."

Popper is led to these difficulties by a combination of doc-

---

[21]Schilpp, op. cit., p. 1,014.
[22]Ibid., p. 1,047.

trines implausible in themselves and even less plausible in combination. He wrote his first book in reaction to the view that the empirical sciences are "reducible" to our sense experiences, and rightly held that this view hardly did justice to objective science. But he jumped to the other extreme, and adopted a largely formal approach to the theory of scientific knowledge. From this approach he developed his main views about the priority of logic over psychology, the rejection of induction on logical grounds, and the discovery of the method of conjectures and refutations as the best, because most "rational," scientific method.

But this unempirical approach, nourished by the horror of all "subjectivism," yields a conception of science and its guiding methods that is utterly inappropriate to its subject matter. As Popper recognizes, science (like the law) is a human activity of problem-solvers governed by critical habits and principles. But these principles have themselves developed by trial and error and may develop further. None of these principles is "intrinsically" or "essentially" rational: Their rationality lies in their success in promoting the ends of inquirers and resolving the problems of scientists. This is clearly seen in the case of induction: Even if there are no formal rules codifying this practice, it hardly follows that it is "arbitrary" or "subjective" (let alone that it does not exist), simply on the ground that it does not conform to the standards of rationality antecedently laid down by Popper.

Instead of espousing a view as riddled with internal flaws as Popper's, we can reasonably continue to believe that there really are inductive practices, that people do discriminate differences of probative weight in evidence and do rely on logically inconclusive evidence for many beliefs they hold, and further that such evidence can, under certain circumstances, genuinely provide *rational* support for our claims to know a great variety of empirical statements. Popper's fear of "subjectivist" views has led him to exclude from the analysis of science not only those judgments correctly described as infected with bias or subjective distortions, but also what is *typical* in science: decisions and cases of deliberation which are not strictly dictated by universal and exceptionless rules, but which require personal judgment; consequently, he leaves outside the scope of critical guidance the practices that most need it.

Popper is indeed a rationalist of sorts—a Romantic rationalist. Throughout his work we find the image of scientists trying to impose their theories on nature and then awaiting the voice of nature in response; an emphasis on fierce competition between theories; a stress on risks, bold conjectures, and imaginative criticism; a hatred of the view that science is nothing more than technological control; an image of science as a never-ending struggle whose mainspring is contradiction, in which we deliberately seek contradictions in our hard-won syntheses and solutions to avoid stagnation and erect fresh hurdles and challenges; an idea of science as a process that pursues an aim that is elusive, perhaps unreachable, a process that counts as much, if not more, than attaining the goal itself, a journey in which we heroically, impossibly, try to narrow the discrepancy between our finite grasp and our infinite aim. This picture has not enjoyed so distinguished (if not more convincing) an adherent since the days when it was applied to the moral realm, and sometimes to the whole of human existence, by many nineteenth-century German Romantic writers. Surely it is a powerful reason for Popper's appeal, probably more so than the arguments that have made him the scarecrow of "inductivists." The image Popper offers of our efforts to acquire the truth about the world may be momentarily intoxicating, and set up unusual and stimulating trains of thought, but, contemplated in a cool hour, it describes a wild-goose chase.

Is Psychoanalysis a Science?

Freud thought that he was the founder of a science. In one of his later papers, he wrote that psychoanalysis is "a part of the mental science of psychology."[1] But his detractors, a number of whom have mounted several sensational efforts to discredit his character, have contended that he did nothing of the kind. For some of them, he is at best a gifted writer whose eloquence concealed the defective reasoning behind his theories and who properly received the Goethe Prize for literature instead of the Nobel Prize for medicine.

It has sometimes been urged, not always without reason, that the question whether psychoanalysis is a science is not especially important, a librarian's concern or falsely implying that only what is scientific can be rationally credible. But if one takes the question seriously, it is readily seen to be far from clear. What is "science"? There seem to be so many kinds of science that it is difficult to extract a common characteristic

[1]*Standard Edition of the Complete Psychological Works of Sigmund Freud,* J. Strachey et al., trans. (London: Hogarth Press, 1953–1974), vol. 23, p. 282.

that would qualify all of them as science. And what is "psychoanalysis"? A theory of mind, and if so, in which formulation? A therapy? A method of investigating mental disorder? In a recent book,[2] Adolf Grünbaum, a philosopher whose most important previous work concerned philosophical and scientific questions of space and time, tries to clarify this question and also to articulate what he calls the "logical foundations" of psychoanalysis. By this he means the logical relations between the hypotheses of the theory and the kinds of evidence that Freud and his followers thought could support the theory. Those familiar with Grünbaum's work will expect a far more fastidious and exhaustive treatment of this subject than is to be found in previous philosophical studies.

Few philosophers have concentrated systematically on psychoanalysis, although there have been some distinguished exceptions, such as Sartre and, lately, Richard Wollheim. Karl Popper sought, some thirty years ago, to illustrate his model of science by showing psychoanalysis to be what he called a "nonscientific" theory. As noted in the previous chapter, according to Popper, a theory is scientific only if it is "falsifiable." By this he meant that the theory must yield some predictions that are observable and could refute the theory if they failed to occur. Popper complained that Freudian theory is not falsifiable in this sense because anything a human being says or does is compatible with it; it can explain everything, and thus explains nothing. He also claimed that psychoanalysts were not especially concerned to test their theory critically, by which he meant that they did not try to falsify it. In 1962, in a forceful paper read at a symposium organized by Sidney Hook, the distinguished philosopher Ernest Nagel put forth a more complex criticism of classical psychoanalytic theory that also emphasized the unfalsifiability of many psychoanalytic hypotheses.

Grünbaum stands apart from this critical tradition. He wishes

[2]Adolf Grünbaum, *The Foundations of Psychoanalysis: A Philosophical Critique* (Berkeley: University of California Press, 1985).

both to acknowledge Freud's accomplishments as a scientific methodologist and to rebut Popper's charges. But he also claims that Freud never succeeded in firmly grounding his theory in empirical findings. His book is a strangely organized, difficult work, unmistakably a string of scholarly articles to which vast accretions of evidence and afterthoughts have been added. It is written so much in reaction to the views of other philosophers and interpreters of Freud that Freud seems at times incidental to Grünbaum's purpose. The book has, for example, a ninety-four page "introduction" (in fact, one-third of the book) in which the "hermeneutic" approach to psychoanalysis (which Freud did not hold) is criticized. This is followed by a chapter on the testability of Freudian theory, which concentrates largely on Popper. Only in the second chapter do we arrive at Grünbaum's positive contribution to the debate about the scientific status of Freud's arguments for his theory.

Grünbaum's views are not excessively complicated, but he presents them in an obscure and frustrating manner. The book is a stupendous rococo construction, a philosophical Nymphenburg divided in parts, chapters, and subchapters. He uses words like "scientophobic" and "psychonoxious"; for him a woman with bad skin has a "dermatological deficit" and a footprint in the sand is a "pedal invasion." The book contains some of the most dreadful and inadvertently funny formulations I have ever seen, as when Grünbaum chastises a philosopher who has "treated us to a procession of logical enormities interlaced with homiletic *ipse dixits.*"

"Psychoanalysis" has generally stood for a psychology of mental functioning, including disorders of functioning, and for a method of treating such disorders. But it has had other meanings. Freud's theory is, in fact, a vast collection of propositions of different kinds. Some of them are abstract and speculative, such as his sketch, completed in 1895, of a theory of mind which sees the mind as a set of elements, each charged with "psychic energy," the system of elements as a whole conforming to various constraints, such as a law of conservation of energy. Freud thought at one time that if these elements could be identified with physical entities in the brain (such as neurons), his theory could provide a physical basis for psychoanalysis. But he let the project languish.

Other components of Freud's thought are remote from observable evidence because they are general propositions about human nature—such as his claim that "the force behind all human activities is a striving toward the two convergent aims of profit and pleasure." Such propositions are on a par with Rousseau's claim that all human beings are basically good, or with the postulation of original sin: Instead of being amenable to empirical confirmation or refutation, such statements are vague principles governing inquiry into human beings.

Still other Freudian propositions (such as his claim that repressed homosexual love is causally necessary for the condition of paranoia) are not in principle untestable, although they may be difficult to test, as we shall see. But given the heterogeneous nature of Freud's thought it is difficult to view it in its entirety as a scientific theory like the standard formulations of statistical mechanics. Accordingly, when the "scientific status" of Freudian theory is discussed by philosophers and others they usually mean a reconstruction of his work that excises some of Freud's ideas, plays down others, and improves or emphasizes still others. For example, few contemporary writers include in Freud's "theory" his comments in favor of telepathy or the inheritance of memory, and they often exclude aspects of his thought that he considered of the greatest importance, such as his "death instinct."

Grünbaum, for his part, generally confines his discussion to Freud's theory of unconscious motivation and personality. He concentrates on Freud's view that ideas can be "repressed" or made unconscious by agencies at work within the mind, and on his belief that forbidden wishes and impulses of a sexual character that are unsuccessfully repressed in childhood can return in later life in the disguised form of psychopathological symptoms. He also discusses Freud's therapeutic method, which tries to undo past repressions and restore conflicts to consciousness by artificially creating a situation in which the patient's unconscious is permitted to express itself through free association, and in which the patient is supposed to work out a mature solution to his previously repressed infantile conflicts. Drawing on Freud's hypotheses about motivation and personality, the psychoanalyst interprets the remarks produced by the patient in free association in order to help him arrive at a solution to his conflict.

Popper wrote that Freudian theory is without empirical content because it does not exclude "any particular person's acting in any particular way, whatever the outward circumstances. Whether a man sacrificed his life to rescue a drowning child (a case of sublimation) or whether he murdered the child by drowning him (a case of repression) could not possibly be predicted or excluded by Freud's theory."

Grünbaum contests Popper's claim by arguing that a number of the hypotheses of Freud's theory are falsifiable (and thus exclude a variety of events); and he adds that Freud was willing to accept the falsification of some of his ideas. He cites the example of Freud's hypothesis that repressed homosexual love is causally necessary for the occurrence of paranoia.[3] In 1915 Freud was consulted by a lawyer whose client, a young woman, had sought his protection from a man with whom she had been having an affair. He suspected she was paranoiac and asked Freud to examine her. Freud found that she showed signs of paranoid delusion, but he also found no evidence of a repressed homosexual attachment.

Grünbaum claims that Freud was prepared to surrender his theory of paranoia, and he quotes Freud's remark that in view of his findings, "either the theory must be given up or else, in view of this departure from our expectations, we must side with the lawyer and assume that this was no paranoic combination but an actual experience which had been correctly interpreted." Grünbaum also claims that Freud's theory of paranoia is not

---

[3]In "A Case of Paranoia Running Counter to the Psychoanalytic Theory of the Disease," in *Standard Edition of the Complete Psychological Works of Sigmund Freud*, vol. 15, pp. 263–272.

empty of "empirical content," as Popper had implied, for it yields the empirical prediction that with the decline of the taboo on male homosexuality in our society—for instance, in San Francisco—there should be a decreased incidence of male paranoia. Moreover, Grünbaum says, Freud showed his willingness to give up a refuted idea when he abandoned his early hypothesis that neurosis originated in the children's actual seductions by adults.

Grünbaum pursues at considerable length the question of whether psychoanalytic theory is "scientific" insofar as it can meet a formal "criterion of demarcation" between "scientific" and "nonscientific" statements. Formulated in this way, the question is not of evident importance. What is important for the scientific status of a theory is the promise it holds to contribute to systematic and controlled knowledge of the world. Even a vague, untestable, or false theory can have such promise if it suggests an interesting path of research to scientists. Moreover, whether or not a theory is itself "scientific" it can be investigated in a scientific spirit. Even if it had no testable claims of its own, psychoanalysis could still be scientific insofar as psychoanalysts made efforts to clarify their hypotheses and submit them to rational criticism.

Of course if a theory is testable, or has some evidence in its favor, its claim to scientific status may be stronger. But this status can depend on numerous other considerations, such as the theory's power to organize hitherto unconnected facts, its scope or range, and the strength of competing hypotheses. Philosophers and sociologists do not know enough about science to compile a full list of whatever considerations would contribute to the scientific status of a theory. The effort to construct a general rule or "criterion" of scientific status remains a dubious enterprise. No firm understanding of science has resulted from the construction of such criteria.

Far more important than his controversy with Popper are the chapters in which Grünbaum tries to identify some of the main obstacles that stand in the way of finding empirical support for psychoanalysis. He largely confines his discussion of this question to asking whether the most important part of Freud's theory—the theory of motivation and personality—can receive support from the kinds of empirical evidence Freud thought could support it. He pays particular attention to Freud's hypothesis that the origin of neurosis lies in repressed fears, wishes, and impulses, noting that Freud called the theory of repression "the cornerstone on which the whole structure of psychoanalysis rests." According to Grünbaum, not only does Freud's theory of dreams (which are held to represent repressed wishes) and slips of the tongue rest on this basic theory, but it is presupposed by the major post-Freudian schools of psychoanalysis, including the "object relations" school derived from the work of Melanie Klein, among others, and the "self psychology" of Heinz Kohut as well. If the repression theory is discredited, then so are other theories.

The repression theory was formulated by Freud in the last decade of the nineteenth century. He administered to patients suffering from symptoms of hysteria a "cathartic" treatment using hypnosis. Each hysterical symptom, he argued, originated in the repression of the memory of a trauma which preceded the appearance of the symptom. By his treatment he sought to lift this repression by bringing to light the traumatic experience. When he did so, he said, the symptom disappeared, so he felt justified in explaining his success by postulating that the uncovered trauma was the cause of the symptom.

Freud later replaced hypnosis by the method of free association, but he retained the view that any therapeutic gain depended on the patient's insight into the causes of his affliction. And he assumed that any lasting success with his method could be held as good evidence that the interpretation he had put to the patient was true. Freud therefore rested his repression theory on what he took to be therapeutic success and thought that this success could be ascertained through "clinical observations"—data drawn from within the psychoanalytic treatment session. Clinical observations, he thought, could both support his theory and give the analyst access to deep aspects of the patient's mind that could not be examined in other ways.

Using clinical observations to test the repression theory and related causal psychoanalytic hypotheses, Grünbaum writes, presented Freud with several difficulties. First, such observations alone could not, logically, support psychoanalytic hypotheses, at least a great many of them. Consider, for example, Freud's celebrated case of the "Rat Man," Paul Lorenz, who suffered from compulsive fears that a horrible punishment involving rats would befall both his father (who was dead) and a woman friend. After examining Lorenz, Freud concluded that he was an obsessive neurotic. According to his theory, the specific cause of obsessional neurosis was repressed sexual experiences in early childhood; he therefore assumed that Lorenz must have had such experiences as infantile masturbation. It so happened that Lorenz did not have any direct memory of them. But Grünbaum argues that even if Lorenz had truthfully recalled that he had had such experiences and had repressed them, such memories would not have supported Freud's hypothesis about the origins of obsessional neurosis. Even if many such neurotics existed, it might also be true that many persons who did *not* have such experiences also turned out to be obsessional neurotics. As Grünbaum writes:

> Suppose it were hypothesized that drinking coffee is causally relevant to overcoming the common cold. Consider, too, the case of a recovered cold sufferer who turns out to have been drinking coffee while still afflicted by the cold. Then such an instance, taken by itself, would hardly qualify as *supportive* of the hypothesized causal relevance.

To gain satisfactory support for Freud's hypothesis, we also need to have evidence of persons whose unconscious was *not* afflicted with repressed infantile sexual activity and who did *not* subsequently go on to develop obsessional neuroses. Such evidence must inevitably be found outside the psychoanalytic treatment session.

But Freud faced a second, equally serious, difficulty in using clinical observations to support psychoanalytic hypotheses like the repression theory. The treatment of a patient could be called a "success" only if the analyst had correctly identified the actual cause of the patient's affliction and only if the symptoms of the patient had disappeared because he gained insight into the cause of his condition. But if the patient accepted the analyst's interpretations, and if his symptoms subsequently went away, is it not possible that they did so because the analyst had unwittingly "talked" the patient into improvement without either identifying the true cause of the patient's condition or guiding him to genuine self-knowledge?

If this were so, of course, then the apparent "success" of the analysis would not be good evidence for the truth of the analyst's various interpretations, or for the theory that lay behind these interpretations. It would only confirm the analyst's skill in inducing the patient to manufacture responses to his questions that validated his interpretations, a skill shared by African witch doctors and Christian Scientists, among others. As Grünbaum expresses the difficulty, such evidence of "success" would be "contaminated" by suggestion. The analysis would be a placebo (though an inadvertent one), like a sugar pill that "cures" a headache because the patient believes that it does. The therapy might "work," but not because of factors that are deemed to be remedial by psychoanalytic theory.

Freud, who was intensely concerned about the problem of the "contamination" of clinical evidence by suggestion, called it "the objection that is most often raised against psycho-analysis." It was raised, indeed, even by his colleague Wilhelm Fliess. Freud sought to minimize the effects of suggestion in psychoanalysis, but at the same time he was forced to admit that a form of suggestion is used in every psychoanalysis. For as an analysis proceeds, and the patient uncovers more and more repressed material, he comes, in Freud's words, to reexperience "emotional relations which had their origin in his earliest object-attachments during the repressed period of his childhood." He relives these childhood situations and uses the analyst as the "object," thus transferring to the analyst the unconscious infantile attitudes he held toward his parents and other "objects."

Freud wanted the analyst to encourage this "transference" because the patient's feelings for the analyst, once marshaled, might help the analyst to draw out memories from the patient and other material useful to the analysis; in doing so, Freud wrote, "the transference is changed from the strongest weapon of the resistance into the best instrument of the analytic treatment." But Freud insisted that this use of suggestion differed entirely from that used in hypnosis, in which symptoms were "forbidden" to exist. In analysis, he said, suggestion functions to educate the patient in uncovering the underlying cause of his symptoms and in achieving insight.

In 1917 Freud gave what Grünbaum calls "a brilliant effort to come to grips with the full dimensions of the challenge of epistemic contamination by adulterated clinical responses." He used evidence of therapeutic success not only to confirm his theory (as he had done before) but to counter charges that this confirmation was spurious because of suggestion.

The analyst, Freud wrote, can make to the patient all sorts of suggestions that influence the analysis. Indeed, he has no difficulty in making the patient

> a supporter of some particular theory in thus making him share some possible error of his own. In this respect the patient is behaving like anyone else—like a pupil—but this only affects his intelligence, not his illness. After all, his conflicts will only be successfully solved and his resistances overcome *if the anticipatory ideas he is given tally with what is real in him.* Whatever in the doctor's conjectures is inaccurate drops out in the course of the analysis.[4]

According to Grünbaum, Freud assumed in this argument that the patient cannot conquer his illness without insight into its causes, and that he cannot get insight into its causes by hypnosis or any other therapy than psychoanalysis, with its method of unlocking repressed ideas by "free association." So if an analysis is successful, and if the patient's symptoms go

[4]*Standard Edition of the Complete Psychological Works of Sigmund Freud,* vol. 16, p. 452; italics added.

away and new ones do not appear, then it is good evidence that the doctor's conjectures did indeed "tally" with what was "real in him" and are therefore *true*. To be sure, suggestion was used in the analysis, but the analysis was not in its entirety a matter of suggestion, for if the symptoms disappeared—were in "remission"—then the patient must have had insight into his affliction, an insight arrived at with the help of the analyst. Therefore every *successful* analysis is evidence of the truth of the analyst's interpretation—and indirect evidence both of the truth of the theories that have guided the analyst in arriving at these interpretations and of the validity of the method of free association.

Grünbaum carefully shows why this argument is flawed. He casts doubt on Freud's premise that a variety of mental disorders and the symptoms accompanying them cannot be conquered unless the patient gains psychoanalytic insight into the causes of his condition. This premise is vulnerable, Grünbaum argues, first, because durable remissions of symptoms may be "spontaneous"—by which he means not the disappearance of symptoms for no apparent reason but remissions caused by events outside the psychoanalytic treatment.

Second, the sort of insight given by psychoanalysis is evidently not necessary for curing patients, Grünbaum says, since rival treatments (like behavior therapy) can yield results as impressive as those of psychoanalysis, if not more so. Grünbaum also writes that Freud recognized some of the flaws in his argument and by 1937 had surrendered his claim that psychoanalytic insight is necessary for the cure of psychoneurotic illness. But he complains that although Freud gave up the "tally argument," he never replaced it with another way of supporting his theory or of purifying clinical evidence for it. So the charge of what Grünbaum calls "epistemological contamination" of clinical observations through the analyst's suggestions remains. As a result, such observations cannot be legitimately used to confirm psychoanalytic hypotheses. Nor can the method of free association, whose credibility as a method lay in its alleged

ability to uncover repressions, be supported unless some substitute for the "tally argument" is found.

Grünbaum claims, therefore, that the central hypotheses of
psychoanalytic theory are devoid of evidence of the kind Freud
thought could support them. Indeed, he goes further: "The
seeming ineradicability of epistemic contamination in the clinical data, adduced as support for the cornerstones of the psychoanalytic edifice, may reasonably be presumed to doom any
prospects" for the cogent testing by clinical observations of
Freud's major tenets.

Important as this conclusion may be, it is a restricted one.
Grünbaum does not claim that there has been, or can be, no
evidence, clinical or otherwise, for Freudian theory. According
to Grünbaum's argument, it remains possible that what Freud
described as a "tally" between the analyst's interpretations and
the patient's psychic "reality" does occur. The problem is whether
that "reality" has not itself been determined by the analyst's
suggestions. Grünbaum's book is for the most part confined to
creating serious doubt that *one* kind of evidence—"clinical observations" from the analytic session itself—which Freud thought
could be used to support his theory, is capable of doing so.
This conclusion does not rule out the possibility that methods
of verification other than Freud's might confirm psychoanalytic
theory.

For example, psychoanalytic hypotheses about the causes of
illnesses like paranoia or obsessional neurosis might be partly
tested, at least in principle, in the way epidemiologists try to
test their hypotheses about the causes of diseases like lung
cancer or malaria by studying the incidence of the illness in a
population and inquiring whether the conditions under which
it occurs match those postulated by psychoanalytic theory. Freud's
hypothesis that the specific cause of paranoia is repressed
homosexual love, which is cited by Grünbaum, is an illustration
of a psychoanalytic hypothesis that might be studied in this
way. It yields, as we saw, what Grünbaum calls a "statistical
prediction" that "the decline of the taboo on homosexuality in

our society should be accompanied by a decreased incidence of male paranoia." Such a prediction can be tested in principle, and in doing so one need not appeal to any data drawn from the psychoanalytic interview. Indeed, Grünbaum says that researchers might even now "begin garnering appropriate statistics on the incidence of paranoia with a view to ascertaining in due course whether these epidemiologic data bear out the psychoanalytically expected decline."

In some cases, researchers might even be able to test the causal claims of psychoanalysis experimentally, by deriving from them hypotheses that can be tested in a laboratory. Such experiments have been attempted, and I shall discuss one of them below. But Grünbaum neither systematically assesses the body of evidence that has been thought by some experimental investigators and others to bear on Freudian theory nor explores ways of testing the theory that might be developed in the future. Of course standard experimental procedures comparing people who are and are not undergoing analysis generally are not applicable to the psychoanalytic interview between analyst and patient, but even "clinical observations" might confirm Freudian theory if some way of "purifying" them of the possible effects of suggestion could be found.

Nor is Grünbaum's conclusion as controversial as he sometimes suggests, for he tells us that an orthodox analyst, Kurt Eissler, has said that "future validation and/or disconfirmation of Freudian theory will come very largely from extraclinical findings." And if findings drawn from outside the psychoanalytic interview eventually prove to be the only ones capable of testing Freudian theory, that should not be so surprising, as Philip Holzman, an analyst who teaches at Harvard, has pointed out in a recent paper.[5] Psychoanalysis is a speculative theory that does not make many specific predictions and, as Holzman says, many such theories in the history of science have not been

---

[5]Philip Holzman, "Psychoanalysis: Is the Therapy Destroying the Science?" *Journal of the American Psychoanalytic Association* (Spring 1985).

testable by the methods from which they arose. The theory of natural selection, for example,

> is probably *not* capable of being tested by the same method from which it arose—that of observation of continuities, discontinuities, and diversity among species. To test ideas about how species evolve requires experimentation within a sphere different from the one that led to the hypothesis included in the theory of natural selection. It requires controlled experiments in genetics and in biochemistry, fields that were not even known to Darwin.

At best, Holzman writes, "the psychoanalytic situation is an admirable one for generating ideas about human conduct that would not occur in a psychology laboratory," but it is not the place to test whether these ideas are true.

Grünbaum writes that the validation of Freudian theory outside the psychoanalytic session is "largely a task for the future." In fact there have been a great many efforts made during the past half-century to apply scientific methods to test the theoretical and therapeutic claims of psychoanalysis.[6] But these studies and experiments—which have sought to find empirical evidence for the psychoanalytic theory of dreams, repression, paranoia, personality types, and other phenomena—have been controversial. Some students of such experimental studies of Freudian theory, like the English psychologist Hans Eysenck, have argued that they provide no strong evidence at all for any Freudian hypothesis. Why is this so? For one thing, investigators have not agreed on what standards of experimental design and justification of results should be employed in such tests. Secondly, even if uncontroversial standards of testing are used, they are extraordinarily difficult to apply in testing the psychoanalytic theory of therapy. To construct a controlled test

[6]Two large surveys of such results are S. Fisher and R. P. Greenberg, *The Scientific Credibility of Freud's Theory and Therapy* (New York: Basic Books, 1977), and Paul Kline, *Fact and Fantasy in Freudian Theory*, 2nd ed. (London: Methuen, 1981).

of the therapeutic efficacy of psychoanalysis by classical scientific standards, for example, two groups of persons would have to be matched for both the nature and the intensity of their condition and then randomly distributed into a "treatment" and a "control" group. An analyst must be "randomly" selected. The life of the "control" group must be regulated so that no "psychotherapy" is inadvertently given it. Criteria of "cure" or outcome should be specified in advance.

All of these conditions have been exceptionally hard to obtain. How can it be shown that two persons have the same psychological problem and in the same degree of intensity? How would the problem be defined, and what constitutes "psychotherapy"? Is "cure" to be construed as "insight" or as symptom remission? There are numerous other conditions that must be met if such tests are to have validity, such as arranging for follow-up studies to ascertain the durability of successes or failures of treatment.

But even if the conditions of controlled experimentation could be realized, tests of Freudian claims are often impossible to design because of the loose texture of the claims themselves. S. Fisher and R. P. Greenberg, in their book on the scientific status of psychoanalysis, speak of the complexity of the Freudian theory of how "personality defenses" are organized: "Freud, in describing such defenses, suggests that a wish may variously express itself in direct pursuit of the goal of the wish or in outright denial of the wish or even in the defensive pursuit of goals that are the direct opposite of the wish. How, ask many analysts, can you put this brand of complexity into an experimental design?" Because of this inaccessibility to experiment, many alleged "tests" of Freudian theory are not really tests of the theory at all.

In his careful book, which covers much the same ground as Grünbaum's and more, the Oxford philosopher B. A. Farrell cites one experiment he found "impressive" because he thinks it went some way toward testing Freud's theory of repression by finding evidence of it in perception and recognition:

Dixon used an apparatus which allowed him to present stereoscopically two spots of light—one brighter than the other—to the left eye of the subject and stimulus words, subliminally presented, to the right eye. The apparatus enabled the subject to control the brightness of the two spots, and he was instructed to work it continuously so that he could "just see the brighter of the two spots but never the dimmer one." It was found that when emotionally disturbing words (whore and penis) were presented subliminally to the right eye, the visual threshold went up and the subject had to increase the brightness of the spot shown to the left eye.

If the experiment is "firmly replicated, it suggests very strongly that some internal control machinery is at work of the sort described by the theory of repression."[7]

But another student of experimental work on psychoanalysis, the philosopher Edward Erwin, claims that Dixon's experiment fails to support Freud's theory of repression, not because it is poorly designed, but because it does not really test that theory; it is thus an example of what, to use Farrell's own distinction, is a test of a claim "suggested" by Freudian theory but not of the theory itself. This is because Dixon shows only that there can be "discrimination without awareness which affects recognition thresholds." But Erwin claims that this could not test the Freudian theory of repression, which postulates an unconscious mind that is performing the repression:

the mere fact that there is discrimination without awareness and that this discrimination affects recognition thresholds does not establish that any subject has defended against threatening material by incorporating it into his unconscious. Repression could be the cause of perceptual defense effects, but there is no firm evidence so far that it is.[8]

[7]B. A. Farrell, *The Standing of Psychoanalysis* (Oxford: Oxford University Press, 1982).

[8]Edward Erwin, "Psychotherapy and Freudian Psychology," in S. Modgil and C. Modgil, eds., *Hans Eysenck: A Psychologist Searching for a Scientific Basis for Human Behavior* (Philadelphia: Falmer Press, 1985).

Criticisms such as Erwin's support Grünbaum's view that the testing of Freudian theory outside the clinical setting is largely a task for the future. But this is because tests of psychoanalytic hypotheses have proved so difficult to design and to conduct. The claim that there is "no evidence" for psychoanalytic theory is frequently meant to convey not that positive evidence has been found that decisively runs against the theory, but rather that investigators have been unable to invent good tests of it and therefore no strong evidence exists for or against it.

There is no reason to suppose that better tests might not be invented in the future, although such tests might confirm or disconfirm a number of competing theories, not just Freud's. Will psychoanalysts be indifferent to the outcomes of such tests, as Popper and others have implied? Again, although some psychoanalysts have ignored or treated capriciously considerations of evidence, we need not suppose that all have behaved in this way, or that they must do so, now or in the future. One of Grünbaum's contentions, after all, is that Freud did not behave in this way. He was, indeed, scornful of religion and of obscure occult theories—which he spoke of as a "black tide of mud"[9]—for their insensitivity to questions of evidence. Grünbaum says that he has found "ample evidence that Freud's successive modifications of many of his hypotheses throughout most of his life were hardly empirically unmotivated, capricious, or idiosyncratic."

If psychoanalysts wish to respond to criticisms like Grünbaum's, it would seem appropriate that they systematically attempt to clarify and test their hypotheses. Have they failed to do so because of a blind, dogmatic adherence to their views? Some may have done so, but this path of research has been blocked for other reasons as well. For one thing, psychoanalytic theory is still in a process of development, so that there is no one clear research tradition to follow or to test. For example, the supporters of the "object relations" school have contested

---

[9]Elliott Oring, *The Jokes of Sigmund Freud* (Philadelphia: University of Pennsylvania Press, 1984), p. 89.

Freud's claim that all behavior and all aspects of personality, including psychopathology, express efforts to satisfy or discharge innate drives like those of sex and aggression. They deny that social relations with others are secondary, a derivative of the expression of these drives.

The analysts of the object relations school have therefore either abandoned or supplemented Freud's view. The English psychoanalyst John Bowlby, for example, wrote that the child's tie to his mother is not secondary to basic drives; it does not result from the fact that the mother provides the child a way of gratifying his need for nourishment or contact. Rather, he argued, the need for attachment in human beings is primary; it is an instinctual need independent of such drives as sex and aggression, and all children have an innate propensity to establish such ties of attachment.[10] The difference between the views of orthodox Freudians and object relation theorists might lead them to hold entirely different hypotheses worthy of being tested.

Even if there were a clear research tradition to test, there is, as Holzman points out, an insufficient number of scientists who wish to devote their time to testing psychoanalytic hypotheses. This is so not only because few medical and other scientists have shown strong interest in Freud's ideas, but also because, as Holzman expresses it, "in some quarters, the appropriate career goal of a psychoanalyst is one that emphasizes clinical psychoanalysis *only,* undistracted by the siren call of laboratory or other empirical research, university teaching, or other nontherapeutic but scholarly pursuits." Holzman suggests that even if psychoanalysis is scientific in its approach to its problems, it will not advance to the stage of testing its ideas and becoming a mature science if its institutions remain exclusively concentrated on psychoanalytic therapy. The question

[10]For an account of the object relations school, see Jay R. Greenberg and Stephen A. Mitchell, *Object Relations in Psychoanalytic Theory* (Cambridge, Mass: Harvard University Press, 1983). Morris Eagle, *Recent Developments in Psychoanalysis* (New York: McGraw-Hill, 1983), is the clearest book on its subject that I have seen.

of whether psychoanalysis is likely to become a science is therefore largely an "institutional" one. The "emphasis on maintaining a cadre of exclusive practitioners, or practitioners of an exclusive therapy, produces advocates with vested interests in maintaining the therapy against all change, influence and criticism." And he places the responsibility for the shortage of scientists working on the testing of psychoanalytic theory "at the doorstep both of the psychoanalytic institutes who focus only on teaching the therapy, and on the universities who shun the psychoanalytic data."

These institutional questions Grünbaum mostly ignores, but he does discuss another force within psychoanalysis that arrests the clarification and testing of Freudian and other psychoanalytic theory: the recent vogue among some psychoanalysts and philosophers to complain that Freud misunderstood his own enterprise when he claimed scientific status for it. In their view, psychoanalysis should not be regarded as a science, or as a "proto-science," or even as scientific. It is a "hermeneutic" enterprise which does not discover the causes of mental affliction but analyzes their "meaning" through a collaboration between patient and analyst, whose task is to create a more satisfactory "story" of the patient's life.

In his "introduction" Grünbaum attacks the view of such "hermeneutic" interpreters of psychoanalysis as Paul Ricoeur and the late George Klein; especially effective is his discussion of Jürgen Habermas, who holds that psychoanalysis is an instance of what he calls "critical" science, which aims at the "emancipation" of human beings. Grünbaum shows how Habermas and others trivialize psychoanalysis by removing its claims to scientific status; and he shows as well how most of their objections to seeing it as science—such as their claim that the concern of psychoanalysis with the "meaning" of symptoms or illnesses excludes it from being a causal science—rest not only on logical mistakes and ignorance about psychoanalysis but on misconceptions about the scope of natural science. One could add that the hermeneutic position is a retreat to the line of greatest safety by those psychoanalysts and philosophers who have been unduly impressed by the arguments that psycho-analysis cannot attain scientific status.

For those who believe that the "tally argument" is sound, Grünbaum's account of its defects should be clarifying and challenging. One frequently feels, however, that his book pursues the wrong questions to ask about psychoanalysis today and that, like many philosophers, he is too impatient with unclarity and fumbling attempts to articulate obscure ideas. Since psychoanalytic theory is not a discrete story like a myth or a novel, but might, like other theories, be further developed, and since new experimental designs might be able to test some of its claims in the future, one wants to ask how much is gained by examining its "logical foundations" in the way Grünbaum does, however useful it may be to know what Freud and some of his followers conceived them to be. Instead of ferreting out the methodological flaws in Freud's way of testing his theory within the psychoanalytic treatment session, Grünbaum might profitably have examined in greater detail, as Farrell tries to do, the full range of efforts that have been made to test the main hypotheses of psychoanalysis outside the clinic, and to specify what obstacles must be surmounted by similar tests in the future if they are to yield strong confirmations or discon-firmations of that theory.

It is true that psychoanalysis was created at the turn of the century and has not yet fulfilled its scientific promise. It may never do so. But many theories in the history of science took a long time to acquire a reputation for being "scientific." As Farrell remarks, "Harvey's theory of the circulation of the blood remained very unsatisfactory until the capillaries were discovered. Prout's suggestion—that the atomic weights of elements could be exhibited as multiples of hydrogen—was only taken up and appreciated later on. Newton's theory of matter and his corpuscular view of light had to wait for a couple of centuries before they could be handled by science with some confidence."

It is also true, however, that many theories, after much de-velopment and patient attention from scientists, have failed to yield confirmed hypotheses and have either collapsed under the weight of repeated disconfirmations or have been rendered obsolete by new theories. It is possible that psychoanalysis will have this fate. The profession has become increasingly isolated from organic medicine; it has found no new Freud; its theoretical development has been stagnant. It is arguable that what seems evidently true in Freud, such as his notion of repression or his emphasis on the unconscious and on the irrational springs of much of human behavior, has long been known and that Freud introduced an unnecessary technical language and a dubious metaphysical backdrop to describe these phenomena. And it is possible that psychoanalytic theory will be replaced in time by shorter therapies of various kinds and by psychopharmacology derived from new developments in the neurosciences.

Nevertheless, there is something to psychoanalysis, and to the insights of what Grünbaum calls "Freud's brilliant intellectual imagination" (such as his theory of repression), and our attitude toward psychoanalysis might prudently be one of benevolent skepticism. It would be unwise to judge it finally as a theory at the present time, or to foreclose the future of scientific invention. However imperfectly formed and unsupported some of its hypotheses may be now, they may be improved; and even if they are eventually falsified or otherwise discredited, they may stimulate the imagination of scientists working in other fields to incorporate what seems true in them into more satisfactory and confirmed theories. Farrell is not wrong in claiming that many of Freud's ideas may be "pointers to the truth—signposting the avenues to pursue if we wish to get at a reasonably definitive account of human nature."

Paul Valéry

Although he is unfamiliar to most younger Americans today, and even half forgotten by some of those who once read him, Paul Valéry was seen forty years ago by many European intellectuals as among the most important intellectual personalities of the preceding half-century and ranked among such men as Einstein, Bergson, Proust, Picasso, and Freud. They thought of him as a sage who wrote prophetic essays about Europe and the Orient and whose obscure and rapturous poems had been praised by Joyce and Rilke and Eliot, who called him "the representative poet, the symbol of the poet, of the first half of the twentieth century." Valéry was praised by Santayana and Bernard Berenson, by Auden and Stravinsky, by the New Novelists and Borges and Jacques Derrida; Cyril Connolly called him "the most dazzling of European intellectuals."[1]

Valéry made his contemporaries familiar with his ideas about everything, often expressing them in extravagant and imprecise ways. His ideas on philosophy, which have not been taken up or even mentioned by many commentators on his work, are, I think, worth looking into, and in this essay I propose to explain why. Valéry tried to demolish existing philosophy by invoking the positivist principles of his day and to transform philosophy into an instrument of self-realization, which he held to be the final goal of all human activity. I do not think that he made a good case either for the death of traditional philosophy or for its reform into self-help. Still, when his views are modified to remove exaggerations and errors, there is something to be found in them. He saw, I think, something important about the way philosophers formulate and advertise their problems, and if he was right most popular conceptions of philosophy need to be amended or thought through anew.

I

Paul Valéry was born on October 30, 1871, in Sète, near Montpellier, on the Golfe du Lion in southern France. His father, Barthélemy Valéry, was of Corsican origin; his mother was Fanny de Grassi, whose father had been consul in Sète of Sardinia and subsequently of Italy. Barthélemy Valéry owned a navigation company and at his death in 1887 was also the head clerk of the Douanes Impériales at Sète.

When Valéry was still a boy, the family moved to Montpellier, where he attended a *lycée* and took a *baccalauréat* in 1888. He formed friendships there with André Gide and Pierre Louÿs, who introduced him to the poetry of Gautier and Herédia and the other "Parnassians." At this time, Mallarmé[2] was consolidating his attack on aesthetic naturalism and developing his own view, which came to be known as "Symbolism." Poetry, he thought, should suggest or evoke mental states without directly describing them; it should be neither the social propaganda of the naturalists nor the conversational *vers libre* of the *décadents*. He further urged the artist to be a priest of beauty who should lead a distinctive way of life, subordinating everything to the search for "purity" in art.[3]

After seeing Mallarmé's name in Huysmans's *À Rebours*, Valéry began to read the poet's work and was at once impressed with his technical skill. He wrote to him, enclosing some of his own poems, and on October 24, 1890, he received a message

from the poet that noted Valéry's gift of "musicalizing"; in a
later message, Mallarmé urged the younger man to "gardez ce
ton rare" ("preserve that precious tone"). But it soon became
apparent that Valéry could not conform to Mallarmé's religion
of art and that the search for "purity" had, for him, the effect
of suffocating all desire to write poetry. In 1891 he passed his
law examinations after serving for a period of time in the army,
but he had little interest in becoming a lawyer. He seems,
indeed, to have had no interest in doing anything except analyzing his own mind. He wished, he wrote around this time,
to explore and define his "intellectual powers" and to discover
ways of developing these powers, but he had little or no idea
of the general direction his life would take.

He fell in love with a Mme. de Rovira, whom he had seen
only a few times and to whom he had never spoken, and this
episode seems to have precipitated a crisis of will. On October
4, 1892, when he was barely 21, he says, he passed a night of
immense anxiety in Genoa and shortly thereafter entered into
a "great silence," in which he did not write poetry for twenty
years. In 1894 he moved to Paris, where he lived in a spare
room on the Rue Gay-Lussac and soon was in touch with the
Mallarmé cénacle, including Henri Regnier and Marcel Schwob.
They met regularly at Mallarmé's house on the Rue de Rome,
where, Valéry's daughter Agathe Rouart-Valéry writes, "devant un paysage de Claude Monet, une esquisse d'Hamlet, et
le portrait de Mallarmé par Manet, dans un brouillard de fu-
mée, se distillent les plus rares et précieux entretiens" ("Beneath a Monet landscape, a sketch of Hamlet, and Manet's
portrait of Mallarmé, the most singular and precious discussions
are distilled within a cloud of cigarette smoke").[4]

The question of a career persisted, however. Unlike his friend
Gide, he was not well-to-do, and unlike Mallarmé (who taught
English and wrote English manuals) he had not acquired the
certification necessary to become a teacher. Huysmans suggested that he apply for an appointment at the War Office, but
nothing came of it at first. Valéry was asked to write as part of
his application a composition on how the army could take part

in the life of the French nation. His examiners were unfavorably impressed by the result. In the catalogue of books, manuscripts, photographs, and other items pertaining to his life that was published by the Bibliothèque Nationale in 1956, one can find the appraisal of one of them: "Jamais je n'ai lu pareilles choses, c'est simplement monstreux" ("I have never read such things in all my life—monstrous is the word"). The examiners concluded that "le candidat est un esprit absolument nuageux qui ne sera un rédacteur. Sa place est dans un mauvais journal. C'est un vulgaire décadent, un Paul Varlaine [sic] en prose dont l'administration n'a que faire" ("The candidate's mind is so utterly vague that he will never make a good editor. He belongs in the yellow press—he is a vulgar decadent, a Paul Varlaine [sic] in prose who will be of no use whatever to the administration").[5]

Valéry went to London in 1896 to work in the offices of the Chartered Company of Cecil Rhodes, whom he greatly admired. The company was trying at the time to annex the Transvaal and the Orange Republic to Rhodesia. Valéry was assigned to the company's press departments; he writes that his "duty was to watch over the relations of these departments with the French press."[6] The next year, he applied once more to the Ministry of War and this time was accepted. Within four years, however, he left this position and became secretary to Édouard Lebey, director of the Havas press service. Lebey suffered from Parkinson's disease, and Valéry's job, which was to give him financial security and a good deal of leisure for twenty-two years, was to serve as companion and counsel to the old man and to keep him informed of the press accounts of current events.

In the late Nineties, Valéry wrote the two prose works for which he was to become famous, *Introduction to the Method of Leonardo da Vinci* (1895) and, in the following year, *Monsieur Teste*. Both of these works were portraits of men who had developed their "intellectual powers," an aim or condition that, as we shall see, Valéry never succeeded in clearly describing. *Teste*, which Valéry called a "roman d'un cerveau" ("novel of a mind"), described a man who liberates himself from everything that is not directly related to his aim of "self-mastery"—material possessions, sexual entanglements, conventions of society, vanity. The character was partly based on that of Dégas, whom Valéry admired and a number of whose paintings of dancers he was to own, and certainly derived also from the detective Auguste Dupin in Poe's *Murders on the Rue Morgue.* (As if to confirm the accuracy of the description of his character in the novel, Dégas refused to be the dedicatee of Valéry's book.)

In London, Valéry had met Aubrey Beardsley, Edmund Gosse, and others, including William Henley, who edited the *New Review,* which had recently published a series of articles on the threat posed to British industry by German competition. As Valéry later described them, these articles argued that "in every economic field, thanks to the scientific organization of production, consumption, means of transportation and publicity, and to very precise and searching procedures centralizing innumerable bits of information, this enterprise was systematically evicting British products from world markets, even taking over the markets in the British colonies themselves."[7] The articles only stated facts, however, and Henley asked Valéry to contribute an essay "in the French manner," describing the larger significance of these facts. This essay was to become Valéry's well-known "Conquest of Method," which eloquently expressed the fear that civilized values and cultures might be destroyed by rational economic (and military) warfare of the kind he saw practiced by the Germans.

Mallarmé died in 1898, and two years later Valéry married Jeanne Gobillard, the niece of Manet's sister-in-law, the painter Berthe Morisot. They were married for over forty years and had two sons and a daughter, but their marriage does not appear to have been especially animated or passionate.*

Valéry's "great silence" came to an end in 1913, when he

---

* During the marriage, Valéry had an affair in the Twenties with a surgeon's daughter, Catherine Pozzi, and in the Thirties with Renée Vaultier, a sculptress. He does not seem to have been tutored in intimate matters. He kept lists not only of mental exercises but also of sexual encounters, which he would grade "potential," "semi," or "complete."[8]

was already forty-two. André Gide and the publisher Gaston Gallimard had founded the *Nouvelle Revue Française*, and had asked Valéry in 1912 if he would consent to a republication of some of his early poems. Valéry demurred. Gide asked again, and finally, Valéry tells us, after much inner torment, he consented. He also began to revise a number of these poems. In 1920 he published them in a collection, *Album des Vers Anciens*, which had a modest success in the Parisian literary world. In 1913 he began to write a new poem, one that he estimated would run to thirty or forty lines. Over the course of the next five years, however, it grew in length until it ran to 512 alexandrines. This was the famous "La Jeune Parque"; it was followed by the equally well known "Le Cimetière Marin" in 1920. Unlike Valéry's early poems, these poems were not heavily derivative from Mallarmé but represented something of a new development. Both had an extraordinary, incantatory power and seemed to carry profound metaphysical implications. The "Jeune Parque" has no clear-cut subject but invokes large themes—death and non-being, destiny and sexual desire—in an obscure but suggestive way, evoking exquisite visions of color and light, sea spray, moonlight, gold and purple, sleeping women. The "Cimetière Marin" is a complicated, extended philosophical speculation in which the poet confronts existence by contemplating a cemetery high above the sea at noontime. Valéry seems to use the sun, the sea, the graveyard as symbols of life, mind, and death; the poem, in one familiar reading, seems to suggest that excessive contemplation—the life led by Teste, for example—leads to a kind of stultification and immobility; the poet realizes that this excludes life itself and that he must break free and write his poem and return to life. (According to Valéry, the "Cimetière Marin" was never finished but was seized from his desk by Jacques Rivière, the editor of the *Nouvelle Revue*, and published in the state in which Rivière found it.)

After these poems appeared, Valéry began to acquire the fame that was to accompany him for the rest of his life. In 1923 T. S. Eliot began his campaign to bring new readers to Valéry's work by publishing a translation of one of the poems in the *Criterion*. In Germany, Rilke translated Valéry's poetry. The French journal *Connaissance* published a poll of readers in 1921 which found Valéry the greatest of contemporary poets.* Lebey died in 1922 and to make money Valéry took to giving lectures and writing essays and testimonials and introductions and prefaces to luxurious editions of classical authors. He wrote memorials and tributes to Racine, Descartes, Goethe, Swedenborg, Bossuet, Stendhal, Baudelaire, La Fontaine, Bergson, Poe, and Poincaré, among others. He would later insist that these pieces were "made to order." The text of an essay on architecture, for example, "was to be magnificently printed in an infolio, and had to be exactly adjusted to the decoration and pagination of the work. I was therefore asked to make my contribution exactly 115,800 letters long, that is, 115,800 printed characters." Valéry also wrote on a variety of aesthetic and political concerns. Some of these writings were essays on off-beat subjects—the dance, women's vote, photography, technology. Valéry acquired a reputation for prophecy in some of these essays; the "Conquest of Method," mentioned earlier, which predicted in 1897 the rationalization of warfare in both the economic and military sphere, was one example. His essay on the "ubiquity" of art, in which he predicts that art will become like gas or water, instantly accessible like other consumer products, is another.

But rereading the large corpus of Valéry's writings that originate in the period after Lebey died, one feels that he published far too much. He permitted the publication of one book after another of aphorisms and anecdotes, many of which are trivial. "The 'natural' is boring,"[10] runs one, "idealism is a kind of sulks,"[11] another. "A truly 'exact' mind can understand only

---

* He was greatly admired by younger writers like Soupault, Aragon, and Breton. In the journal *Littérature* of March 1921 there appeared an evaluation of some two hundred writers from Alcibiades to Zola, rated on a scale from −25 to +20, with 0 indicating absolute indifference. Breton gave Valéry +15, higher than his grade of Apollinaire, Max Ernst, Duchamp, and other heroes of surrealism and Dada.[9]

itself and only in certain states."[12] "Optimists write badly." One feels that every little thought he has is taken seriously by its author, and that only an uncritically admiring observer of his own mind could allow these thin ideas to be published. There is also a somewhat superior tone that exhibits itself from time to time in these essays: Valéry is constantly assuring us that he is accustomed to being "interpreted" and that he is familiar in advance with the objections to his ideas that critics raise. He is more than a little condescending and pompous— *de haut en bas*—alternately arrogant and embarrassingly self-critical—an egoist who begs your indulgence because he is unworthy of addressing you, a trait he shared with his admirer T. S. Eliot. At the same time, he is maddeningly proud that he has nothing to do with the "world," with journalism, or politics, or the academy, and his essays are often written as if they were peremptory communications from a distant, superior intelligence. These pieces often have an elegant surface, but when one has scraped off the literary caramel on them and tried to find out what they are about, one usually sees that the ideas in them are quite crude. Valéry tends to make very large claims without examining their basis in fact or theory. He is perfectly content to use vague abstractions and grandiloquent turns of phrase, as is evident in the titles of some of the essays— "Crisis of the Mind," "Politics of the Mind," "The Outlook for Intelligence," "Our Destiny and Literature," "Notes on the Greatness and Decline of Europe," "America: A Projection of the European Mind." He constantly speaks, for example, of the need for "reason" in politics, but he never tells us what it is or what steps must be taken in order to introduce it into politics.

At the same time, however, he presents himself to the reader as a skeptic who has no truck with the "impure" of any kind, especially with ill-defined or vague expressions such as "State, Democracy, Freedom," which are "idols." In this mood he displays an overdeveloped, self-conscious and excessive fastidiousness and whittles away his subject until nothing is left, until everything that is "impure" is subdivided to infinity. Understandably, little of practical guidance emerges from this process. Indeed, it encourages an absence of any fixed opinion, as is evident, say, from an overview of Valéry's political convictions.

In the Nineties he was a fierce anti-Dreyfusard, not surprising in a patriot who grew up after the Franco-Prussian war of 1871 and the defeat at Sedan—his son François says that "at the sound of a military band passing in the street he would fall into step."[13] In 1898 he wrote to Gide, "What does this devouring of insects matter? Let us seek true freedom, the kind to be furnished to a man with the burden of State."[14] When the forgeries of Colonel Henry were exposed in the same year, demonstrating that the alleged proofs of Dreyfus's guilt were without foundation, and Henry committed suicide, Valéry contributed to a subscription—"pas sans réflexion" ("not without reflection"), he said—organized by *La Libre Parole*, the organ of the right-wing anti-Semite Émile Drumont, to aid Henry's widow. François Valéry says that if his father had been killed in the First World War he would have been thought a rightist with views not far from those of Charles Maurras or Albert Sorel, for whom human nature was permanently and incurably fractious and had to be controlled by a strong central state. Democracy, he wrote at the turn of the century, is "une terrible affectation, une pose. Rien de moins vrai" ("a dreadful affectation, a pose. Nothing is less likely").[15] He admired masterful, "benign" dictators like Salazar and for a while Mussolini, whom he met in Rome in 1924 and again in 1933. In the Thirties, however, he came to give up his admiration for the modern State and indeed for all politics, which he found corrupt and irrational. He asks himself in 1931 what his political opinions are: "Je n'en ai pas. Mais si j'interroge mon instinct—je trouve la contradiction est dans tous. Anarchie–Monarchie. À la réflexion—je *deviens* aristocratique et oligarchique. . . . Je haïs la confusion, le Dêmos informe et ce qu'on est obligé de lui dire. Pour moi, monarchie est democratie, *contre* aristocratie. L'Église est un beau type de gouvernement" ("I have none. But if I question my instinct—I find all of them harbor contradictions. Anarchy–Monarchy. Upon reflection—I *become* an aristocrat, oligarchic even. . . . I detest confusion, the shapeless Demos and all it must be told. For me, monarchy is democracy, *against* aristocracy. The Church is a fine type of government").[16] But he is unable to form any clear political view even at the age of sixty. Among the papers found after his death was a manuscript entitled "Principles of Planned Anarchy."

In the Twenties Valéry settled carefully into the part of a great man. In 1924 he became president of the PEN club. In the following year he was elected to the French academy.* He also became a member of the Committee on Intellectual Cooperation of the League of Nations. He was received by the Belgian royal family and by Gustave V of Sweden, and met other great men—Conrad, d'Annunzio, Stefan Zweig, Einstein, Ortega y Gasset, Berenson, Tagore, Bergson. In 1927 he described his day to Gide: "I arise between five and six. I find a confused mass of 'necessary' things, of promised and claimable foolishness, and I work without stopping, against these works of boredom and command. At eight o'clock the cursed mailman. The mail of a prime minister, but with no desk, no secretaries. If I had begun to get excited by my work, this shock of letters would stun me, pulverize my mind. The visits begin at 10 o'clock. Until 1 o'clock, I must receive, talk, talk, talk. By lunch time I am dead. One must run, afterwards, since one must 'live'—and I fly from publishers to libraries, etc. At this point I am *finished*, and it matters little whether I go into society"[17]—which he did a good deal, attending the salons of the Comtesse Joachim Murat and Mme. Muhlfeld, and befriending the Duchesse de la Rochefoucauld and Lady Colefax, in whose houses he met distinguished scientists like Émile Borel and Perrin or military men like Joffre and Foch.

---

* He was expected, as part of an old custom, to deliver an encomium to his predecessor in the chair, in this case Anatole France. Instead, he made unfriendly allusions to France, reviving the quarrel that had begun when France, as editor of *La Parnasse Contemporain*, had rejected Mallarmé's "L'après-midi d'un faune" in 1874.

"Society" helped him a good deal. *Le Crapouillot* ran a piece in 1927 entitled "Le Génie Commercial de M. Paul Valéry," which said that "M. Valéry eut l'idée assez nouvelle pour un poète (formé, il est vrai, à l'Agence Havas) de mettre sa valeur littéraire en société anonyme. De bénévoles courtiers volaient de salon à salon, brandissant les bulletins de souscription. Une petit société fût alors constituée de quelque vingt bibliophiles, qui pût être certaine de recevoir tous les livres sans exception de M. Valéry en un format spécial, et servait une rente annuelle au poète pur" ("M. Valéry had the rather novel notion, for a poet [though a poet trained in the Havas Agency], of incorporating his literary capital. Volunteer brokers flew from salon to salon, brandishing stock options. A small company was then constituted, some twenty bibliophiles who could be sure of receiving, without exception, all of M. Valéry's books in a limited edition, and who afforded the pure poet an annual income").[18]

In 1931, Valéry received an honorary degree from Oxford University and two years later was made administrator of the Centre Universitaire Meditérranéen de Nice. In 1937 he was elected to a Chair of Poetics that had been created for him by government decree at the Collège de France. When the Germans occupied Paris he fled to Brittany but returned some months later. When he gave a speech defending Bergson to the Academy he was dismissed from his post at Nice. A vigorous opponent of the Vichy government and of Pétain, whom he had once admired, he was able to see the liberation of France by de Gaulle's forces. His death on July 20, 1945, was marked by a State funeral, and the Rue de Villejust, on which he had lived from 1900 until his death, was renamed after him.

II

Many descriptions of Valéry's personality and appearance by those who knew him mention his wit and refinement. Count Harry Kessler met him at Roger Martin du Gard's in 1926 and described him as "a short, meagre man with artistically disarrayed strands of grey hair, fine deeply-set eyes, and a quiet, musical intonation." A year later, he saw him again, this time to try to persuade him to translate Virgil's *Georgics*: Valéry, "with his carefully parted silver-grey hair, smart black suit, and the Legion of Honor in his lapel, looks like an old French marquis."[19] When Stravinsky met him around 1921 Valéry seemed to him "quick, quiet (he spoke in rapid, *sotto voce* mumbles), and extremely gentle. He seemed a terrible dandy at first sight because of his monocle and *boutonnière*, but that impression dissolved as soon as he began to talk. Wit and intelligence were in everything he said, though not merely in what he said: They were manifest in his whole person."[20]

Others have emphasized Valéry's hauteur and superior tone. Gide said that he was "incapable of real sympathy,"[21] and Nathalie Sarraute spoke of "la hauteur, l'ampleur de ses dédains" ("the haughtiness, the breadth of his disdain").[22] Eliot[23] and Julien Benda[24] described his mind as destructive and nihilistic. According to Salvador de Madariaga, Valéry had an "easily contemptuous nature": he was an "aristocratic, lofty but also haughty kind of man, apt to find the odor of the crowd too strong for his sensitive nostrils."[25]

Valéry frequently described himself in his notebooks as an ascetic who has given up everything to lead a life of art, and whose life has therefore been less "interesting" than those of his friends Gide and Louÿs. Like Teste, he suggests, he has cultivated detachment from conventional life, to the extent that he sometimes wonders whether he is "human." But he also constantly expresses dissatisfaction with himself. He says that he is really "nothing" and has done nothing. Whenever something he has said or written has been praised by someone he admires, such as the mathematician Émile Borel or Henri Bergson, he carefully notes the praise in his diaries with childlike astonishment. He insists that he should not be given responsibility for what has been published under his name, for it was extracted from him by others and presented to the public in an unfinished state. "I have never written anything," he says, "and I never write anything, save under compulsion, forced to, and cursing against it."[26] In the foreword to the first edition of his *Analects*, [27] he says that the book was composed at the "invitation of certain amateurs of the unfinished" and contains "notes written *for myself*: random jottings, ideas or germs of ideas that took me by surprise" and which he has presented "in all their confusion, their scrappiness, their embryonic or sketchlike state as casual ideas."* When Gide asked whether he had stopped writing for pleasure, he said that his "pleasure consists precisely in writing *nothing*."[28]

He says that he has, and has had, no "career," no "métier" or "profession." He loathes the idea of a specialty and says he is content to work on his "self-analysis." He is indignant when he reads Gide's *Journals*, which accuse him of "playing his life like a game of chess that it is important to win, and as he writes his poems, placing just the right word, as one moves up a pawn, in just the right place." Valéry criticizes Gide's self-dramatization, his desire to impress the young, his tendency to confess and preach. How could Gide, his closest friend, have so fundamentally misunderstood him? He cannot be held responsible for the central events of his life. If he has played his life like a chess game, "voilà un échiquier où tout le monde a mis le main, excepté moi" ("Here is one chessboard on which everyone has made a move but me"). Pierre Louÿs, he says, "m'a suborné vers la Poésie. Mon développement 'en profondeur' fût une réaction contre la tyrannie de la crédulité littéraire, et autre. Huysmans m'a précipité dans une carrière administrative. Mon ami André Lebey m'a tiré de là et m'a valu 22 ans d'Havas avec beaucoup de loisir. Mon mariage est l'oeuvre conjugée des dames Mallarmé, de Monsieur Dégas et de l'atmosphère Berthe Manet. Ma 'Jeune Parque' fût conséquence inattendue de la fondation de la librarie NRF" ("suborned me into dealings with Poetry. My development 'in depth' was a reaction against the tyranny of literary credulity, and not only

---

* This remark, as Auden suggested (Introduction to *Collected Works*, vol. XIV, p. ix), "does not quite ring true, especially when one finds him writing privately to a friend (Paul Souday) that he considers his notebooks his real *oeuvre*."

literary. Huysmans thrust me into an administrative career. From which my friend André Lebey extricated me, a benefaction of 22 years at Havas with a good deal of leisure. My marriage was the conspiratorial work of the Mallarmé ladies, of M. Dégas, and of the atmosphere around Berthe Manet. My 'Jeune Parque' was the unlooked-for consequence of the establishment of the Librairie NRF").[29] He continues: "Je n'ai jamais solicité ni décorations, ni présidences, ni doctorats Honoris Causa" ("I have never sought decorations, nor official rank, nor doctorates *honoris causa*"). Toward the end of his life he wrote: "Tous mes événements, carrière, mariage—etc., tout fût l'oeuvre des *autres*. Ma seule politique n'a jamais été que de défendre ma recherche infinie, comme j'ai pu—aux dépens de bien de choses et au prix d'une médiocre vie" ("All the events of my life, career, marriage, etc.—everything was the work of *other people*. My one policy was always, and only, to protect my endless investigations, my research, as best I could—at the expense of many other things and at the cost of a mediocre life"). Valéry was able to see his life as a story of a pure "self-analyst" forced to acquire worldly success by his more sophisticated and practical friends.

It is easy to suppose that this is an elaborate story that Valéry created to convince his readers of his otherworldliness and seriousness. In fact, he had gained from his days at the Chartered Company and at the Havas agency some understanding of how people become famous, enough to write ironically that "genius is a habit some people acquire"[30] and that "fame and glory depend not on effort, which is generally undetected, but on proper staging."[31] He knew how to stage his life, one feels, for example, by choosing to describe his "crisis" of 1892, when he stopped writing, as the central intellectual event of his life, when he renounced all "idols"—the best face, no doubt, to put on what was probably a nervous collapse brought on by sex frustration and envy of Mallarmé. (Such silences were fashionable at the time: Rimbaud and Mallarmé had both had them.)

But the more familiar one becomes with Valéry's "analysis" of himself, the more one becomes convinced that the examiners who called him "nuageux" were right and that despite an orderly and successful public career as an intellectual and administrator, and a reputation for being able to address himself to any subject, his inner life was bleak and unfocused. In his diaries he repeatedly admits to an inability to adhere to a single path or to locate himself against the activities of those around him. At the age of forty he is able to write that "ma caractéristique est peut-être: l'impossibilité de me tenir tout entier dans quelque objet . . . ou sujet" ("perhaps it is characteristic of me that I find it impossible to invest myself entirely in any object . . . or subject").[32] He is incapable of sticking to anything, he says, and his interests are incompatible and lead him in different directions. As a result, he says, he is not a single organic being but a series of "grafts," of mathematics on poetry and logic on superstition. He confesses that he finds himself "too much" of everything: "Je suis toujours trop jeune et trop vieux—trop moi, trop toute chose. Il faut pourtant organiser ce trop" ("I am always too young and too old—too much myself and too much everything else. Yet this *too much* has to be organized").[33]

Why, then, does he not do so? He does not seem to want to. He prefers perhaps to be defined by others. In his most intimate thoughts, moreover, one feels that he is, and wishes to remain, marginal, *à côté de tout*. He says that he has "an instinctive horror of anything that defines me to myself," and that he is someone "who will never adapt himself to the idea of being what he is, at a certain moment."[34] "J'ai reculé devant les actes qui donnent à *l'essence*, l'idée d'une définition de soi. J'ai reculé devant le poète, le philosophe, l'homme d'une profession qui étaient possible en moi. Je ne veux être personne" ("I shrank from the actions which produce an *essence*, the notion of self-definition. I retreated from the poet, the philosopher, the professional who were possible in myself. I want to be no one").[35] He would prefer, he admits, to always remain in "reversible equilibrium," by which he means in a state of potentiality, so that he could easily shift from one task to another. To be capable of anything seems to be Valéry's ideal. He also had, one suspects, a kind of longing to occupy a position contrary to, or different from, his own: Fame as a writer led him to deny that he was a writer at all; acquiring a reputation as a poet induced in him a desire to become known as an essayist; the attractions of anarchism became evident to him the moment he began to consider himself a monarchist. In his rationalist mood, he writes of Nietzsche with a sneer: His was a mind, he says, which was unable to "leave the unprovable alone."[36] But his own rationalism, as we shall see, coexisted in his temperament with an unprovable metaphysics of the self, and also, it seems, with a fascination with the irrational and mystical, with theosophy, symbology, the occult, with views of the universe as a story or a hieroglyph interpretable by signs or keys, or by a secret code. He was drawn to visionaries like Gerard de Nerval and to Swedenborg,[37] who at the age of forty made a transition from being a man of science to espousing a mysticism which held that there are two "realities"—one visible and one spiritual—and complicated "correspondences" between them.

When one considers this attraction to opposites and avoidance of self-definition in Valéry's thought, it seems altogether typical of him to say—at the age of sixty-five—that he was "afraid" of both philosophy and common sense and had "no preference" between them.[38] "Mon sentiment," he wrote only a few years earlier, "fût de n'être pas semblable. N'être pas poète, écrivain, philosophe selon ces notions; mais si je le devais être, plutôt *contr'elles*. Et même—n'être pas *homme*. Ceci est le clef de moi" ("My feeling was to be none of a kind. Not to be a poet, a writer, a philosopher according to such notions; but if I had to be such a man, at least *against them*. And even—not to be a *man* at all. This is the key to me").[39] It is therefore disingenuous of him to ask how he could have come to be an "outsider."[40] He made himself one.

It seems to me that Valéry suffered—at least for long stretches of his life—from a condition that is difficult to describe but common enough. We occasionally speak of one who has had a transforming intellectual or emotional experience—usually described as religious—in which his entire life has been clarified and redirected as (in the expression of William James) "twice-born."[41] His talents, capacities, abilities, however genuine, have hitherto been dispersed and uncrystallized, but now they seem to have been "realized," and to work together harmoniously. But what of those who have *never* been "born" in this sense, let alone twice-born? The unborn person, as I shall use the expression, lacks fundamental convictions or commitments—whether it be a concern for social or political justice, or a belief in God or democracy or immortality—of the kind most people seem to require if they are to define or understand themselves and the world and to act coherently and effectively. Whether he is aware of it or not, the unborn type lacks something like an internal picture of himself that gives direction to the projects he undertakes in life and continuity to the choices he makes among competing projects. In extreme instances of this condition, every significant proposition, every issue and value, every self-description, is open to a continuous and debilitating interior debate.

The unborn person is not merely, or always, someone who is skeptical of general beliefs and values and principles, or who happens to have many interests, or who is impractical or indecisive, nor even someone who has not experienced a sense of belonging to a religious or political group, or who feels "alienated" from his society. The point is, rather, this, that people who are exposed and attracted to many sides of life (for whatever reason) may not be able to form stable inclinations or preferences, or may develop incompatible ones that may grow in urgency if they are kept alive and may indeed keep one another in check. The desire to indulge in free and extravagant images and experiences, for example, may call forth a desire to be constrained and disciplined by logic or some other branch of rigorous thought; the two desires cannot be made identical; one cannot be subsumed under the other; wholeheartedly following one may lead a person to become a poet, the other to a career as mathematician. Someone for whom this kind of conflict is real may be quite unable to form a single picture of himself, or he may create several such pictures and be unable to identify with any one of them. Or, again, he may identify now with this, now with that picture and never enjoy a continuous history as a person. For an unborn person, each side of a fundamental issue may be equally alive; he finds that he cannot come down on either side; he lacks what political parties, or political personalities, possess when they have an "ideology," in the sense of a guide to, or a basis for, political or moral action, like Bolshevism or Zionism.*

Many young people are unborn in this sense for a brief period; then some opinion or value takes hold of them—a stake is driven into the sand—and the structure of identity is slowly established. Others are chronically unborn and likely to experience acute episodes of their condition throughout their lives. Some are ignorant of, or inarticulate about, their condition. Among those who are aware of it, some hope that by changing the circumstances of their lives their condition will subside or disappear; they consequently spend a good deal of energy trying to squeeze themselves into patterns of life in which their uncertainties cannot arise; they become followers of a religious leader, a psychoanalyst, a political or aesthetic savior, someone who will make up their minds for them. Others try to justify their condition by claiming that their lives are superior to those of other people because they have not confined themselves to any rigid style of life but appreciate, indeed embody, a diversity of lives. Some of these go so far as to *disidentify*, as it were, with the conventional categories of life; they are not, they claim, poets or mathematicians or Jews or

---

* Of course such ideologies may be dogmatic, or self-deceptive, or destructive: They may close off, or imprison, those who hold them, or be used to sanction monstrous actions. The point I wish to make is only about the value of having a personal ideology, not about the value of any particular personal ideology.

heterosexuals or political radicals; these, they say, are admittedly *possible* self-descriptions, but no more. They suppose that by withholding their commitment from any of them they have succeeded in stepping outside all restrictions that membership in ordered society can impose upon their inner lives. At the same time, they usually long for a fuller involvement in life and in the lives of others; they feel unused-up, underemployed; the temporary projects they are able to undertake with confidence are too fleeting to give them a sense of purpose or consecutiveness. In many societies, they are pressured by parents, teachers, friends to choose a path and to sharpen themselves into a shape that is more familiar and acceptable, even though it is often unclear to what extent the causes of the unborn state lie within their control.*

* In my view, there is no general answer as to what causes this condition: a physical cause—a brain lesion or a particular diet—may be present in some cases, whereas in others the predominant cause may be a defect in the will, a neurotic inability to choose a fork in the road, and in still others a principal refusal to choose (based on a theory like philosophical skepticism). We are accustomed to saying that certain people are "born" to certain occupations— we speak of a "born" athlete or diplomat or actor—and we mean that by good fortune they possess the gifts or abilities that happen to be those required by a profession that already exists. But most people are not lucky in this respect, either because no such profession exists or because they do not know what talents they have (and thus what they are "fitted" to do) or how to identify them, and consequently they do not make use of their actual talents or gifts; they often accomplish too little, or unsuccessfully try to do too much. For example, William James, who suffered from numerous crises of self-identification in his youth—at various times he thought of himself as a painter, a philosopher, a psychologist—told his sister that "the constitutional disease from which I suffer is what the Germans call *Zerissenheit*, or torn-to-pieces-hood,"[42] and wrote in his *Principles of Psychology*: "I am often confronted with the necessity of standing by one of my empirical selves and relinquishing the rest. Not that I would not, if I could, be both handsome and fat and well-dressed, and a great athlete, and make a million a year, be a wit, a *bon-vivant*, and a lady killer, as well as a philosopher, a philanthropist, statesman, warrior and African explorer, as well as a 'tone-poet' and saint. But the thing is simply impossible. The millionaire's work would run counter to the saint's; the *bon-vivant* and the philanthropist would trip each other up; the philosopher and the lady killer could not well keep house in the same

When Valéry began his "self-analysis" and ran up against the question of what he was to be or become, he did not treat it merely as a problem of finding a career or profession. He became peculiarly attached to it; one senses that he prized the question or problem of self-definition for its own sake and that it became part of his character, a lens through which he viewed the world. He pursued this problem throughout his life in his private notebooks without ever arriving at a firm definition of his inner life. At the same time, his official career as a poet, essayist, and intellectual passed alongside this self-questioning like the scenery in a cyclorama. In 1892, he wrote in a memoir, "Even I did not know where I was headed. No profession, no regular studies, nothing produced, not even any projects."[44] He wrote that "I lived waiting for I do not know what incident to turn up and change my life. My trunk was always at the foot of my bed as a symbol of the departure I was ready to take upon the slightest token by Fate. I held myself in readiness to obey any call or external intervention giving me the signal to transform this stagnant life."[45] He was already twenty-one when he wrote this, however; and thirteen years later we still find him in a similar mood, writing to a friend, "Je travaille peu. Je ne lis pas. J'attends je ne sais quel messie." ("I work little. I don't read. I await some unknown messiah.")[46] It seems clear that even at this late date Valéry had not been able to commit himself to a fixed point of view about the world or human beings or human values, something that is commonly thought to be necessary if one is to lead an ordered life. It also seems, however, that, in time, he accepted this state of affairs and, as we shall see, convinced himself that it was a kind of virtue. Since he was unable to choose a path, "versatility" and "reversible equilibrium"—the capacity to believe this or that, or to act this way or that, at will—became his central aim. What he called his "inner 18 brumaire," his "revolution d'esprit"[47]—

tenement of clay."[43] What James is describing is the impossibility of being too many things. The unborn has not been able to fashion himself into anything at all; he stands frozen before the horizon of possibilities that he could individually, but not severally, make actual.

his "crisis" of 1892—did not create any new convictions but issued in the adoption of a kind of skepticism, a philosophical theory that justified his having no convictions at all and engaging permanently in self-analysis.*

He came to be proud to discover that in him there was "always *reason for not* preferring a solution" to a problem. While he was pleased to reject one image of himself after another, other people—Gide, Louÿs, Rivière—became responsible for "arranging" his public career—as if it were the creation of the publicity department of a Hollywood studio— and still others—readers, literary critics, university professors—became responsible for discovering the "meaning" of his poems and inferring his opinions from his half-written, "unfinished" aphorisms.

III

In Valéry, the inability to be anything in particular led to a desire to be everything at once, or at any rate to being capable of becoming anything at all. He was preoccupied as a young man with the question of what a human mind can do. If not all human minds seem to be capable of producing great works of art or important scientific hypotheses, he wondered, might they nevertheless become so if their native mental powers were "released" or "realized" by some system of rigorous training? He was fascinated by Poe's suggestion in the *Domain of Arnheim* that "many far greater than Milton have contentedly remained 'mute and inglorious' " and that "the world has never seen—and that, unless through some series of accidents goading the noble order of mind into distasteful exertion, the world will never see—that full extent of triumphant execution, in the richer domains of art, of which the human nature is absolutely capable."[49] After reading Baudelaire's translation of Frances

---

* In 1920 he summarized this theory: "*J'ai eu foi dans le scepticisme*, ma devise étant *Faire sans croire* ou Analyse d'abord." ("*I had faith in skepticism*, my motto being *Do without believing* or Analysis first.")[48]

Osgood's memoir of Poe, which mentions the "brilliant imaginings which passed through his ever-vigilant mind,"[50] he became convinced that Poe had realized his own possibilities and that he might be able to do the same. Henceforth he appraised all the activities in his life by whether they advanced or retarded this aim. The aim of his life, he said, was to "exhaust" his possibilities, to carry his mind to the limits of its powers by setting it problems and difficulties to overcome.

This was the idea of "self-possession" or self-mastery, perhaps the cardinal idea of Valéry's thought. "Le problème capital dans la vie," he wrote, "est celui de l'ascèse, que j'entends comme possession de soi" ("Life's crucial problem is that of asceticism, by which I mean self-possession").[51] As with other terms that he used, he was not consistent in his usage of "possession de soi." In some places he speaks of it as the *identification* of "intellectual" powers we might currently have—the ability, say, to tell a valid argument from an invalid one, or to point out whether one idea is compatible with another, or to exercise taste in appraising the aesthetic merits of a painting. In other places, the phrase seems to refer not only to self-knowledge (in this sense) but also to an active effort to develop and organize each of our intellectual powers to the maximum and to combine them in such a way that they give rise to new powers. On this conception, we not only recognize or master a power we already have—like the capacity to count, or to type, or to swim or play the piano—but we seek to deliberately expand our powers and create in ourselves the capacity to acquire other powers—like the capacity to learn things like typing or playing the piano more quickly or efficiently. In this latter sense, indeed, "possession de soi" seems to be a misnomer, since it is used to refer to a *change* of self, not knowledge of the current self.* In still other places he again shifts

---

* Our aim, he says, should not be to create "telle *oeuvre*, mais de faire en *soi-même* celui qui fasse, puisse faire—cette *oeuvre*. Il faut donc construire de *soi*, en *soi*, ce *soi* qui sera l'instrument à faire telle *oeuvre*" ("any specific *work*, but to create in *oneself* the being who makes, who can make, such a *work*. Hence one must construct out of the *self*, in the *self*, that *self* who

to a different meaning of the expression, speaking of "possession de soi" as a form of versatility, the power to turn with ease from one skill or capacity to another.

Valéry frequently speaks of dancers or athletes who were once thought to possess some fixed range of capacities but who, upon taking some regime of exercise or training, discovered that they could do much more than they hitherto suspected. The same is true of the mind, according to Valéry. If we set it problems and exercises—whether logical puzzles or demanding restrictions on the composition of a poem—we may discover mental powers we had not thought we had. "Happy people"[54]— people without problems of this kind—"have no mind," he wrote, in words that might have been written by an American pragmatist; conversely, we might be able to "create" a mind by posing it difficulties.*

Valéry thought that this method of discovering our intellectual powers needs to be guided by a theory of what human minds are capable of becoming and how our mental powers arise, develop, and act together in the human organism. The problem is to discover "la gamme et le système d'accords dont la pensée sera la musique" ("the scale and tuning whose music will be thought").[57] He is led by this concern to stupendous speculation covering hundreds of pages in his notebooks, in which he considers the physical basis of mental life and postulates principles of a science of mind. He did not actually

will be the instrument of making any specific *work*").[52] Judith Robinson describes Valéry's idea of self-possession simply as "une éthique de l'esprit, qui a pour but suprême de développer jusqu'à leurs dernières limites les pouvoirs intellectuels propre à chaque individu" ("a morality of the mind whose supreme goal is to develop to their ultimate limits the intellectual powers suitable to each individual").[53]

* "More than once," he wrote, "I have been taken with the idea of writing a kind of 'Treatise on the Training of the Mind.' I called it *Gladiator* after a famous race horse."[55] Judith Robinson notes that a book by General L'Hotte, *Un Officier de Cavalerie*, was one of Valéry's favorite books; what especially impressed him, she says, is "le parallèle entre l'entraînement du cheval pur sang et l'éducation de l'esprit" ("the parallel between the training of the Thoroughbred horse and the education of the mind").[56]

create such a science. But he repeatedly tried to create what he called his "système"—a formal representation or geometry of the "operations" of the mind, not the *content* of mental states or their physical structures, only their "formal relations" with one another. He is also concerned, as might be expected, to criticize the vocabulary of psychology, which he says has been disfigured by a "cortège" of "impurities"—words like "soul," "consciousness," "will"—that are impregnated by ancient and erroneous assumptions. Psychology, he writes, is still in "l'époque où le sec, l'humide, le feu et l'eau étaient les constituants de la physique" ("the period when the moist and the dry, fire and water, were the constituents of physics").[58] He will use in his own system only "des notions nouvelles, pures, vierges, fondées directement et visiblement sur l'expérience et l'observation" ("new, pure, virgin notions, based directly and visibly on experience and observation").[59]

His central idea, he tells us, is that the mind is a "closed system"—distinct from the "system" of the body but produced by it—that obeys laws of conservation similar to those that hold in the case of energy or heat. He hopes to show that our minds can be analyzed with the help of the mathematical devices so successfully used in thermodynamics to represent the laws by which energy is conserved and transformed in physical systems, and to do so without specifying in detail the "elements" of the system. The mind runs through "phases" or "cycles," he says, and he speculates that the transition from waking to sleeping might be represented in the same way that thermodynamics formally represents the cycle through which a solid can be converted into a liquid and can then be frozen back into a solid. He thinks that what we call "thought" and "sensation" is produced by a "disequilibrium" in the system of the mind. His "originality" as a thinker, he says, consists in seeing "la conscience et ses formations comme une système fermé quasiphysique, à deux variables" ("consciousness and its formations as a quasi-physical closed system, with two variables")—the sensory and the psychic aspects of mental functioning—"en concurrence et en composition toute soumise à une loi de changement" ("entirely governed by a law of change in their opposition to one another and in their composition").[60] Unfortunately the "système" is too vague to be of much interest. Valéry never explains what it is that is "conserved" in mental events or processes like imagining, desiring, or forgetting. He asks us to judge his theory by its "utility" but never explains in what way it is supposed to be useful or how we are supposed to judge its usefulness. Moreover, he does not make it clear whether the "système" should be taken as a scientific hypothesis or in some other way. In some places he seems to regard it as an objective scientific hypothesis that might be helpful in justifying anyone's effort to acquire "possession de soi." In other places he seems to see the theory as one that is "utile" for him alone.* On still other pages he is inclined to see the theory as the basis of an important discovery about the human mind—any mind—that might lead to a new understanding of it. In this mood, he coyly admits that "mon devoir n'est pas facile" ("my task is not an easy one") and without irony suggests that "je tente à mes risques et périls ce qu'on tenté et accompli Faraday en physique, Riemann en mathématiques—Pasteur en biologie—et d'autres"—Wagner no doubt—"en musique" ("I am attempting at my own risks and perils what Faraday attempted and achieved in physics, Riemann in mathematics—Pasteur in biology—and others . . . in music").[64] This was written when he was a young man, but forty years later he is still praising himself as a scientific thinker: "Il est

---

* "Mon but principal," he wrote, "a été me figurer aussi simplement, aussi nettement que possible mon propre fonctionnement d'*ensemble*—monde, corps, pensées" ("My main goal has been to conceive as simply, as clearly as possible, my own *total* functioning—world, body, thoughts").[61] Later he asserts that "le système—n'est pas un 'système philosophique'—mais c'est le *système de moi*—mon *possible*—mon va-et-vient—ma manière de voir et de revenir" ("The system—is not a 'philosophical system'—rather it is the *system of myself*—my *possibilities*—my vacillations—my way of seeing and of repeating").[62] And toward the end of his life he wrote that the main idea of the "système" was "hardie, neuve, feconde pour moi (seul), peu soutenable, imaginaire au regard des tiers" ("bold, new, fruitful for myself [alone], scarcely defensible, imaginary in the eyes of outsiders").[63]

temps de se vanter un peu. Je me vante ou m'accuse d'avoir—
le premier, peut-être—essayé d'introduire dans l'étude ou connaissance de la pensée—de ses produits et valeurs—une con-
sidération *quantitative*" ("It is time to boast a little. I boast—
or accuse myself—of having been perhaps the first man who
tried to introduce into the study or knowledge of thought—of
its products and values—a *quantitative* consideration").[65]
It is therefore unclear in what spirit we are to take the "système." There are some stimulating suggestions and a good deal
of interesting introspective reporting in the pages of his notebooks devoted to it. But in contrast to what one sympathetic
interpreter says—that Valéry was a precursor of Norbert Wie-
ner's "cybernetics"—I cannot see (apart from the virtues I have
already noted) much more in these hundreds of pages than a
kind of doodling in scientific terms and imagery. A topic is
taken up and casually examined and then dropped, usually after
an obscure opinion about it has been expressed, and then another topic is taken up and treated in the same way. Valéry
rarely looks at an issue with any great care or attention; he
does not draw out the conflicting considerations that make it
up or try to respond to it by a dialectical effort to find what
truth lies in these opposing views. He prefers to announce a
grand generalization that, it frequently seems clear, he probably knows is false but which he allows himself to express since
he is only writing in a notebook. Days later, these notebooks
show, without explicitly renouncing his earlier view, he may
discover its opposite. He is made giddy by the excitement of
large claims. But he rarely returns to the same problem to try
to carry through a tentative solution to it or to combine his
ideas or relate them to one another. He just moves on to
something more interesting. In particular, he never asks whether
his own hypotheses conform to the conditions of verifiability
or testability he lays down for "legitimate" science. It should
be little surprise that the "système" has not been taken up by
neurobiologists or psychologists.

Even though he was unable to provide a scientific basis for
his idea of "possession de soi," Valéry wrote that "toutes mes

vues, mes sentiments, mes répulsions, sont dominées, en-
gendrés—par la manie de l'accroissement de l'esprit, et je ne
considère la vie que sous cet aspect" ("All my views, my feelings, my repulsions are dominated—engendered—by the mania
of mental growth, and I consider life only in this aspect").[66]
He convinced himself, for example, that art, music, science,
religion, education, philosophy, among other activities, might,
if suitably interpreted or reformed, contribute to the self-possession of someone who studied them. He even goes so far as
to find "possession de soi" in romantic love, which he calls a
"disease" and a "mystification of the sex act." When two people are said in popular usage to fall in love, he writes, they are
usually doing little more than reaffirming their self-love; their
love is what Mme. de Staël called "self-love à deux."[67] Still,
he thinks that love can be morally justified by what it can do
for the lover: "la valeur vraie—(c'est-à-dire utilisable) de l'a-
mour est dans l'accroissement de vitalité générale qu'il peut
donner à quelqu'un" ("love's true [that is to say, utilizable]
value is in the growth of general vitality it can afford someone").[68]

Valéry shows by his frequent description of his idea of "possession de soi" as a "myth" that he was aware, at least sometimes, of the compensatory value of the idea, whose origins he
ascribes to the convulsive experiences of 1892. Valéry's unborn
state, one might say, gave rise to a need to see himself as
integrated, whole, complete, a need given intellectual form in
a romantic theory of self-realization. On the other hand, Valéry
also professed to be an enlightened positivist, a follower of
Poincaré and Claude Bernard, someone who distrusted "idols"
of all kinds and who demanded verifiable hypotheses and clear
definitions of terms he used. He found "possession de soi" and
science everywhere he looked. For example, poetry was to
make use of scientific effects and yet also be an instrument of
personal development.[69]

Poetry, he thought, should be "pure"—that is, drained of
all prose influences and of all factual, personal, or emotional
elements. Moreover, he had learned from Poe's *Rationale of*

Verse and *Philosophy of Composition* that literature can be
"scientific." In Valéry's view, it should be the product of a
general mechanical procedure, without considerations of
"thought" or "content"; it need not have any single "meaning."* He sharply distinguished between the author of a poem,
the poem itself, and its readers. The poet, he wrote, should be
an "engineer" who creates a "machine" for producing a "poetic
state of mind by means of words."[71] The poem is a self-con-
tained linguistic object that has the power to suggest things
and qualities to the reader, and to create what he called
"ravissement sans référence" ("delight without reference").
"Inspiration" or "enthusiasm" or "sincerity" or some other
psychological state plays no necessary part in the creation of a
poem, he wrote; to suppose it does is to reduce the author of
a poem to an observer of something that is going on inside
him. Creating a poem, he said, is a matter of "calculation."
The poems for which he was famous, he says, were "calculated."

   The final end of poetry, like so much else, was for him the
exercise of his own intellectual powers. The poet should submit
himself to strict metrical schemes and stanzaic forms, and to a
small vocabulary, for this makes the problem of creating poetry
harder and therefore more rewarding for him. "La poésie même,"
he said, "ne m'a intéressé comme sorte d'instinct de rossi-
gnol;—mais *surtout* comme problème et prétexte à difficultés—
ou comme construction bien définie; à conditions psycholo-
giques et physiques imposées; comme exercice des ressources
d'un certain genre et une dialectique non pour convaincre mais
pour enchanter" ("Poetry itself has been of no interest to me
as a sort of nightingale instinct; but *particularly* as a problem
and a pretext for difficulties—or as a well-defined construction,
subject to certain imposed psychological and physical conditions; as an exercise in resources of a certain kind and as a

---

   * When Gustave Cohen or Alain "interpreted" his poems, Valéry said
that his "verses have the meaning that people attach to them" and did not
attempt to correct them.[70]

dialectic not to convince but to enchant"). [72] This indeed is how he distinguished himself from Mallarmé, for whom the creation of a poem—the linguistic construction—was "the essential and unique object." [73] For Valéry writing a poem was "a particular application of the mind's powers."

If one looks at Valéry's thought as a whole, one sees that he was constantly trying to promote two incompatible views: the romantic theory of self-realization that allowed him to suppose that he could acquire unity, harmony, coherence, and completeness—attributes he lacked—and to see everything he touched as part of a single stream of meaning; and a skeptical and positivistic philosophy of life according to which all genuine problems or issues are empirical and soluble, a philosophy that excludes from rational analysis much of what passes as morals, religion, politics, history, psychology, and a good deal more, including the notion of "possession de soi." The result of trying to combine these conflicting ideas created an internally divided body of thought that had little practical content and that, one suspects, did nothing to guide his daily life. The overwhelming impression one receives of him is that of a brilliant but fundamentally colorless and chilly personality unable to form a controlling image of itself and retreating into a snobbish and haughty detachment, a *grand seigneur*, as Count Kessler described him, with "a gleaming surface of manners and intelligence over an abyss of obscurity which is difficult to define and perhaps deliberately veiled." [74]

IV

Valéry's views on philosophy illustrate the tension between romanticism and positivism in his thought that I have just described. On the one hand, the classical problems of philosophy seemed to him figments, myths, linguistic fairy tales; at the same time he was attracted to them as puzzles or obstacles the study of which might improve his mental power.

A person like the young Valéry who is profoundly concerned with what he shall be or do is likely to be familiar with some

of the problems of philosophy long before they are explained
to him by teachers of philosophy, for these problems are often
only precise formulations of doubts and questions that have
already suggested themselves. It is natural for him to ask himself such questions as: Which way of life should I choose? Which
is the best? Is it the one that brings me the most money, or
the most power over others, or the greatest amount of physical
pleasure? What is it that is good in itself—my own happiness,
the welfare of the human race? Are there universal standards
of right and wrong, good and evil? This series of questions,
which could be multiplied indefinitely, often suggest themselves
to intelligent and inquisitive people. They are not formulated
as philosophical problems as they have been stated here, but
these are the kinds of questions that give rise to such problems
when they are accompanied by arguments that show what conflicting philosophical principles are at stake in them. Once one
has asked such questions, one might go on to ask others: Are
values such as good and evil discovered or invented? Is there
an objective reality that is independent of the knower? If so,
how do we know anything about it? How do we know such
propositions as "2 plus 2 equals 4" or "I see my hand"?

In 1894, Valéry began to rise before dawn and write down
his thoughts in notebooks that he left on his death and that
were published posthumously in France. The full set of *cahiers*—261 volumes—covers some 26,600 pages in the 29-vol-
ume facsimile edition published between 1957 and 1961 by the
Centre National de la Recherche Scientifique.[75] James Lawler,
a close student of Valéry's thought, has written that these notebooks were "the mainspring of his creative life, of comparable,
but more oblique, importance for the origins of his work than
were *Jean Santeuil* and *Contre Sainte-Beuve* for Proust's mas-
terpiece."[76] Valéry conceived the notebooks, he continues, as
"the record of his mental exercises, his logbook compiled in
the name of self-control, the disport of his detachment, clarity,
precision." Valéry called the *cahiers* the principal work of his
life; "mon vrai moi est là" ("my real self is therein"),[77] he
wrote to Gide. He wrote in them on biology, history, mathe-

matics, poetry—whatever happened to interest him—and did
not edit himself or try to transform his ideas into the ironic
velvet style of his published work. Like much of Valéry's work,
these notebooks have been dealt with in a large critical literature.[78] But his comments on philosophy, which occupy some
three hundred pages of fine print in the Pléiades edition of the
Cahiers edited by Professor Robinson, and which provide a
much fuller sense of Valéry's views on philosophy than his
previously published work, have hardly been touched on by
specialists in Valéry's work or by philosophers. These remarks
are not written in the style of the pulseless treatises of philosophy's dead giants, or the informal contemporary fashion among
philosophers of constructing cobwebs of queries, jokes, and
hypotheses around some plausible assumption, suggesting unlimited complications beneath its surface. They are, instead,
hurried, colorful, and informal observations and fragments of
arguments, *aperçus*, reactions to a wide and varied reading and
to extensive thought on philosophy.

Teachers of philosophy frequently encounter at least two
attitudes—by no means the only attitudes—toward philosophy
among their students. The first is practical and constructive. It
finds philosophical problems unreal, and disposes of them
whenever possible by challenging their premises or by drawing
distinctions that dissolve them. The problem of the external
world—is there an objective reality independent of the knower?—
is altogether silly to them—"external" to what? is the knower
"external" to the world? they ask. They have no sympathy with
the student who, like Descartes, is genuinely concerned to
know whether he exists; who is asking the question? they say.
Very little is left of philosophy after this kind of temperament
has examined it. The other sort enjoy philosophical problems
the way some enjoy crossword puzzles or parlor games; they
derive pleasure from trying to solve them, and are fascinated
by arguments for their own sake. Truth for its own sake is
rarely what they value about philosophy; they study it for the
pleasure of acquaintance with large and exciting claims and the
stimulus of paradoxes. Valéry alternated between these atti-

tudes, as we shall see. Traditional philosophy, he thinks, is a mass of confusions; if philosophers were to define their terms, their problems would vanish. Philosophy should be reformed into an instrument of self-development; the problems of philosophy should be of use; they should serve as stimuli to thought. The greater part of Valéry's efforts are devoted not to answering philosophical questions, but to showing that traditional philosophy as a project or discipline—its problems and methods and "results" taken together—has been fruitless and should be reformed into such an instrument. He is therefore less concerned with solving any particular problem, such as the problem of the external world or the mind-body problem, than with the rationale or "justification" of philosophy and its methods.

Valéry's notebook entries on philosophy are those of an amateur who has found himself puzzled by philosophical problems and who is trying to make his way around a difficult subject. He exaggerates a good deal and often fails to support his judgments or to defend them against competing claims. He feels—perhaps wrongly—that he must provide a reason for studying philosophy before he actually begins to do so, but he does not know where to look for such a reason. The notebook entries are sharply formulated, in striking contrast to the somewhat affected and overwritten prose one associates with Valéry. He writes here with a sense of discovering something for himself; his ideas have a wit and bluntness that are usually absent, moreover, from the writings of philosophers, many of whom have rendered themselves incapable of expressing themselves clearly. Valéry asks himself what impulses drove him to study the subject; he tries to explain to himself his desire to study philosophy by what he knows of his own character. He does not succeed, in my opinion, in bringing any particular philosophical problem closer to a solution—this was not really his aim, as we noted above—but he sets down hundreds of propositions, many of them vivid and brilliant, that express in amusing and provocative formulations a description of the activity of philosophers that is at once more suggestive and straightforward than most descriptions of philosophy offered by philosophers themselves.

"I am not at ease with philosophy," he wrote. "I know that it is inescapable, and that we can hardly open our mouths without paying tribute to it. But how can we help that, when philosophy itself cannot tell us precisely what it is? It is almost meaningless to say, as people often do, that every man is a philosopher without knowing it, since the very man who takes it up consciously is unable to explain exactly what he is up to."[79] The behavior of philosophers fills him with suspicion. They seem to him to have toiled for thousands of years without ever explaining what it is they want to accomplish; their problems seem false, their speculations frivolous; they have by their own account achieved few results and made little progress. It is (not surprisingly) unclear to him why philosophy has any importance.

In 1917, Valéry listed in his notebook a number of classical philosophical problems that he considered to be "false": the "reality" of the external world; the immortality of the soul; Zeno's paradoxes of motion; the reality of time and space; free will versus determinism. Elsewhere he explained some of these and similar judgments. "Toute l'affaire du Zénon," he wrote in 1937, "repose sur cette curiosité . . . philosophique: *S'efforcer d'imaginer impossible un phénomène* (vol de flèche, etc.) *d'observation constante et banale*" ("Zeno's whole case rests upon this 'philosophical' oddity: *to compel oneself to consider impossible a phenomenon* (an arrow's flight, etc.) *of the most regular and ordinary observation*").[80] After all, he continues, "nous savons que la flèche vole et qu'Achille attrapera la tortue—mais nous savons aussi que si nous pensons vraiment à la flèche, nous perdons aussitôt le vol. Nous savons qu'il n'est pas vrai que le mobile parcoure d'abord la *moitié* du chemin, la moitié de la moitié etc. Car moitié est un arrêt qui exclut le mouvement" ("We know the arrow flies, and that Achilles will catch up with the tortoise—but we also know that if we really think of the arrow, we immediately lose its flight. We know it is not true that a moving body first covers *half* its course, half of that half, and so on. For half is a stop which excludes movement"). Our daily observations show that something must be wrong with the philosophical problem, which is just a fabrication so clever that it has hypnotized generations of philosophers. Again (to use an example we have already mentioned), he asks, what kind of problem is the so-called difficulty of the "external world"? If it is a scientific question, then we should be able to investigate it by probabilistic or statistical methods, but to ask what is the probability of the existence of the external world is absurd. In fact, the question is an "invention gratuite";[81] parler de la réalité du monde extérieur, c'est demander si le mètre étalon est un mètre" ("gratuitous invention; to speak of the reality of the external world is to ask if the standard meter is a meter at all").[82] In other places he thinks that he can dispose in a similar way with other philosophical problems. The famous mind-body problem—what is the relation between these seemingly quite different things that coexist in the human being, and perhaps in other species?—rests, for Valéry, on a trick, since mind and body are "relative terms."[83] "La distinction de l'âme et du corps est impossible dans le détail. Dès que l'on précise il y a inextricable mélange" ("The distinction between body and soul is impossible in detail. As soon as there is any attempt at precision, there is an inextricable mingling").[84] At best, one can draw a functional distinction between them; there is, moreover, no independent entity named by the word "mind." Only philosophers hold that mind is *opposed* to body: they have defined it so—that is all. Or consider the question of the origin of the world. "Parler de l'origine du monde, c'est le considérer comme objet fabriqué. Parler du 'monde,' c'est supposer un objet qui se tient dans la main" ("To speak of the origin of the world is to consider the world as a manufactured object. To speak of the 'world' is to posit an object to be held in the hand").[85] And to ask *who* created the world is not to ask a question but to state a dogma.

Such philosophical problems, he says, are "gaping mouths" into which "we go on pouring fatuous answers, and with them our mind's self-respect."[86] To discuss the truth or falsity of philosophical theories and systems—"machines d'opéra intellectuel" ("intellectual wind machines")[87]—leads only to a dialectical contest in which "l'échange des propositions antinomiques entr'elles est devenu un régime permanent" ("the interchange of contradictory propositions has become a steady diet").[88] These problems are "false" and "unreal," he says, and must be set aside and replaced by real ones if philosophy is to be of any use.

As we shall see, he does not use the idea of a "true" or "real" problem consistently. When criticizing philosophical problems as "unreal," however, he often uses a positivist criterion according to which an "unreal" or "false" problem is one that rests on an "abuse of language." As early as 1901—many years before the publication of Wittgenstein's *Tractatus* or the formation of the Vienna circle of positivist philosophers, who also made this point—he writes that "any problem which leads to antinomies"—contradictions between apparently rational principles—"is constructed by means of an abuse of language."*[89] In 1913 he wrote that "il n'y a de vrais problèmes que ceux dont nous savons d'avance la classe de la réponse" ("The only real problems are those whose class of answers we

---

* Many philosophers, he says, assume that each element of ordinary speech is a *name* of something—a point later made by Wittgenstein and Gilbert Ryle. He says that philosophers take words in themselves to be problems, as if they were essences to be discovered instead of conventions created to deal with specific interests or needs. They treat concepts formed in other places and times as if they were appropriate to our present circumstances, forgetting that "la philosophie et ses mots et ses problèmes se sont faits dans des époques où la physique et la physiologie étaient enfantines" ("Philosophy and its words and its problems were created in periods when physics and physiology were in their infancy").[90] This is why "le métaphysicien qui parle de Dieu, du Monde, des essences, etc. est comparable à un homme qui imprimerait des billets de banque sans encaisse ni garanties—et par consequence qui pourrait en faire de cent milliards, d'une infinité de francs, etc." ("The metaphysician who speaks of God, of the World, of essences, etc. is comparable to a man who prints banknotes without capital or collateral—and who consequently might produce billions—an infinite number of francs, etc.").[91]

know in advance").[92] A quarter of a century later he is able
to say flatly that "tout problème dont la solution est indifférente
à la pratique ou insoluble par elle est ou—inexistent—ou pure-
ment verbal, du à langage, ou—mal énoncé" ("any problem
whose solution is either indifferent to practice, or cannot be
solved by the latter, is either nonexistent or purely verbal—
due solely to language—or else ill-stated").[93] On this view, all
human knowledge is verifiable, as is made clear by the progress
of science; only observation and other real effects in the world
can certify a body of hypotheses. If the principle of verifiability
were applied to philosophy, it would sweep away its phony
problems like a broom. For example, Valéry invites us, in an
essay on freedom,[94] to consider the celebrated problem: Are
we able to choose to act according to our own will or are all
events, including our choices, predetermined by causes? He
characteristically says that the word "freedom" has no precise
meaning except in physics. The opposition drawn by philosophers between freedom and determinism he finds entirely unclear: the philosopher's notion of freedom as a "first cause" is
obscure—what is such a cause and how could we know that it
is the absolutely first, or initiating, cause of an event?—and his
idea of determinism seems to presuppose that if we knew everything we could predict any action (including our choices) from
laws and initial conditions, but it is senseless to say that we
could ever "know everything." Furthermore, there are obviously many *kinds* of freedom—physical liberty, freedom of
thought, freedom *from* interference by others, freedom *to* do
what one wishes—and restrictions on liberty that are both external (laws, the police) but also cultural and psychological.
Everything about the so-called problem of freedom looks absurd, he thinks, once we "squeeze" the vagueness out of terms
like "freedom," "cause," and "determinism." There is therefore no problem here that can be put in a clear or soluble form,
and therefore—this is the positivist's conclusion—no problem
at all. (He admits, however, that there is still a problem of
"human action": Is choice a myth? Is the self that makes a
choice a cause in itself?)

Most philosophical problems are like that of liberty, Valéry thinks, and he cannot satisfy himself that prolonged study of them over hundreds and hundreds of years has produced any important results. Indeed, he says, philosophy has not arrived at a single item of knowledge that it can call its own; as Descartes noted, "no single thing is to be found in it which is not subject of dispute," even though "it has been cultivated for many centuries by the best minds that have ever lived."[95] Philosophy seems to be an endless argument about problems whose importance—indeed, whose existence—has not been established. The daily life of philosophers seems to consist in contradicting other philosophers, or in advancing banal propositions—the "proof" that I can see with my eyes or that I have a hand or that it is impermissible to eat children. Unlike in biology or physics, nothing seems to change in philosophy except the choice of problems to argue about.

Even if philosophers have created fascinating hypotheses and images—Plato's cave, the river you cannot cross twice, Achilles running after a tortoise he cannot overtake—they have not, Valéry claims, developed any methods of verifying them. How, he asks, could you verify either contention in the debate over free will? Philosophers seem to have laid down no rules of their game, no controls over the formulation of their problems or the appraisal of tentative solutions to them. As a result, he suggests, they indulge in irresponsible speculation, an accusation that many others before him have made.* And since

---

* The most memorable expressions of this charge have been made by philosophers. Cicero claimed that "there is no statement so absurd that no philosopher will make it," and was approvingly cited by Hobbes and repeated by Descartes, who is cited with admiration by Karl Popper. Voltaire said that "metaphysics contains two things: the first, that all men of sound sense know anyway; the second, that they will never be able to know." Hume and Kant said similar things, the latter speaking in the *Critique of Pure Reason* of the "anarchic dialogue" and "ill-applied industry" of metaphysics, calling it "a dark ocean without beacons," with "no standard weight or measure to distinguish sound knowledge from shallow talk."[96] It may be wondered whether there is another discipline whose legitimacy has been so often called into question by those who have described themselves as belonging to it.

there is so little critical control over these speculations, he adds that philosophers have been set free to make silly and exaggerated claims for their work.* In fact, he says, not only are philosophical problems usually artificial, but answers to them, especially philosophical systems, are equally so—they are lyric poems, dreams, "mots musiques" ("words for music").[98] Metaphysics, he wrote in 1900, is "astrologie de mots" ("word astrology");[99] the metaphysician is the man who speaks "too soon."[100] After a lunch with the theologian Teilhard de Chardin in 1932, he noted maliciously that "tout ce qui est métaphysique me semble ce qu'il y a de plus *léger* et devoir être traité à la Banville, à la Rossini" ("Everything metaphysical seems to me what is lightest of all, even frivolous, and should be treated à la Banville, à la Rossini").[101]

Like Hobbes, or Descartes, or Russell and Carnap, Valéry believed that philosophers write nonsense because they fail to begin their inquiries with clear definitions of terms. What they need, he says, is "une Science des énoncés, et donc une épuration des questions" ("a Science of statements, hence a purification of the questions"),[102] which can be accomplished only by constructing a new language in which "false" problems cannot be formulated. The difficulty, for example, with the problem of free will is that philosophers can create what seems to be a problem by using words and expressions that are entirely unclear. Philosophers could adopt such a language if they wished and confine themselves to "real" problems, but they have not.

Why not? Valéry thinks that they do not because they do not really wish to solve their problems or to submit their claims

---

* There are plenty of examples. Kant wrote in the *Critique of Pure Reason* that "in this inquiry I have made completeness my chief aim, and I venture to assert that there is not a single metaphysical problem which has not been solved, or for the solution of which the key at least has not been supplied." Wittgenstein claimed to have solved all the major problems of philosophy in his *Tractatus*, and Descartes wrote in his *Principles of Philosophy* that "every phenomenon of nature is described in this book." This is the sort of thing that led Whitehead to say that "the chief error of philosophy is overstatement" and Popper to call megalomania the "occupational disease" of philosophy.[97]

to empirical test. Instead, they enjoy doubting and the activity
of creating problems. This is an aspect of philosophy that Valéry stresses again and again. False, unempirical, irresponsible
as they may be, these problems, he thinks, have been the motor
of philosophy, its answers and systems secondary. "C'est la
question qui fait la philosophie" ("It's the *question* that makes
philosophy"),[103] he writes; it is a mistake to assume that philosophers are mainly concerned with the business of settling or
resolving ancient problems—as if these problems simply occurred to everyone and did not owe their existence largely to
the efforts of philosophers. In fact, he says, philosophers struggle hard to invent these questions, or to make them apply to
new social or historical circumstances, and the questions they
choose to pursue, he thinks, are "choisies de manière [à] n'avoir
pas de solution" ("chosen in such a way as to have no solution").[104]

The philosopher has a "mania for interrogation"[105] and his
"trade" is "unlimited interrogation in the interrogative infini-
tive."[106] He carefully monitors and studies "common sense,"
science, and other ways in which we think about the world,
looking for vulnerable elements in them, and then attacks where
our concepts are imprecise, ambiguous, or weakened by mis-
use. To create his problems, he turns concepts that however
loose have served their purpose in everyday life into obstacles,
into instruments designed to "torment" our ruling ideas. The
philosopher transforms "toute réponse en demande" ("every
answer into a question") and "inserts a thousand difficulties
into a common expression in which those who invented the
expression could see none whatever;"[107] he "creates doubts
and perturbations" and paradoxes. This, he says, is what the
philosopher has done with the words "cause," "liberty," "objective." The great philosophical systems are based on the rein-
terpretation of words. The universal statements of Hegel or
Leibniz or Kant—that Reality is Rational, that Man is Free—
are only universal "par écriture" ("by writing")[108] and the elegant symmetries they find in nature are "purely nominal."[109]
He is appalled by the "pseudo-ideas" of Being, Essence, Sub-

stance and "la logique du vide" ("the logic of the void")[110] he finds in Spinoza. The "apparent rigor"[111] of Kant annoys him: "tout Kant suppose, en réalité, une croyance latente à la valeur absolue, surnaturelle du *langage*. . . . Il ne se demande pas si les termes ont un sens, mais cherche un sens idéal de ces termes et croit que ces sens sont des *réalités* transcendentales" ("all of Kant presupposes, in reality, a latent belief in the absolute, supernatural value of *language*. . . . He does not ask whether the terms possess meaning, but rather seeks an ideal meaning for the terms and believes that these meanings are transcendental *realities*").[112] Kant's celebrated laws of morality and beauty are just his personal preferences imposed on all rational beings; indeed, it is "comique de voir Kant qui devait avoir un goût de chien chercher le beau" ("comical to see Kant, who obviously had rotten taste, searching for beauty").[113] Moreover, he is constantly discovering "necessities"[114] in our thought when all that he has done is to point out features of the language we happen to have. He never asks himself whether a judgment that is "necessary" in one language (like "All bachelors are male") may not be contingent in another language. Yet Valéry says that he can imagine a language in which the idea of weight is logically inseparable from that of body, so that "all bodies have weight" is a necessary truth.

Philosophers "doubt" propositions most of us take for granted in order to advance their problems, even though there is rarely any genuine *occasion* for doing so. Descartes, for example, "introduit ce qu'il lui faut pour suivre son raisonnement—il *doute*. Tout est perdu. Il pose *Dieu*. Tout est sauvé. Il écrit *Dieu*—ce qu'il faut pour m'ôter d'un doute" ("introduces what he needs in order to follow his reasoning—he *doubts*. All is lost. He posits *God*. All is saved. He writes *God*—what is needed to remove my doubt").[115] This kind of "philosophical doubt," he says, is an "opération fictive"[116] and "une sorte de pantomime ou comédie qui se joue de telle heure à telle autre" ("a kind of pantomime or comedy performed between fixed hours");[117] it issues in "problèmes de théâtre,"[118] "enfantines—c'est-à-dire posées sans égard aux moyens d'y répondre, et

répondues en conséquence—c'est-à-dire par des moyens dé-
rivés des questions mêmes—dont ils ne sont qu'une autre
expression" ("childish—that is to say, posed regardless of the
means to answer them, and answered consequently, that is to
say, by means derived from the questions themselves—of which
they are merely another expression").*[119]

Once we understand that philosophical problems are constructions created by philosophers, and that even their "pro-
fundity" is a contribution of the philosopher, we must surrender
the uncritical assumption that the "business" of philosophy is
to come up with answers to its questions. This could not be
the business of the many philosophers who have devoted themselves at one time or another to creating difficulties for popular
ways of thinking about the world, and actively preventing them
from being resolved. If Valéry is right, philosophy could not
be what many have thought it to be—a key to the riddles of
existence or some other intellectual construction designed to
bring peace to the soul: something that settles doubts and orders conflicting desires and beliefs. Instead, Valéry suggests,
philosophy, when carefully studied, usually has the effect of
opening up what had previously been regarded as settled and

---

* Exercising philosophical doubt and trying to answer the problems it
gives rise to, Valéry argues, can induce in us an "ivresse théorétique"
("theoretical intoxication").[120] This emotional and instinctual appeal of
philosophy is for him the distinguishing mark of some philosophers, like
Pascal, for whom he conceived a dislike as violent as that felt by Herder for
Voltaire or by Bradley for John Stuart Mill. Pascal is an "excitant," he says,
"une sorte d'agitateur, de turbulent," not an "*aliment*. La différence est
grande. L'excitant se substitue à la fois au *moi* et au monde extérieur—
Consume—amène les réactions. L'aliment reconstitue, recharge, fournit aux
réactions" ("stimulant . . . a kind of agitator, a disturber of peace, [not a]
nourishment. There is a huge difference. The stimulant substitutes both for
the *self* and the external world—consumes—brings about reactions. Nourishment reconstitutes, recharges, provides for reactions").[121] He repeats
Nietzsche's charge that Pascal could have given France the calculus but instead sank into what he calls "raisonnements insupportables—vomissement
total et amer aux pieds de Dieu" ("unendurable reasonings, a total and bitter
vomit at God's feet").[122]

creating an accumulation of doubts and problems. Moreover, in his view it could never have been, and is not now, an enterprise in which "philosophers" as a body try to bring closer to resolution those immensely difficult questions that bedevil us—the mind-body problem, the foundations of ethics, the reality of the objective world—the way, say, a group of oncologists try to conquer cancer, each researcher working on his share of the larger problem that will not be solved unless all work together in a suitable division of labor. The image of this kind of science is in Valéry's view an inappropriate one to use as a model of the activities of philosophers (and perhaps of much science); a better one would be that of a contest or a game played by those who invent—and those who try to solve— "philosophical problems."*

Yet philosophers continually insist that they are engaged less in the creation and promotion of problems (if at all) than in finding the "truth," that is, "solutions" to their problems. The model of their activity, at least for many of them, is science. But this is a false analogy, made by philosophers who don't wish to know what they do every day in their philosophy classes. What "truth" is to be discovered—what "solution" is to be found—when the problem one is trying to solve has been formulated by other philosophers so as to have no solution? This is what Valéry means, I think, when he writes that "ce qui le plus a nui à l'avancement de la philosophie a été (et est encore) la méconnaissance plus ou moins voluntaire de la nature de cette activité-attitude" ("what has done most harm to the advancement of philosophy has been [and still is] the more or less deliberate failure to recognize the nature of this activity-attitude").[124] The result of this self-deception is that it has

---

* Valéry writes: "*Metaphysical controversies*: whether space is finite, whether similar figures can exist—and so forth. Such discussions, when pressed to their extreme limit, have the exciting qualities and sterile outcome of a game of chess. All they prove, when the game is ended, is that A's a better player than B. Sometimes they also teach us that such and such a move should be avoided in future. It's a sure way of losing the game. Or else that we should take such and such precautions."[123]

remained "imparfait, toujours critiqué dans son faux objet et non dans son vrai; jamais poussé à sa perfection propre, mais tendu hors de son vrai domaine" ("imperfect, invariably criticized in its false object and not in its true one; never taken to its own perfection, but extended outside its true realm").[125] Philosophers complain how difficult their problems are, forgetting that it is they who have made them so by progressively closing off one avenue of solution after another. Valéry would have agreed with Santayana that some philosophers "are keenly excited at not knowing where they are. They are really here, in the common natural world, where there is nothing in particular to threaten or to allure them; and they have only to remove their philosophical bandages to perceive it."[126]

If philosophy has been, and is, conducted in such a mistaken manner, how might it be improved? What direction should it take once its false problems and imprecise terminology and florid speculations are removed from it? Like so many other reformers of philosophy—Descartes, Bacon, Spinoza—or William James and Schopenhauer—Valéry hoped that philosophy could be remade so as to give those who study it some self-knowledge, freedom from superstition, and respect for reason; he hoped that it could improve our habit of thinking for ourselves and our appreciation of argument and criticism, as well as to widen our range of emotion, sympathy, and imagination. According to Valéry, philosophy should become an art of "possession de soi." It will never be a science—his positivist teachers have taught him that whatever is not verifiable is a game of words—"jeux de mots"—but it can become an "art" that will improve our lives. And the first step in allowing it to become such an art, he thinks, is confining the work of philosophy to "real" problems, not merely "real" insofar as they do not rest on abuses of language—the positivist criterion of a "real" problem we have mentioned earlier—but "real" also in that they are "mine." True problems, he says when discussing the reform of philosophy, are those which "tourmentent et gênent pour vivre" ("torment and embarrass in order to live").[127] The classical problems of philosophy were nonsense because they were based on obscure concepts, but in addition they were foreign to him and he never understood them "en ce sens que je ne les aurais pas inventés" ("insofar as I had not invented them").[128] We see here that Valéry's allegiance to both a positivist philosophy and a demand for self-realization expressed itself in his thought in two distinct (and conflicting) senses of the "reality" of a problem or concern.*

As in his theory of poetry, much of Valéry's view of a reconstructed philosophy is expressed in positivist language even though the end of philosophy is self-realization. So, for example, he tells us that philosophy needs a "new language" that will purify philosophy of impure concepts and false problems. But Valéry does not believe that this new language is a universal one such as that sought by Ramon Lull or Leibniz or Wittgenstein. Part of the "méconnaissance" philosophers have of their activity is that it is universal and impersonal and scientific. In fact, Valéry says, it is inescapably personal. Even though philosophical systems claim to explain everything in the universe and yet also "pretend to have no author,"[129] he writes, philosophy is nothing but "the product of the philosophical temperament."[130] So even though he uses the positivist's language, Valéry thinks that philosophy must be "reformed" by each person in his own way. "In my opinion," he says, "every philosophy is a question of form. It is the most comprehensive

---

* Valéry never seems to consider the possibility that these criteria of "real" problems might conflict. Yet a problem that I have invented for myself may rest on "abuses" of language, and conversely a problem that does not rest on such abuses may not be "real" for me. Removing all problems that are "unreal" in the linguistic sense from philosophy may not remove all problems that are "unreal" in the other sense. His criteria, moreover, are far from clear. What exactly is an "abuse" of language? Which language is it an abuse of? How does one tell if one "could have invented" a given problem? Valéry constantly implies that science provides the best examples of "real" problems that "il n'y a de vrais problèmes que ceux dont nous savons d'avance la classe de la réponse," as we have seen him say. If that were true, such questions as how gravity and other forces act across empty space would not have been "scientific" or "real" questions when posed in the time of Newton, and Valéry would have urged scientists not to ask them.

form that a certain individual can give to the whole of his internal and external experience—and this without respect to the learning and accomplishments he might possess."[131] Philosophy should not be thought of as a discovery about the universe but as an instrument or device like a piece of clothing or a pair of shoes. It must serve us, "et n'être pas une simple possibilité de discourir—selon un langage special—à côté de la vie, une manière de penser apprise et sans application" ("and not be a simple possibility for making speeches—in a special language—alongside life, a learned way of thinking, and one without application").[132] Otherwise, to adopt a celebrated image of Schopenhauer's, it is nothing more than a wax nose or an artificial limb that must constantly be refastened.

Philosophy should be a form of "possession de soi," he insists. "Une vraie philosophie serait la reconnaissance, l'éducation et la possession de tous les organes spirituels—l'étude de chacun, de leur force ou faiblesse personnelles et leurs suppléances mutuelles" ("A true philosophy would be the recognition, the education, and the possession of all the spiritual organs—the study of each one, of their particular strengths or weaknesses and their mutual substitutions").[133] It should be "*un art de penser* qui soit à la pensée naturelle ce que la gymnastique, la danse, etc. sont à l'usage accidentel et spontané des membres et des forces" ("*an art of thinking* that might be to natural thought what gymnastics, dancing, etc. are to the accidental and spontaneous use of one's limbs and strength"),[134] "une attitude et une tendance au dressage, une volonté vers l'homme dressé par soi-même" ("an attitude and a tendency toward training, a will toward the training of man by himself").[135] The object of philosophy will be "l'accroissement des potentiels, le capital de precision, de force, de réactions justes et rapides" ("the growth of potentials, the capital of precision, of strength, of exact and swift reactions").[136] Leonardo, Descartes, Wagner have used philosophy this way; they are, he says, "men I consider prodigiously more universal than the Aristotles and Platos and the Kants and the Hegels, because they were masters of the means that make it possible to manipulate that in which man can *feel*, with precision, that he is richer and vaster than necessary for individual life—and what more can philosophy want that is not absurd?"[137] The model of a philosopher is Descartes, who created, or wished to create, a "philosophie de puissance réelle" ("philosophy of real power")[138] that would be a genuine method for discovering facts rather than an extension of the impoverished scholastic and medieval logic of science. He "wanted us to discover in ourselves what he had found in himself."*[139] He was not really a "philosopher" in the popular sense. His famous *cogito ergo sum* has no sense.[144] The method of doubt is pointless, he says, and the principles Descartes offers as results of this method are "insignificant."[145] In fact, Valéry says, Descartes is an "anti-philosopher."[146] The true aim of the *cogito* is to do away with philosophy; it means only "j'ai confiance en moi" ("I rely on myself"),[147] and proves nothing, being only "un mot de drame, un mouvement littéraire" ("a theatrical password, a literary movement").[148] The method of doubt in Descartes marks the freedom of his mind, whereas when used by others it becomes "le doute de perroquet" ("parrot doubt").[149]

---

* Valéry writes that "si puissante, si profonde, si seduisante, que soit une philosophie et même une religion, il est impossible qu'elle satisfasse un esprit puissant/actif qui ne l'a pas inventée" ("however powerful, however profound, however seductive a philosophy and even a religion, it is impossible for it to satisfy a powerful/active mind which has not invented it").[140] This is the basis for Valéry's hostility to traditional ways of teaching philosophy, which he thinks "répugne à l'enseignement organisé" ("detests organized instruction").[141] He is horrified at the thought that students might get degrees in philosophy and become professional philosophers: "que la philosophie soit devenu chose scolaire, chose distincte du philosophe, chose professionnelle, chose de mémoire—cela est dérisoire. Car elle ne s'explique que par l'existence individuelle, centrale" ("that philosophy might become an academic matter, something distinct from the philosopher, something professional, a matter of rote—how absurd! For philosophy is accounted for only by an individual, central existence").[142] He exclaims, "quoi de plus laid que la philosophie, ou la chose soi-disant telle, depuis qu'elle s'enseigne à titre de valeur de carrière et comme une specialité professionnelle?" ("What could be uglier than philosophy, or what calls itself philosophy, once it offers its teachings as a career value and a professional specialty?")[143]

What are we to make of Valéry's proposed reform of philosophy? For one thing, the project of reform is unclear because Valéry never seems to have formed any definite idea of "possession de soi" and never clearly explains what is involved in the development of a person's "powers." His discussion of both points is superficial. Despite his constant reference to obstacles that release powers, we are not told *how* such latent powers are to be identified in a person or how to identify *which* obstacles will release *which* powers; indeed, his account of this question is entirely schematic and abstract: He never offers a concrete description of his methods of "dressage," nor does he apply his theory of how to acquire "possession de soi" to any personal or social questions we are familiar with or show how the practical concerns of men like Leonardo or Wagner contributed to their self-realization. Moreover, whatever Valéry means by a "power," the "development" of these powers must surely depend on a number of conditions that he never discusses or mentions. The potentials I have realized may come into conflict—my moral sense may come into conflict, for example, with the way I earn a living; I must also have the stamina, will, and organizational ability to realize my potentials. In addition, much depends on luck—that we are not struck by lightning on our way to an important event in our lives, such as our marriage or an interview for a job. Furthermore, it is impossible to develop *all* of our powers, and the cultivation of some powers brings others into existence and suppresses or inhibits the development of still others. We may learn how to count, which allows us to develop other powers, such as that of counting prime numbers, but in concentrating on acquiring mathematical skills, we may neglect the cultivation of other skills or powers, such as physical strength or a wide knowledge of painting. We must therefore choose *which* powers we wish to develop—our powers of aesthetic appreciation or of physical force or of rational criticism—and the extent to which we wish to develop them. Stated as a problem of choice among powers in this way, the question of "possession de soi" is a version of a central problem of morals, namely, the choice of what kind of self I shall be. Valéry provides no moral criterion of choice among powers, or among alternative conceptions of the "economy" of powers, to be developed by philosophy (or poetry or education) and thus contributes nothing to this ancient question. It may be that this is because he does not believe in "morality" and never broke free of a childish Nietzschean conception of it. Even though he says he should obey the golden rule and not increase suffering in the world, he thinks that morality is "subjective" and "personal"* and that—this is his usual refrain—it too should be made an instrument of "possession de soi": What is moral is what increases my intellectual powers. But this egoistic position is of course a repudiation of morality, which inescapably implies that in a variety of circumstances I may have to modify, or give up, my own desires and interests, or delay their satisfaction, in order to do what is right.

V

If Valéry's proposed reform of philosophy seems unpromising, what of his criticism of traditional philosophy? It, too, seems flawed. His claim that the problems of classical philosophy are not "real," because based on "abuses of language," is a positivist dogma, as is his view that philosophy will progress if we alter and refine the language we use, or confine our talk to propositions in an ideal language in which philosophical problems cannot arise (because they cannot be expressed). No plausible language of this kind has ever been proposed by anyone; those that were could not be used by human beings to communicate with one another. Moreover, his claim that "philosophers," with their "mania for interrogation," have devoted their best energies to "tormenting" us with "purely verbal" problems depends greatly on how such problems are formulated—as is evident if one tries to express the problem of free

* It is entirely characteristic of him to write that "la moralité tombe devant la clarté comme le vêtement dans un pays de soleil" ("morality falls before clarity like a garment in hot countries"), and that it is "imprecise" and "impure."[150]

will or causality or the relation between mind and body or any of the other problems Valéry believes are "false." This hardly justifies us, however, in calling the problems themselves "purely verbal" or "nominal." The categories in which we think, and perhaps the features of the world which they name, if any, are themselves puzzling; one cannot go backward in time, for example, by deciding to use the word "time" in such a way that it is possible. Moreover, not *all* philosophers could be described as concerned with raising intransigent problems, at any rate not all the time. There have been different kinds of philosophers—systems-builders like Hegel, radical critics of systems like Nietzsche, dogmatists like Maistre, skeptics and problem-raisers like Hume or Socrates. To say that some philosophers raise problems some of the time is one thing; it is quite another to claim that all philosophers do so all the time. To try to answer a philosophical problem is not an activity "subordinate" to, or "derivative" from, that of inventing problems. The desire to give an inspiring picture of the world, or to dramatize hopes, ideals, and values in a coherent way is as distinctive of philosophy as are criticism and argument. Philosophers like Aristotle or Spinoza, one feels, were really trying to give a picture of the universe as a whole, to arrange the facts as they knew them in a comprehensible manner, and to help scientists to explain traits, events, and processes in the world.*

If we prune Valéry's stated views of these errors, however, we can formulate the rudiments of a picture of philosophy that is more adequate than the textbook account of philosophers as members of a brotherhood trying to resolve ancient puzzles and instructing us about right conduct and the meaning of life. In a revised version of Valéry's view, we could say that some philosophers invent and promote problems—try to make them profound and insoluble—whereas others try to resolve them;

---

* At the same time, however, what looks like answering problems might have a different source. We can learn the limits of a problem by trying to answer it. When we try to answer problems we are sometimes trying to understand the problem better (by constructing and testing in imagination possible answers to it) or creating a platform, as it were, for a deeper problem.

the activity (and history) of philosophy may be seen as a kind of contest between them. The exaggeration and absurdity for which philosophers have often been criticized is frequently, in this view, a product of the competition between problem-raisers and problem-solvers. The lack of "results" or "progress" in solving philosophical problems—long regarded by many historians of philosophy as a scandal—is no more a deficiency of philosophy, on this view, than it is a deficiency of chess that one side must always lose in a completed game.*

Nor are most calls for the "reform" of philosophy appropriate on this view. The claim, for example, that some method or rule—a priori insight or linguistic analysis or empirical observation—would settle the problems of philosophy is found in Descartes, Hume, Locke, Husserl, Russell, Carnap, Dewey, Wittgenstein. It is interesting to read Mill's contention that Jeremy Bentham "introduced into morals and politics those habits of thought and modes of investigation which are essential to the idea of science; and the absence of which made those

---

* According to William James and Bertrand Russell, it is true, philosophy has had "results," but the credit never goes to it, but rather to the science to which the solution is assigned. Astronomy, for example, was once part of philosophy, as was physics (and linguistics and formal logic), but once repeated and repeatable confirmations of conjectures about material bodies were obtained, the results were termed "scientific," no longer philosophical. But this point is no objection to the view we are describing. It only raises the further question: What a mysterious form of problem-solving philosophy must be if each problem it solves is immediately deprived of its philosophical status.

Once we acknowledge the part played by problem-raising in philosophy, the notion of progress in philosophy must be correspondingly modified. If philosophy is an activity of raising as well as responding to problems, "progress" in it cannot be confined to success in solving problems. It is also progress of a kind when philosophers succeed in bringing out what is involved in an obscure problem or in exposing errors in alleged "solutions" to it. Progress in philosophy can consist in strengthening problems in this way or in binding them more tightly to other problems, thereby protecting them as a group against solution. But progress can also occur if better answers are found to these same problems. The matter hinges on how much, and how fruitfully, the game of philosophy is stimulated and advanced.

departments of inquiry, as physics had been before Bacon, a field of interminable discussion, leading to no result." Philosophers, he continues, are now "forced to understand one another, to break down the generality of their propositions, and to join a precise issue in every dispute. This is nothing less than a revolution in philosophy."[151] The way the game of philosophy has been played has certainly changed over time. But reforms such as the one Mill is proposing, which try to divert the essentially antagonistic forces that keep philosophy in motion into a single line of motion or direction, have always failed; that such a reform would be voluntarily adopted by philosophers would seem as unlikely as all buyers and sellers in a free market agreeing to further the interests of a single firm.*

Valéry's simple but interesting point is that philosophical problems such as the problem of free will differ from mere questions in that philosophers have made such problems "difficult" and in many cases insoluble by protecting them with supporting argument until all avenues of solution are closed. He saw that such problems are not formal or empirical: The problem of free will, for example, cannot be solved by invoking empirical observation or the calculi of mathematics or logic. He also noted that such problems have been discussed for hundreds of years without resolution. The "ontological" argument for the existence of God—that reflection upon the concept of God is sufficient to logically demonstrate that something corresponding to that concept must exist—because He is perfect and existence is one of the "properties" of anything that is perfect—was stated by Anselm in 1060, "refuted" by Gaunilo in the thirteenth century, revived by Duns Scotus, reaffirmed by Descartes, modified by Leibniz, "refuted" by Kant, reaf-

---

* The effort to kill off the whole of traditional philosophy, to "dissolve" its problems, whether led by Comte or Richard Rorty, is a case in point of a failed reform. The "death of philosophy" anxiously awaited never occurs; the old problems simply rearise in new and more respectable formulations. And when philosophers congratulate themselves on "bypassing" certain problems, they usually have succeeded only in abandoning philosophy, not reforming it.

firmed by Hegel, and is still discussed today.[152] Such problems, Valéry seemed to say, are open in the special sense that we have not only not been able to solve them, but we do not know how to go about solving them, or what a satisfactory solution would be. We also have no evidence that we will ever arrive at a solution, or that continued discussion of them will advance us toward a solution. Even if a solution to such a problem were found, it would usually presuppose a solution to other problems of the same sort, so that trying to solve one problem would appear to carry a need to solve others belonging to the same group. (So, for example, solving the problem of free will requires us to solve the equally difficult problem of specifying what relation holds between two events by virtue of which one brings about, or causes, the other.) When one considers that these problems have remained relatively the same over many centuries and have earned the attention of brilliant minds throughout this period, without a single solution to any of them appearing, the suggestion that they are not soluble seems plausible.

But how have they become open in this way? Valéry suggests that philosophers have played a large part in their becoming so, by trying to make them difficult, the way lawyers try to make a case for their client's position. It does not follow, however, that because such problems might once have been simpler and perhaps easier to solve than they are now (as is suggested by the assertion that they have been "made" difficult to solve by philosophers) that we could "make" them easier to solve once again. For what we call "philosophical problems" are problems that have been promoted by exceptionally clever philosophers who have strengthened them with objective arguments that have survived the opposition of common sense and of science, as well as the counter-arguments of lesser or ungifted philosophers; because of the efforts of these outstanding philosophers—Descartes and Hume and G. E. Moore and Russell (to select a few at random)—these problems are today objective constructions that are for all practical purposes really insoluble. But if we have good reasons for believing that they are most likely insoluble, why should we not set them aside? Why study them at all? The fact is that we are entirely unable to follow this policy of suspending judgment. We cannot be indifferent in this way, for example, to the question of why we should be moral or whether we exist. We cannot wait until new evidence comes in to support our view that we should help others in distress. These problems inevitably ensnare us because—soluble or not—they concern our most intimate and deepest convictions, beliefs, and attitudes. They are problems, as Kant noted, that "human reason is not able to ignore" and yet is also unable to answer.[153] We must *respond* to these problems—make up our minds about them—without *solving* them in the sense that a solution would remove the puzzlement entirely, as a vaccine might remove a disease once and for all. And since these problems are generally never really solved, they arise again and again in new and troubling variations as our circumstances change and we acquire new information about the world. The business of responding to them is therefore never finished, and has to be done over and over again.

Other philosophers, perhaps, have suggested that philosophy changes over time in considerable part because of the efforts of philosophers to invent and promote problems. Russell wrote in one phase of his career that "the point of philosophy is to start with something so simple as to seem not worth stating, and to end with something so paradoxical that no one will believe it."[154] The British philosopher H. H. Price noted that the philosopher "deliberately and methodically [causes] the headaches which he is subsequently going to cure."[155] John Dewey claimed that the value of philosophy "lies not in solutions (which only action achieves) but in defining difficulties and methods" and that "the chief role of philosophy is to bring to consciousness, in intellectualized form, in the form of problems, the most important shocks and inherent troubles of complex and changing societies."[156] But few, if any, of them have made this suggestion with such subversive charm and liveliness—or with such carelessness of formulation and indifference to the opinions of teachers, historians, and others who professionally study philosophy—as did Valéry. His contempt for philosophy, as well as his fascination with its reform, gained in expressive fluency and in vehemence, one feels, because they were both so closely bound up with his search for a solution to his own profound lack of self-definition and to other problems encountered by the unborn personality.

Notes

1. T. S. Eliot, "Leçons de Valéry," in *Paul Valéry Vivant* (Cahiers du Sud, 1946), pp. 74–81. Cyril Connolly, *Enemies of Promise* (New York: Doubleday, 1960), p. 419. For biographical information on Valéry, I have drawn on: Alastair Thomson, *Valéry* (London: Oliver & Boyd, 1965); Henry Alexander Grubbs, *Paul Valéry* (New York: Twayne Publishers, 1968); Charles G. Whiting, *Paul Valéry* (London: The Athlone Press, 1960). The biographical introduction to *Paul Valéry: Oeuvres*, 2 vols. (Paris: Gallimard, 1957, 1960), by his daughter Agathe Rouart-Valéry is the best and fullest biography of Valéry so far available. Valéry's works have been translated into English. See *The Collected Works of Paul Valéry*, general editor Jackson Mathews, Bollingen Series, published first in New York by Pantheon Books and subsequently by Princeton University Press. Fifteen volumes were published between 1956 and 1975 in the following order: Vol. IV, *Dialogues*; Vol. VII, *The Art of Poetry*; Vol. III, *Plays*; Vol. XII, *Degas, Manet, Morisot*; Vol. X, *History and Politics*; Vol. XIII, *Aesthetics*; Vol. V, *Idée Fixe*; Vol. IX, *Masters and Friends*; Vol. XIV, *Analects*; Vol. IX, *Occasions*; Vol. II, *Poems in the Rough*; Vol. I, *Poems*; Vol. VIII, *Leonardo, Poe, Mallarmé*; Vol. VI, *Monsieur Teste*; Vol. XV, *Moi*. See also *Paul Valéry: An Anthology* (selected by James R. Lawler), Bollingen Series XLV, Princeton University Press, 1976.
2. For Valéry's friendship with Mallarmé, see *Collected Works*, Vol. VIII, pp. 215ff.
3. See Valéry on his friendship with Pierre Louÿs, written in 1925: "Thirty years ago, the word 'artist' meant us, someone who lived apart, a dedicated person, at once victim and priest, a person who was singled out by his gifts and whose virtues and weaknesses were not those of other men." *Collected Works*, Vol. IX, p. 287.
4. Introduction to *Oeuvres*, vol. 1.
5. Paul Valéry, exposition 31 janvier–31 mars 1956, catalogue prepared by Marcel Thomas, Gerard Willemetz, and Jacques Suffel, preface by Julien Cain, Bibliothèque Nationale, Paris, 1956.
6. *Collected Works*, Vol. XV, p. 52.
7. *Collected Works*, Vol. XV, p. 57.
8. Grubbs, op. cit., p. 38.
9. "Paul Valéry," *Yale French Studies*, vol. 44, 1970.

10. "Bad Thoughts and Not So Bad," in *Collected Works*, Vol. XIV, p. 480.
11. "Rhumbs," in ibid., p. 195.
12. Ibid., p. 37.
13. François Valéry, Preface to *Collected Works*, Vol. X.
14. Letter to Gide, February 14, 1898, in *Collected Works*, Vol. XV, pp. 195f.
15. Paul Valéry, *Cahiers* (2 vols.), edited and annotated by Judith Robinson (Paris: Gallimard, 1973). Henceforth, in referring to items in the notebooks of Valéry, I shall refer to this edition by volume, page, and date of entry thus: I,300;1914 indicates that the cited statement is from volume I, page 300, and was written in 1914. The statement referred to in the text is II,1448;1897–1900.
16. II,1491;1931.
17. *Collected Works*, Vol. XV, p. 263.
18. *Le Crapouillot*, described by André Berne-Joffroy, *Valéry* (Paris: Gallimard, 1960), p. 35.
19. Harry Kessler, *In the Twenties* (New York: Holt, Rinehart and Winston, 1971), pp. 300, 327.
20. Igor Stravinsky and Robert Craft, *Memories* (New York: Doubleday, 1962).
21. André Gide, *Journal* (Paris: Gallimard, 1939), Vol. II, entry, May 8, 1927.
22. Sarraute, in Berne-Joffroy, op. cit., p. 287.
23. Eliot, op. cit.; introduction to *Collected Works*, Vol. VII.
24. Julien Benda, in Berne-Joffroy, op. cit., p. 282.
25. Introduction to *Collected Works*, Vol. X.
26. Gide, op. cit., Vol. III, entry, Oct. 28, 1929, fn. 23.
27. *Collected Works*, Vol. XIV, p. 265.
28. Gide, op. cit., Vol. III, entry, Oct. 28, 1929, fn. 23.
29. I,1448;1943.
30. *Collected Works*, Vol. XIV, p. 128.
31. Ibid.
32. I,59;1912–13.
33. I,60;1912–13.
34. *Collected Works*, Vol. XV, pp. 217, 340.
35. I,64;1913.
36. *Collected Works*, Vol. IX, p. 260.
37. See Valéry's brilliant essay on Swedenborg (1936) in *Collected Works*, Vol. IX, p. 110.
38. *Collected Works*, Vol. XV, p. 397.
39. I,113;1928.
40. *Collected Works*, Vol. XV, p. 309.

41. William James, *Varieties of Religious Experience*, lecture 8.
42. Elizabeth Hardwick, ed., *Selected Letters of William James* (Boston: David R. Godine, 1981).
43. William James, *Principles of Psychology*, Vol. I (Cambridge, Mass.: Harvard University Press, 1981), pp. 295–96.
44. *Collected Works*, Vol. XV, p. 8.
45. Ibid., p. 50.
46. Introduction to *Oeuvres*, vol. 1.
47. *Collected Works*, Vol. XV, p. 7; I,154;1937.
48. *Oeuvres*, Vol. 2, p. 1489.
49. Edgar Allan Poe, *Domain of Arnheim* (New York: Library of America, 1984), pp. 858–59.
50. I,175;1939; also I,1442, editor's note.
51. I,338;1917–18.
52. I,368;1935.
53. Judith Robinson, *L'Analyse de l'esprit dans les Cahiers de Valéry* (Paris: Corti, 1964); also Robinson, "Valéry's conception of training the mind," *French Studies*, July 1964.
54. *Collected Works*, Vol. X, p. 110.
55. *Collected Works*, Vol. XV, p. 325.
56. Judith Robinson, *Cahiers de l'Association Internationale des Études Françaises* (Paris: Société d'Édition "Les Belles Lettres," No. 107, March 1965), p. 287.
57. I,334;1915–16.
58. I,807;1921.
59. I,783;1902–03; I,806–807;1921.
60. I,864;1944; I,854;1942.
61. I,793;1914.
62. I,841;1935.
63. I,854;1942; see also Whiting, op. cit., p. 8.
64. I,782;1902–03.
65. I,856;1942–43.
66. I,84;1919–20.
67. Louis Kronenberger and W. H. Auden, eds., *Viking Book of Aphorisms* (New York: Penguin, 1961), p. 181.
68. II,404;1918–19.
69. Jean Hytier, *La Poétique de Valéry* (Paris: Colin, 1970); also James R. Lawler, *The Poet as Analyst: Essays on Paul Valéry* (Berkeley: University of California Press, 1974).
70. "Concerning 'Le Cimetière Marin,' " in *Collected Works*, Vol. VII, pp. 140–52.
71. "Poetry and Abstract Thought," in ibid., pp. 52–82.
72. I,244;1915.

73. I,303;1942.
74. Kessler, op. cit.
75. See Judith Robinson's introduction to her edition of the *Cahiers* (I,xi).
76. Lawler, op. cit., p. xviii.
77. Grubbs, op. cit., p. 108.
78. See A. James Arnold, *Paul Valéry and His Critics. French Language Criticism 1890–1927* (Charlottesville: The University Press of Virginia, 1970); also his bibliography of Valéry in *Critical Bibilography of French Literature*, Vol. VI, *The Twentieth Century*, Douglas W. Alden and Richard A. Brooks, eds. (Syracuse, N.Y.: Syracuse University Press, 1980).
79. *Collected Works*, Vol. IX, p. 12.
80. I,702;1937–38.
81. I,686;1935.
82. I,559;1918.
83. I,700;1937.
84. I,495;1905–06.
85. I,604;1925.
86. *Collected Works*, Vol. XIV, p. 442.
87. I,545;1916.
88. I,545:1916.
89. I,481;1901.
90. I,594;1924.
91. I,765;1944.
92. I,513;1913.
93. I,709;1939.
94. "Fluctuations on Freedom," in *Collected Works*, Vol. X, p. 251.
95. René Descartes, *Discourse on the Method of Rightly Conducting Reason and Seeking for Truth in the Sciences*, Part I.
96. Cicero, *De Divinatione*, cited by Hobbes in *Leviathan*, chap. V; Descartes, op. cit., cited by Popper in *Conjectures and Refutations: The Growth of Scientific Knowledge* (New York: Harper & Row, 1963) p. 312; Voltaire, cited in John Herman Randall, *The Career of Philosophy* (New York: Columbia University Press, 1962), vol. 1, p. 858; Kant, Introduction to *The Critique of Pure Reason*.
97. A. N. Whitehead, *Process and Reality*; Karl Popper, "How I See Philosophy," in Charles Bontempo and S. Jack Odell, *The Owl of Minerva* (New York: McGraw-Hill, 1975), p. 43.
98. I,516;1913.
99. I,479;1900.
100. I,580;1922.
101. II,651;1932–33.
102. I,591;1923.

103. I,646;1929.
104. I,677;1934.
105. *Collected Works*, Vol. XIII, p. 204.
106. Ibid., p. 202.
107. *Collected Works*, Vol. VIII, p. 140–41.
108. I,568;1921.
109. I,581;1922.
110. I,749;1943.
111. I,743;1942–43.
112. I,744;1942–43.
113. I,636;1928–29.
114. I,744–45;1943.
115. I,638B;1929.
116. I,727A;1940.
117. I,518;1913.
118. I,509;1912–13.
119. I,663;1931–32.
120. I,739;1942.
121. II,1199–1200;1925.
122. II,666;1936.
123. *Collected Works*, Vol. XIV, p. 307.
124. I,586;1923.
125. I,579;1921.
126. George Santayana, "Soliloquies in England" and "Later Soliloquies," in I. Edman, ed., *The Philosophy of Santayana* (New York: Random House/Modern Library, 1936), p. 363.
127. II,1567;1940.
128. I,652;1930.
129. *Collected Works*, Vol. VIII, pp. 17–18.
130. I,534;1915.
131. *Collected Works*, Vol. VIII, p. 116.
132. I,710;1939.
133. I,326;1902.
134. I,361;1929–30.
135. I,339;1918.
136. I,352;1926.
137. *Collected Works*, Vol. VIII, p. 349.
138. I,583;1922–23.
139. *Collected Works*, Vol. IX, p. 10.
140. I,599;1924.
141. I,708;1938.
142. I,589;1923.
143. II,1565;1939.

144. I,714;1940.
145. I,673;1933.
146. I,717;1940.
147. I,701;1937.
148. I,518;1913.
149. I,657;1931.
150. II,1383;1918. See *Collected Works*, Vol. XIV, pp. 46–90; also Édouard Gaède, *Nietzsche et Valéry* (Paris: Gallimard, 1962).
151. John Stuart Mill, "On Bentham" in *Utilitarianism*.
152. Alvin Plantinga, *The Ontological Argument* (Garden City, N.Y.: Doubleday, 1965).
153. Kant, Preface to first edition of *Critique of Pure Reason*.
154. Bertrand Russell, *Logic and Knowledge*, Robert Marsh, ed. (London: Allen & Unwin, 1977).
155. H. H. Price, "Clarity Is Not Enough," *Proceedings of the Aristotelian Society*, Vol. 19, p. 3.
156. John Dewey quoted by John Herman Randall in P. A. Schilpp, ed., *The Philosophy of John Dewey* (Evanston, Ill.: Northwestern University Press, 1939).

Part Three

Part Three

Clifford Geertz: The Aims of Anthropology

According to Clifford Geertz, anthropology—"long one of the most homespun of disciplines, hostile to anything smacking of intellectual pretension and unnaturally proud of an outdoorsman image"—has, together with much else in social science, been changing in recent years. He says that its golden age, when there was widespread agreement on the general aim of the social sciences—"to find out the dynamics of collective life and alter them in desired directions"—is over. Today, he says, "calls for 'a general theory' of just about anything social sound increasingly hollow, and claims to have one megalomaniac." Social scientists no longer feel the need to mimic the methods of physicists and other natural scientists. Social thought is being "refigured," and the exploration of new metaphors for understanding social and cultural life drawn from the humanities has produced new and unfamiliar "blurred genres"—scientific speculations resembling belles lettres, histories resembling mathematics, and, as we shall see, anthropology resembling literary criticism.

A learned anthropologist who has written books on Bali, Java, and Morocco, and essays on many other issues, including economic development, religion, and "third world" politics, Geertz has for many years been articulating and promoting a theory of culture and a method for understanding it, most effectively in his collection of essays, *The Interpretation of Cultures* (1973). Cultural anthropologists try to understand the workings of the religions, myths, rituals, kinship systems, of other cultures (or of our own). But what is a "culture"? And in what does such "understanding" consist? How should cultural anthropologists see their task? And what methods promise to assist them in accomplishing it?

I

In a review of the work of Lévi-Strauss published some years ago, Geertz wrote that the anthropologist's

> personal relationship to his object of study is, perhaps more than for any other scientist, inevitably problematic. Know what he thinks a savage is and you have the key to his work. You know what he thinks he himself is and, knowing what he thinks he himself is, you know in general what sort of thing he is going to say about whatever tribe he happens to be studying. All ethnography is part philosophy, and a good deal of the rest is confession.[1]

For Geertz, human beings are not finished products of biological evolution, but "symbolizing, conceptualizing, meaning-seeking" animals, who wish to "make sense out of experience, to give it form and order." Not only is this desire "evidently as real and as pressing as the more familiar biological needs," it has causally affected them. Geertz's view of human nature contrasts sharply with the claim that human culture is an off-shoot of biology, a spark thrown off by some underlying physical or biological process and possessing no causal powers of its own. He thinks that evidence about the evolution of man from apes and other hominoids suggests that "culture, rather

[1]Clifford Geertz, *The Interpretation of Cultures* (New York: Basic Books, 1973), pp. 345–346.

than being added on, so to speak, to a finished or virtually finished animal, was ingredient, and centrally ingredient, in the production of that animal itself." Especially important in this evolution, Geertz wrote, was "the increasing reliance upon systems of significant symbols (language, art, myth, ritual) for orientation, communication, and self-control."

In a recent collection of essays, *Local Knowledge*,[2] Geertz again emphasizes the importance of these "systems of significant symbols" in the explanation of culture and argues that some celebrated accounts of culture paid too little attention to them and too much to "primitive psychology." E. B. Tylor and J. G. Frazer, the founders of modern anthropology, believed that "primitives" have primitive minds, minds on a lower rung of the evolutionary ladder than ours; these "primitives," they claimed, attempted to do what we do in our science, to explain and order the universe and acquire control of it, but did it miserably because of the limitations of their mental apparatus. They consequently moved about, as Geertz puts the view, in "a hodgepodge of concrete images, mystical participations, and immediate passions." This overly intellectualistic view tended to ignore that much of what not only "primitives" but we ourselves do is not a matter of belief or attempted explanation at all. Puberty initiations, rain dances, cargo cults may be actions expressing values that are cherished or thought worthy of reaffirmation; they may not be protoscientific judgments—any more than an American who sings "That Old Black Magic" is exhibiting his belief that there is such a thing as magic and that it is old and black.

The Tylor-Frazer view, which Geertz says "persists in certain sorts of developmental psychology, certain styles of comparative history, and certain circles of the diplomatic service," has in addition been undermined by the claims of such diverse thinkers as Freud and Skinner and Chomsky that the cognitive processes of human beings are roughly the same everywhere.

---

[2] Clifford Geertz, *Local Knowledge: Further Essays in Interpretive Anthropology* (New York: Basic Books, 1983).

What differs from people to people, these claims suggest, is not psychological processes (like perceiving or imagining) but the vehicles of thought—conceptual "structures," categories, classifications of space and time, plants, animals, colors, sexes—used in such processes.

Geertz's own view of culture underscores the importance of these conceptual "structures" and regards them neither as biological epiphenomena nor as reflections of a group "mentality" nor as patterns of behavior, but rather as a "system of symbols." What he means by this claim is not entirely clear, however, for he also suggests that culture should be understood not as consisting of the symbols themselves, taken abstractly, but as consisting of symbols as they are used to convey meaning in distinct social situations. He seems to suggest that such systems of symbols (most notably, language) are inherent in cultures and that without them there would be no cultural phenomena to describe, for our language and other symbols do not simply describe the "world" we live in: They contribute in some fundamental sense to that "world" being what it is, and may be said, in part, to create it.

Further, these "symbolic forms" are for Geertz not "gauzy mental forms" and not "private" (or in anyone's "head"): They are public "inscriptions" of a "communal sensibility." And he does not mean by "symbol" merely an affective or emotive symbol. For him thinking, for example, is a "manipulation" of symbolic forms; a poem can be "a symbolic model of the emotional impact of premature death"; and "the central rituals of religion—a mass, a pilgrimage, a corroboree—are symbolic models (here more in the form of activities than of words) of a particular sense of the divine, a certain sort of devotional mood, which their continual re-enactment tends to produce in their participants."

What he means by "symbol systems" in use may perhaps be illustrated by his "ethnographically informed" reflections on art in *Local Knowledge*. According to Geertz, art cannot be understood by an approach that locates "aesthetic power" in "formal relations among sounds, images, volumes, themes, or gestures." To study an art form is to study "a collective formation" that makes concrete "a way of experiencing" and brings "a particular cast of mind out into the world of objects, where men can look at it." Furthermore, "it is out of participation in the general system of symbolic forms we call culture that participation in the general system of symbolic forms we call art, which is in fact but a sector of it, is possible." To understand art works we must "place" them among the products of other modes of social activity, incorporate them into

> the texture of a particular pattern of life. And such placing, the giving to art objects a cultural significance, is always a local matter; what art is in classical China or classical Islam, what it is in the Pueblo southwest or highland New Guinea, is just not the same thing, no matter how universal the intrinsic qualities that actualize its emotional power (and I have no desire to deny them) may be.

He draws on Robert Faris Thompson's account of the meaning of line among the Yoruba tribe to give an example:

> It is not just their statues, pots, and so on that Yoruba incise with lines: they do the same with their faces. Line, of varying depth, direction and length, sliced into their cheeks and left to scar over, serves as a means of lineage identification, personal allure, and status expression; and the terminology of the sculptor and of the cicatrix specialist—"cuts" distinguished from "slashes" and "digs," or "claws" from "splittings open"—parallel one another in exact precision. But there is more to it than this. The Yoruba associate line with civilization: "This country has become civilized," literally means, in Yoruba, "This earth has lines upon its face."
> . . . [The Yoruba concern for line] grows out of a distinctive sensibility the whole of life participates in forming—one in which the meanings of things are the scars that men leave on them.

If culture is a set of symbolic forms (as they are actually used), then the task of an anthropologist studying a culture should be to identify its symbol systems. And how is this to be done? As Geertz conceives it, this task involves trying to grasp the "native's point of view," to "determine what this people or that take to be the point of what they are doing." And he believes this also involves a change in method, a turning away from "laws-and-causes social physics," from "a laws-and-instances ideal of explanation towards a cases-and-interpretative one." What is sought, he says, is "interpretive explanation," an explanation which "trains its attention on what institutions, actions, images, utterances, events, customs, all the usual objects of social-scientific interest, mean to those whose institutions, actions, customs, and so on they are." Such explanations do not issue in scientific laws but in "unpackings of the conceptual world"—the symbol systems—in which the native lives.

II

His recommendation that anthropologists seek explanations of culture "connecting action to its sense rather than behavior to its determinants" sets Geertz against those positivists and behaviorists, and others, who claim that the social sciences should use methods of inquiry and patterns of explanation identical, for all practical purposes, with those in other sciences. Human beings, these theorists acknowledge, are indeed more complex than stones or plants, but they claim nevertheless that they are physical systems that are in principle predictable. Causal generalizations about them can be confirmed or disconfirmed, they say, by observations of their behavior in the same way that hypotheses about inanimate objects are. They hope that such causal generalizations will in turn be explained by more inclusive theories which will enable us to explain and predict such human conduct as the behavior of economic markets, kinship systems, crime and deviance, voting patterns, the causes of class conflicts and of war. It is true, they contend, that constructing and verifying these laws and theories is often limited by the frequent impossibility of conducting controlled experiments on human beings, and by the special problems that arise when self-conscious human beings study each other. But, they claim, these obstacles do not necessarily prohibit constructing a science of society.

On Geertz's view, the business of human sciences like anthropology is to study not behavior but *actions* that have meanings for those who perform them, and actions like voting or praying or participating in a strike cannot be understood by causal generalizations, he thinks, but instead require a distinctive "method." The "meanings" that partially constitute human actions are typically elements, on this view, in a configuration of categories and rules embedded in behavior. They are part of "social reality" or a "form of life" discoverable less by empirical observation than by "making sense" of conceptual connections. These rules and conventions "constitute" this social reality in the way the rules of chess "constitute" the game of chess: They define the possibilities and limits of a way of behaving and must be "grasped" if we are even to identify a significant range of actions that occur in it. To understand a handshake, for example, requires that we "see" or "make sense" of the connections between the clasp of hands and such socially recognized concepts as courtesy or forgiveness, but also that we know what can and cannot be accomplished with a handshake, such as that with it we can bring a business transaction to a close, but not, say, create a marriage or vote for a political candidate.

Geertz's view sets him against not only positivists and behaviorists but also the various large general theoretical approaches—"diffusionism," "evolutionism," "biological determinism," "sociobiology" (he calls it a "curious combination of common sense and common nonsense")—that have sought to discover general "laws" of the development or evolution of culture (or at least "patterns" or "regularities" among "culture traits") by cross-cultural studies, or that too confidently have promised to explain such diverse cultural items as marriage rules, folklore motifs, trade patterns, farming techniques, political organization, diet, dress, etiquette, by the influence of "dominant" or "primary" factors like technology, or ecology, or population expansion, or by the invocation of psychological, biological, geographical, or climatological "laws." Far from producing general laws of culture or cultural development, Geertz has remarked, these approaches have provided little more than vague and evasive generalizations about the "unity of man" and his "basic needs" and "their multiple modes of fulfillment."

These views—apart from his current emphasis on "symbol systems"—are mostly critical of anthropological theory. What is Geertz's view about the dominant tradition in anthropology until after World War II, the "functionalism" of Radcliffe-Brown and Malinowski and their respective followers?

Functionalism was a methodological and theoretical view that emphasized not the origin or evolution of particular institutions—customs, rights, myths, political and social arrangements—but the part they play in the working of the "social system" as a whole. It was expressed in at least two influential formulations. Bronislaw Malinowski's "psychological" version of functionalism roughly held that institutions should be analyzed and understood not only as interdependent or interrelated, but primarily through the contribution they made to the "satisfaction" or fulfillment of the biological and psychological needs of people in a society. A. R. Radcliffe-Brown's "structural functionalism," on the other hand, repudiated this psychological approach and sought to establish a "natural science" of society distinct from psychology. On this view, psychology cannot be the foundation of social anthropology, for social arrangements affect the psychology of the members of a society; rather, while Radcliffe-Brown did not entirely reject psychological causes and conditions of behavior, he held that society is something like an entity distinguishable from the individuals who compose it, with needs of its own, and capable of influencing those individuals through its institutions. Social anthropologists, he further held, should analyze "social structures," defined as the relationships among the actions of individuals, and its task should be to arrive at a statement, if possible, of the laws according to which social structures survive or, more generally, "maintain" themselves over time or undergo change.

Geertz's attitude is unclear. Certainly he has criticized the cruder forms of functionalism on the ground that they are too "static," too concerned with how society maintains its "equilibrium" rather than with change of social structure, too ahistorical, too untestable, and of course too insensitive to the place of "symbolic structures" in culture, tending to view symbols as pale reflections of underlying psychological or social structural conditions. But in his earlier work, Geertz sought to develop a "dynamic functionalism" which saw the "meaningful" and symbolic features of culture and the "causal-functional" aspects of social structure not as "mere reflexes of one another" but as "interdependent" variables. "The driving forces in social change," he wrote, "can be clearly formulated only by a more dynamic form of functionalist theory, one which takes into account the fact that man's need to live in a world to which he can attribute some significance, whose essential import he feels he can grasp, often diverges from his concurrent need to maintain a functioning social organism."

According to this "dynamic functionalism," human behavior (as opposed to that of lower animals, whose behavior patterns are largely inherited with their physical structure) is "inherently extremely plastic." On this view, culture provides "controls" on our "general response capacities." It is "a set of control mechanisms" for the governing of our behavior. Cultures are systems of symbols, and symbols are "extrapersonal mechanisms for the perception, understanding, judgment, and manipulation of the world," or "extrinsic sources of information," in that—"unlike genes, for example—they lie outside the boundaries of the individual organism as such in that intersubjective world of common understandings into which all human individuals are born, in which they pursue their separate careers, and which they leave persisting behind them after they die." Symbol systems, in this form of functionalism, are "socially determined" (or "at once a product and a determinant of social interaction").

Does Geertz still hold to the possibility of such a form of functionalism? He seems not to, although he does not explicitly say so; but he clearly rejects the forms of structuralism that have enjoyed a vogue in intellectual life in recent years: The approach of Lévi-Strauss, for example, which seeks to discover invariants of the human mind beneath the diverse cultural codes of different peoples, he calls a "higher cryptology."

III

But to return to our earlier question. How, on Geertz's view, should anthropologists go about "grasping" the native's point of view? Can they acquire this understanding by the customary methods of field study, observation, and verbal interview, or must they engage in some other kind of participation in the native "world"? One celebrated answer to this question is that the fieldworker must immerse himself in the native world, acquire the "world view" of the native through empathy and sympathetic identification, and grasp the "meaning" of native actions by reference to what meaning he would attach to the act in similar circumstances. Geertz claims that this "myth of the chameleon fieldworker, perfectly self-tuned to his exotic surroundings, a walking miracle of empathy, tact, patience, and cosmopolitanism, was demolished by the man who had perhaps done most to create it," namely, Malinowski, who had officially spoken of grasping the "imponderabilia of actual life" through empathy, but who, as was revealed by the posthumous publication of his field diary, did not exhibit much of a capacity to think or feel like a native at all.

Geertz's own view is that anthropologists do not need to possess any special capacity for empathy in order to understand the world of the native: "The trick," he says, "is not to get yourself into some inner correspondence of spirit with your informants," but rather "to figure out what the devil they think they are up to." This does not consist in merely translating what natives tell us, for they might tell us such things as that they are birds or that a witch has pushed them out of a tree. Rather, the "translation" of cultures involves "the reshaping of categories . . . so that they can reach beyond the contexts in which they originally arose and took their meaning so as to locate affinities and mark differences." This is still far from clear, unfortunately.

Geertz's own ethnography, as is shown by his papers on Bali and Morocco, largely consisted in "searching out and analyzing the symbolic forms—words, images, institutions, behavior—in terms of which, in each place, people actually represented themselves to themselves and to one another." Although he acknowledges that the latter task is not, on the face of it, simpler than that of exercising empathy (or, we might add, really any less mysterious), he thinks that he can provide an informal description of something like a "method" for accomplishing it. This is a cultural version of what philologists and textual critics have called "hermeneutics," a process of "tacking" or "hopping back and forth between the whole conceived through the parts that actualize it and the parts conceived through the whole that motivates them." As practiced by Geertz, this "method" generally consists in his selecting some category (categories describing persons in Bali) or practice (the Balinese cockfight) or word (the Indic word *dharma,* or roughly, "duty") and attempting to connect it to "the general views of what reality really is" embodied within it; he then tries to clarify these general views further through their connection with other aspects of native life. For example, Geertz thinks that key words, or categories, when analyzed, can "light up a whole way of going at the world." He writes,

> All Balinese receive what might be called birth-order names. There are four of these, "first-born," "second-born," "third-born," "fourth-born," after which they recycle, so that the fifth-born child is called again "first-born," the sixth "second-born," and so on. Further, these names are bestowed independently of the fates of the children. Dead children, even stillborn ones, count, so that in fact, in this still high-birthrate, high-mortality society, the names do not really tell you anything very reliable about the birth-order relations of concrete individuals.

He continues:

> The birth-order naming system does not identify individuals as
> individuals, nor is it intended to; what it does is to suggest that,
> for all procreating couples, births form a circular structure of
> "firsts," "seconds," "thirds," and "fourths," an endless four-
> stage replication of an imperishable form. Physically men appear
> and disappear as the ephemerae they are, but socially the acting
> figures remain eternally the same as new "firsts," "seconds,"
> and so on emerge from the timeless world of the gods to replace
> those who, dying, dissolve once more into it.

Thus, Geertz thinks that the designation and title systems of
the Balinese suggest that they hold certain metaphysical beliefs,
that "they represent the most time-saturated aspects of the
human condition as but ingredients in an eternal, footlight
present."

Why would they do so? Geertz would argue that it is, in
part, because they see their lives as a kind of pageant or play,
in which the roles, but not the actors, endure, in which each
person is "the temporary occupant of a particular, quite un-
temporary, cultural locus." This "play" is, he says, about hierarchy and status, and Geertz thinks that "the enactment of
hierarchy" is a recurrent feature of Balinese life. In the nineteenth century, for example, Bali

> was a theatre-state in which the king and princes were the im-
> presarios, the priests the directors, and peasantry the supporting
> cast, stage crew, and audience. The stupendous cremations, teeth-
> filings, temple dedications, the pilgrimages and blood sacrifices,
> mobilizing hundreds, even thousands of people and great quan-
> tities of wealth, were not means to political ends, they were the
> ends themselves, they were what the state was for.

The ceremony was not mere decoration, or linked to displays
of force, but the very substance of the state. In *Local Knowledge* (and elsewhere) Geertz argues that this preoccupation
with hierarchy and status is reflected not only in Balinese politics and its aesthetic rituals, with "eleven storey towers, flow-
ered arrows shot into fabric snakes, purple and gold coffins

shaped as lions, incense, metallophones, spices, flames," but also in its darker aspects, in its sorcery (which is "filled with images of perversion and wild brutality"), its cockfights, its funerals, with their "charred bones, entranced priests, somnambulant widows, affectless attendants, dissociate crowds, eerie in their picnic calm."

By this "hermeneutic" tacking, Geertz thinks we might arrive at a "translation" of another culture. We might also, he thinks, thereby provide evidence for reflections on general topics such as the nature of the self, or of justice, or of ideology. In the essays in *Local Knowledge* he tries to do just this. One of them examines the idea of "charisma" and describes some of the symbolic forms that display the fact that a governing elite in a society is truly governing, using as evidence the progresses of Javanese, Balinese, and English sovereigns. The learned title essay on law as "local knowledge" is another "ethnographically informed" essay on a general topic. Geertz argues against the claim that law is a normative system superimposed on a "neutral" or culture-independent body of "facts," and against approaches to comparative law that treat it as an abstract structure of rules (as in some versions of legal positivism) or instruments for maintaining social equilibrium (as do functionalists who see law as "a clever device to keep people from tearing one another limb from limb, advance the interests of the dominant classes, defend the rights of the weak against the predations of the strong, or render social life a bit more predictable at its fuzzy edges").

Instead, he urges comparative lawyers to look into the merits of his "interpretive" methods. Investigating three different "varieties of legal sensibility"—the Islamic, the Indic, "and a so-called customary-law one found throughout the 'Malayo' part of Malayo-Polynesia"—Geertz maintains that "legal thought is constructive of social realities rather than merely reflective of them." Legal "facts" are "socially constructed" and normative from the start. They express a "local" sense of justice and a "way of imagining the real." Laws do not "just regulate behavior, they construe it"; and disputes over what sorts of laws should govern a society are disputes over what sort of society is desired.

IV

Geertz says that his concern with "how meaning in one system of expression is expressed in another" and with the "commensurability of conceptual structures" raises questions of "practical epistemology" and has led him "more complexly" into "relativism" than many other investigators of culture. But this "relativism," it is important to note, is not the kind of relativism that has been recently discussed by philosophers, and that holds that what investigators see, or hear, or expect, is "theory-laden" (or otherwise heavily dependent upon their "background knowledge" or valuations or "conceptual schemes"). According to this notion of relativism, historians examining the assumptions of other periods, or proponents of different inclusive and incompatible scientific theories criticizing each other, or anthropologists trying to understand other cultures, occupy different "theoretical universes." No "neutral" language can be devised in which "objective" empirical tests of competing interpretations can be expressed. We can, for example, describe the properties of virtually any material body anywhere—in Indonesia or Switzerland or Liverpool—in the language of Newtonian physics, but because "forms of life" are not comparable, there can be no neutral language of this kind in which to "translate" or describe the social realities of Indonesian peasants, Swiss mountain climbers, and British factory workers. Thus, according to this relativistic view, while they may discover truths, social scientists cannot be "neutral" and are severely limited in their access to other "theoretical universes."

Nor does Geertz advocate the stronger version of relativism that regards the very application of our standards of rationality and truth to other cultures as "a category error," so that in assessing, for example, whether witchcraft embodies truths or not, we must employ "local" standards of "truth" and "rationality."[3] If either of these relativistic positions were acceptable the work of "interpretive" (and other) anthropology would be blocked from the outset. Despite his acceptance of at least one form of relativism, Geertz speaks of "relativism" (without further qualification) as "a bit of academic neurosis" and characteristically adds that in anthropology "those of us who attend with care to specific cases, usually peculiar, are constantly being told that we are undermining thereby the possibility of general knowledge and should take up instead something properly scientific like comparative sexology or cultural energetics."

On his view, we are neither prevented, on the basis of philosophical arguments about "meaning" and "conceptual schemes," from understanding other cultures nor unable to appraise and judge these other cultures by our standards of rationality and cogency simply because there is no absolutely neutral or "privileged" standpoint for doing so. Acquiring the kind of "understanding" he seeks of other cultures—"determine what this people or that take to be the point of what they are doing"—need not cast into doubt our standards of truth or rationality, or our morals.

If Geertz is not a "relativist" (as this term is sometimes defined), his pluralism, his appreciation of differences, contrasts, conflict, among cultures is refined to an unusual degree. In an essay on common sense, he tells us that the East African tribe the Pokot look on hermaphrodites (or "intersexuals") not with horror but as "errors," rather like "botched pots," whereas the Navajo, while they see hermaphrodites as abnormal, nevertheless regard them with "wonder and awe." Most Americans, he notes, look on them with horror and try to disguise them as "hims" or "hers." "So much for savages," he says. He is amused that what is regarded as common sense or as patently true can differ so widely from one people to another, and recounts that when an old Javanese peasant woman told him

[3] For an introduction to some of the issues about rationality that have been raised recently by philosophers and others, see Martin Hollis and Steven Lukes, eds., *Rationality and Relativism* (Cambridge, Mass.: MIT Press, 1982).

about "the role of 'the snake of the day' in determining the wisdom of embarking on a journey, holding a feast, or contracting a marriage" and he asked her what this snake looked like, she told him, "Don't be an idiot; you can't see Tuesday, can you?"

Among the most acute and sensitive passages in Geertz's writings are those that concern the conflicts that accompany the contact of diverse patterns of life. In *The Interpretation of Cultures,* for example, he described the situation—evidently still with us—of newly independent "third world" countries, in which some reformers believed that the end of colonial rule would be followed by the spontaneous formation of nations that realized the ideals not only of political independence but also of popular rule, rapid economic growth, social equality, and cultural rebirth. But in fact, wrote Geertz, few of these ideals were realized, and in time, the inspiring leaders of the new nations, such as Gandhi or Nkrumah or Nasser, died or were killed off, and the forces of privilege and inequality reasserted themselves, as did divisive "nationalisms" within these nations.

Accompanying these developments, and partly causing them, were fierce and sustained conflicts among the citizens of these new states, and among the most important of these conflicts, Geertz wrote, was that between their desire to be "modern" (for example, to acquire a higher standard of living) and their need to remain themselves. As he described it, the conflict lay between the claims of "primordial attachments"—the claims of blood, race, region, tradition, religion, language, and all else that he called "psychologically immediate"—and the demands of nation-building in our century. Frequently, he said, the end result was a "twisting, spasmodic, unmethodical movement" which turned "as often toward repossessing the emotions of the past as disowning them," a movement in which national leaders behaved like "naive artists," trying now this style and now that—presidential autocracy, party oligarchy, military dictatorship, despotic monarchy—in an effort to "domesticate" or neutralize these "primordial attachments."

Again, in his famous book *Agricultural Involution: The Processes of Ecological Change in Indonesia*, Geertz examined the effects of the superimposition of an alien civil and economic order on preexisting and "psychologically immediate" ways of life, this time the imposition by the Dutch of a capitalist export economy on the subsistence economy of the Javanese peasantry. Geertz noted, as had been pointed out by Dutch economists before him, that far from creating actual economic development in the peasant economy, the result was a "static expansion" of land use over wider areas, with any rise in production absorbed by a rise in population. He added that despite what he claimed was the existence of an ecological symbiosis between the subsistence crops (such as paddy) and the export crops (such as sugar cane), the peasant response to the alien economic order was not only an internal elaboration of traditional techniques of farming, but the enforcement of a peasant ethic of "shared poverty," which in effect obstructed economic efficiency and intervened in the distribution of economic benefits from farming by dividing them into smaller and smaller portions so that all would benefit.[4]

[4]*Agricultural Involution: The Processes of Ecological Change in Indonesia* (Berkeley: University of California Press, 1963). The book stimulated wide comment among those concerned with the economic development of peasant economies in the third world, and some claimed that Geertz had provided good reasons for supposing that merely injecting investment capital (or, for that matter, such technological innovations as high-yield seeds, fertilizers, or insecticides) into these economies would not lead to desirable increases in production unless an alteration in the "world view" of the peasantry was also effected.

The theses of *Agricultural Involution* have, however, also been widely challenged. The most comprehensive review of these challenges, to my knowledge, is to be found in Benjamin White, " 'Agricultural Involution' and Its Critics: Twenty Years After," *Bulletin of Concerned Asian Scholars*, vol. 15, no. 2 (April–June 1983), pp. 18–32. White claims that "almost no element of the Geertzian view of Javanese agrarian change is supported by available evidence," and in particular assails the notion of "shared poverty": "The crucial error" of Geertz's book, he writes, "lies in assigning to this ethic a determinant role in regulating the actual relations of distribution between classes."

In other places, Geertz attacks the familiar social-science doctrine that

> the world is growing more drearily modern—McDonald's on the Champs Elysées, punk rock in China; that there is an intrinsic evolution from *Gemeinschaft* to *Gesellschaft*, traditionalism to rationalism, mechanical solidarity to organic solidarity, status to contract; that postcapitalist infrastructure in the form of multinational corporations and computer technology will soon shape the minds of Tongans and Yemenis to a common pattern.

Instead, he proposes his own "view that things look more like flying apart than they do like coming together (one I would apply to the direction of social change generally these days, not just to law)."

This raises, of course, the further question: If this crazy-quilt pattern of the world's law, customs, practices is the norm and not a passing phenomenon, if "dissensus" is "the hardening condition of things," how will communication (let alone firm action designed to introduce "progress" and "development" —what indeed will be the chosen meaning of these words?) take place in this cacophony? Geertz thinks that we need to create "a novel system of discourse" in order to describe these "abnormal" situations (which, he adds, are not much clearer within other cultures than in ours), although he does not describe this new discourse.

On the other hand, White believes that Geertz's book "has become a rather tired punch-bag, an easy target for criticism which often goes no further than pointing to something wrong in the Geertzian picture, without proposing alternative views of Java's agrarian transition in its place. Researchers might have more usefully applied theoretical advances made in the study of other agrarian transitions, rather than simply taking another bash at Geertz."

It might be added that while certain of Geertz's theories (such as that postulating an ecological symbiosis between subsistence and export crops in Java) may have been refuted by White and others, Geertz's stress on the role played in agrarian change by peasant conceptions of right and wrong has been and remains highly suggestive, although it is not clear to what extent efforts to assign a greater weight to the influence of native ethics (like "shared poverty") as opposed to other factors in the determination of such change can ever be decisive.

Geertz accompanies this persistent stress on diversity and conflict in his work with a warning about the moral role that can be played by cultural anthropology. He acknowledges that anthropology can be morally "broadening" and that one of its functions is to "see ourselves amongst others, as a local example of the forms human life has locally taken." As he wrote some years ago, "the essential vocation of interpretive anthropology is not to answer our deepest questions, but to make available to us answers that others . . . have given." But he also says that

> the image of the past (or the primitive, or the classic, or the exotic) as a source of remedial wisdom, a prosthetic corrective for a damaged spiritual life—an image that has governed a good deal of humanist thought and education—is mischievous because it leads us to expect that our uncertainties will be reduced by access to thought-worlds constructed along lines alternative to our own, when in fact they will be multiplied.

The results of cultural translation are more likely, in other words, to introduce an instability and uncertainty in our moral and epistemological lives and to contribute to what Geertz calls "the sense of believing too many things at once that seems to haunt us," and to "our intense concern with whether we are in any position, or can somehow get ourselves into one, to judge other ways of life at all." He does not wish us to be haunted by this possibility or to surrender our values and standards simply because we have been made familiar with different ones, but rather to acquire a feeling and sympathy for diversity so that we may consult other answers to common problems and other vocabularies in which to express them.

V

Local Knowledge reinforces the impression one has from Geertz's other work that he is penetrating when trying to convey the color and movement of native "worlds"—what he calls the "curve" and "distinctive tonalities" of native existence—

or amusingly breaking down the banal or pretentious generalizations he finds in social science and elsewhere. One's dis-
appointment with the book lies in its lack of clarity and its
failure to develop its central position. In his first book of essays,
Geertz was advancing his theory of culture to a less than sympathetic audience, but as he explains in this new book, to a
considerable extent that battle has now been won, and many
audiences are ready to entertain the idea of an "interpretive"
anthropology. One would expect, therefore, a fuller, more
rounded statement and defense of that general approach in this
book.

Instead of developing that view (or repudiating elements of
it) these "further essays in interpretive anthropology" consist
mostly of general reflections on widely dissimilar topics and
take for granted certain elements of his earlier view while apparently repudiating others (without saying so). No doubt this
inconsecutive character of *Local Knowledge* owes something
to the origin of many of its chapters in addresses to learned
societies. But it is exacerbated by Geertz's prose, which, for
all its irreverence and occasional brilliance, is too often di-
gressive and clotted with metaphor, tending to a self-conscious
virtuosity that is at first immensely attractive but in the end
cute, *voulu*, almost oppressive. Drugged into a kind of exhil-
aration by his racing sentences, which frequently couch criticisms of opposing views in burlesque treatments when a fuller
discussion is more appropriate, one sooner or later realizes that
one has no clear idea of his view; if he has presented a view,
one must reread many scattered passages in order to stitch it
together.

What are we to make of Geertz's central thesis that culture
is a general system of symbolic forms, and that these forms
(and the cultures they make up) must be understood in their
actual practice? We never really learn what Geertz thinks a
symbol is, or how things acquire symbolic value, or vary in
symbolic intensity, let alone how symbols (or symbol systems)
change, or are linked to broader aspects of social existence.
We look to his earlier work for clarification, and there we find

that he defines a symbol as "any object, act, event, quality, or relation which serves as a vehicle for a conception," which is, of course, a somewhat vague conception. But in *Local Knowledge* he nowhere tells us whether he still holds this definition, leaving it to us to guess his current views on the subject. He speaks of "symbol systems," but although this expression has become fashionable among philosophers and others in recent years, it is not clear what it really means.

For example, when Geertz claims that the symbols in our or another culture form a "system," does he mean to imply that they possess the kind of order found in some mathematical symbolic systems in which clearly defined rules of transformation enable one to derive the full symbolic apparatus of the system from some small basic group? It would appear that this sense of "system" would be altogether too restrictive for Geertz's purposes. Again, is Geertz claiming that in order to form a "system," symbols would have to interact regularly or be sufficiently interdependent to form some sort of unity or whole, so that a change in one would affect the others? If symbol elements or symbols could be altered without a change in the others, the collection of symbols would hardly merit the name of a "system" in this sense.

But once more I do not think that this is Geertz's understanding of "symbol system," for it seems to imply that the symbols themselves causally interact, whereas this is generally not so. The written notes of music, or the numerals of mathematics, are symbols, but they do not causally influence one another. The composer or mathematician manipulates them according to the system he follows. What, then, might Geertz mean? Unless I am mistaken, he means that if symbols form a system they do not only denote objects in regular ways but also embody some set of common attitudes and values, and that when they are used, they "express" these attitudes and values.

But what gives him confidence that we, or anyone else, are "trafficking" in "symbol systems" in this sense? What kind of evidence would support such a claim? In our ordinary lives, I think, we encounter a fluid and not wholly determinate collection of particular symbols used in various and not always consistent ways, which suggests that while symbols may be used systematically by some people (or by the members of some part of a culture) it may yet be that our culture as a whole has nothing like the cohesiveness of a "symbol system" in the sense that I have attributed to Geertz. The symbols we use are frequently ambiguous both in public use and personal association—as in color symbolism, in which black can symbolize evil as well as the "beauty" of "black literation"; or dependent for their meaning on circumstances on one's role or one's group membership (bread and wine may symbolize nothing to a Catholic in a restaurant). Moreover, the symbols we use often change (sometimes radically) over time. And sometimes symbols are confused with signs, or function as both (darkening skies generally do not symbolize anything, but rather serve as a sign: They portend the imminent presence of something else, namely rain).

Although it would be unfair to hold him responsible for the work of other ethnographers, we may use his example of the Yoruba in order to illustrate some of the obscurities that attach to his view of symbols. The Yoruba, he tells us, "associate line with civilization." But what is the line that symbolizes civilization—an abstract line or some concrete instance of a line? Is just any drawing of a line a "symbolic action" for the Yoruba? Is a line slashed in a cheek one symbol and a line scratched in the earth a second symbol, or are these one symbol "used" in different ways? Is a line in the face symbolic if acquired by accident? What is their "symbol system" a system of?

The moment one trains one's attention on Geertz's use of "symbol" and "symbol system" and "symbolic action," one is prompted to ask a host of such questions. But so far as I was able to tell, all that we learn in his work about how to answer them is something along the lines of Geertz's claim in *Local Knowledge* that analyzing symbol use as "social action" is "an exceedingly difficult business at which everyone from Kenneth Burke, J. L. Austin, and Roland Barthes to Gregory Bateson,

Jürgen Habermas, and Erving Goffman has had some sort of pass." We are not told what views these very different thinkers have held or whether they have clarified "symbolic action."[5]

The same lack of clarity is found in Geertz's discussion of the thesis that gives his book so much of its stimulus: his "interpretive turn." When he wrote some years ago that he takes the "analysis" of culture to be "not an experimental science in search of law but an interpretive one in search of meaning," or suggests that anthropologists "turn from trying to explain social phenomena by weaving them into grand textures of cause and effect to trying to explain them by placing them in local frames of awareness" (to take but two statements among many of their kind) what exactly does he mean?

Presumably Geertz does not mean to imply that anthropological investigations of culture should be confined exclusively to "interpretation," for that would result in a factitious closure of inquiry. It is a commonplace that the "meaning" of an action to the actor may not coincide with its significance when considered in the light of what we know about human behavior; and there are numerous examples of proposed explanations of actions that make no reference to the actor's own understanding of his action (and that indeed might be rejected by him). Thus, for example, Durkheim's explanation of the conditions under which people will commit suicide (which, for all its flaws, remains of interest to students of social pathology) makes no reference to how suicides or would-be suicides construe their acts: It explains their actions as undertaken by them when social ties or bonds do not provide them with sufficient sources of

[5]For the work of an author whom Geertz mentions but whose formal analysis of symbol systems he does not explicitly use, see Nelson Goodman's books, *Ways of World-making* (Indianapolis: Hackett Publishing Co., 1978), and *Of Mind and Other Matters* (Cambridge, Mass.: Harvard University Press, 1984). See also the preliminary and suggestive development and extension of Goodman's ideas to the understanding of ritual symbolism by Israel Scheffler in his essay "Ritual and Reference," *Synthèse*, vol. 46, no. 3 (March 1981), pp. 421–437, and Scheffler's reply to comments by Gareth Matthews on pp. 445–448.

attachment or control and their moral health is correspondingly weakened.

To take another example, it has been argued that the post-partum taboo observed in some parts of the world can be explained less satisfactorily by the rationale offered for it by those who practice it (who might say, for example, that it is "immoral" to have postpartum sexual relations) than by what we know to be its role in prolonging the infant's nursing period and protecting it from nutritional deficiency diseases, or in protecting the mother from infection.

Or again, it may be that our "understanding" of the periodic depredations of one tribe on another is augmented not only by learning that the tribe members themselves construe their behavior as placation of a war god, but also by taking into account considerations that they may not know of or acknowledge— say, those that have been stressed by cultural ecologists like Julian Steward, whatever one thinks of the ambitious programs of research of these thinkers. Such work might lead us to discover that the wars coincide with crop failures or with population pressures that stimulate competition for scarce resources and thus in turn bring into existence militarism and conquest.

Criticism of those like Lévi-Strauss (although he officially says otherwise) who do not act as if they are obliged to learn the "native point of view" may be just; for when we describe actions as insults or religious ceremonies or suicides, we thereby attribute certain beliefs to the actors, and if we fail to identify these beliefs we might miss altogether the significance of the actions. But it would be equally objectionable to jump to the other extreme. The understanding of culture proceeds not only by acquiring familiarity with the "world" of the native, but also from asking whether the native point of view is true or not, what its sources are, and what consequences its acceptance has upon the native society, matters with which the natives themselves may not be conversant. We wish, for example, to know *why* natives hold the "symbol system" they do, and why this symbolism alters over time. This latter inquiry (to which such anthropologists as Victor Turner, Mary Douglas, and Raymond

Firth have contributed) involves situating their myths, rituals, cults against the configuration of knowledge we have acquired about the psychology, biology, and sociology of human beings generally.

Perhaps, then, Geertz wishes to claim (as his remarks suggest) that his "interpretive" methods are especially promising in the effort to understand culture and that other methods, while they need not be repudiated, may be set aside. In some places indeed, Geertz seems to claim just this, on the ground that other, better known, methods have not succeeded. He writes, for example, that his proposal that "cultural phenomena should be treated as significative systems posing expositive questions" has become less alarming to social scientists in recent years, in part because of "intellectual deprovincialization" and in part because of the "growing recognition that the established approach to treating such phenomena, laws-and-causes social physics, was not producing the triumphs of prediction, control, and testability that had for long been promised in its name."

But, if this is Geertz's argument, it seems to me to be mistaken. For one thing it rests on a caricature of "laws-and-causes" method. Geertz writes that "mainstream" social science, in seeking laws of "social physics," has held to such ideas as "the strict separation of theory and data, the 'brute fact' idea; the effort to create a formal vocabulary of analysis purged of all subjective reference, the 'ideal language' idea; and the claim to moral neutrality and the Olympian view, the 'God's truth' idea." But apart from what some social scientists infatuated with a "philosophical reconstruction" of social science method (such as crude behaviorism or reductionism) have said or written, which social scientists really ever adhered to such methodological restrictions in practice?

As Geertz himself might agree, adherence to these views is not revealed in the practice of many contemporary anthropologists. But was it implied or revealed in the practice of older anthropologists like S. F. Nadel or Gregory Bateson or Max Gluckman, or even of still older ones like Franz Boas or A.

L. Kroeber either? It seems to me that none of these anthropologists needs to be interpreted as manifesting in his practice
a belief in "brute data" or "ideal languages" or "moral neutrality" (despite the emphasis some of them may have placed
on "value-free" science—which is in fact a form of moral non-
neutrality). Accordingly, it is not clear among whom the views
Geertz describes were "established."

Nor is it fair to link "laws-and-causes" methods with the
search for the laws of "social physics" and then suggest that
the failure to find such laws somehow supports the espousal of
"interpretive" methods. "Laws-and-causes" methods seek to
discover the conditions of dependence between events through
controlled observation and inquiry. "Social physics" presumably seeks laws distinctive of society or culture (of the kind
that Radcliffe-Brown or Malinowski or "culturologists" like
Leslie White hoped to find). The two are not the same, and
giving up the search for "general laws of culture" does not
provide any substantial reasons for surrendering the search for
regularities and laws in the sphere of human action and behavior (let alone endorsing "interpretive" methods). Franz Boas,
who began his career with a firm belief that cultural laws existed, came in time to suspect that they did not; yet he did not
give up "laws-and-causes" methods, or the search for laws of
human behavior.

Moreover, as Geertz suggests, there may be no interesting
general laws of culture, or of anthropology, or sociology, to
discover; and in any case, it may be that the part played by
laws in many social scientific explanations is unlike that played
by them in other sciences. If a sociologist wishes to explain a
rise in juvenile crime he does not need to discover a distinctively
sociological law (let alone a law of juvenile crime), nor does
he usually try to; in general, he will try to explain the phenomenon in question by borrowing laws from other sciences
such as psychology or economics or genetics. He may succeed
or he may not. But if he does not, that in itself does not provide
good grounds for espousing "interpretive" methods in cultural
anthropology; for it may be that such knowledge as we discover

about human behavior and action may still be pertinent to the explanation of cultural phenomena when placed at the service of anthropologists. There is, of course, no way in advance of inquiry to claim with confidence that any "method" is promising or obstructive, but Geertz has not shown that the interpretive methods he recommends are uniquely suited to contributing to our understanding of culture. Other methods (such as that of "laws-and-causes") may usefully cooperate with those he espouses, and may perhaps contribute to our understanding of the "sense" of actions (as when, for example, we use controlled observation to find out whether or not one thing, a flag or a line or a bone, is regularly taken by members of a tribe to stand for another thing).[6]

VI

For these reasons and others, Geertz is best understood as holding that his interpretative methods constitute one way among others for acquiring one form of "understanding" among others. Anthropologists and social scientists might well acknowledge that this is an unexceptionable position. There are, however, difficulties in appraising the precise value of Geertz's methods, because it is unclear what kinds of results we might expect from them.

Consider Geertz's celebrated "reading" of the Balinese cockfight as a "cultural document." According to him, these fights are "at least as important a revelation of what being a Balinese 'is really like' " as Balinese art or social organization or mythology. Usually held in a large square in the late afternoon, and lasting some three or four hours, the fights are made up of nine or ten matches between cocks, and are played in accordance with "extraordinarily elaborate and precisely detailed rules," written down in palm-leaf manuscripts. The participants are

[6]For further discussion of the notion of "understanding" in the human sciences, see my review of W. G. Runciman, *A Treatise on Social Theory*, vol. 1, *The Methodology of Social Theory*, in the *New York Review of Books*, November 8, 1984.

always men—women are "totally and expressly excluded"—
and usually are (at least in major fights) "solid citizenry around
whom local life revolves." For these men, says Geertz, the
cocks are "symbolic expressions of what the Balinese (who are
"oblique, subdued, controlled, masters of indirection and dis-
simulation" and "shy to the point of obsessiveness of open
conflict") revile, namely animality.

Cockfight wagering is complex: "There is the single axial bet
in the center between the principals, and there is the cloud of
peripheral ones around the ring between members of the audience." On the basis of an analysis of these central and peripheral bets, Geertz claims that cockfighting for the Balinese
is not like roulette for us. It is, rather, often a form of "deep
play," play that seems on the surface irrational to engage in
because the stakes are so high, but that is persisted in because,
although "the amounts of money are great, much more is at
stake than material gain: namely, esteem, honor, dignity, respect—in a word, though in Bali a profoundly freighted word,
status." In the cockfight owners and their backers "put their
money where their status is." The cock is the medium for
placing their status on the line, and for those who are able to
bet considerable sums, "what is really going on in a match is
something rather closer to an *affaire d'honneur* . . . than to the
stupid, mechanical crank of a slot machine." For Geertz, then,
the cockfight is "a mock war of symbolical selves" conducted
through a "simulation of the social matrix" in which its devotees
live, and the deep cockfight is "a dramatization of status concerns."

Geertz's "reading" of the cockfight is a composite pageant
of erudition and insight, and is deservedly famous as an example of what skilled "interpretive anthropology" can be. But
it displays not only the imaginative use of interpretation by
Geertz but also some shortcomings of that method. For his
thesis about the cockfight is not simply that the Balinese see
the fight as "a mock war of symbolical selves" or as "a dramatization of status concerns." His central claim is that it is a
mock war that is "read" *by* the Balinese as "saying" something

about their society in general. The fights, he says, are a "medium" through which the Balinese "reflect" on themselves and their society. "Every people, the proverb has it, loves its own form of violence," he writes, and "the cockfight is the Balinese reflection on theirs: on its look, its uses, its force, its fascination." The fight is a form of self-interpretation:

> What sets the cockfight apart from the ordinary course of life, lifts it from the realm of the everyday practical affairs, and surrounds it with an aura of enlarged importance is . . . that it provides a metasocial commentary upon the whole matter of assorting human beings into fixed hierarchical ranks and then organizing the major part of collective existence around that assortment. Its function, if you want to call it that, is interpretive: it is a Balinese reading of Balinese experience, a story they tell themselves about themselves.

Geertz presents much evidence in favor of this view, and claims that the Balinese are themselves "quite aware" of this evidence: "Fighting cocks, almost every Balinese I have ever discussed the subject with has said, is like playing with fire only not getting burned. You activate village and kin group rivalries and hostilities, but in 'play' form, coming dangerously and entrancingly close to the expression of open and direct interpersonal and intergroup aggression . . . but not quite, because, after all, it is 'only a cockfight.' "

But how far does this go toward establishing his view? We may agree that some Balinese view the fights as a means of "activating" rivalries and hostilities without "getting burned"— something which is no doubt prized in a society "shy to the point of obsessiveness of open conflict." But that the Balinese see the fights as an occasion for acting out such hostilities in "play" form is quite different from claiming that they "read" the fights as analyses or interpretations of their social order, or that the fights are "reflections" on violence or on "the whole matter of assorting human beings into fixed hierarchical ranks and then organizing the major part of collective existence around that assortment."

It is one thing to claim that devotees of the cockfight attribute deep significance to it because it serves as an opportunity to express and dramatize their individual status conflicts and rivalries; it is another to describe the cockfight as a "commentary" by the Balinese on the social order and organization that makes these conflicts possible. The latter claim, which makes the Balinese seem to be attending the cockfight as social analysts, Geertz does not seem to have established. Thus, for all its suggestiveness, Geertz's view of the cockfight as a "metasocial" story the Balinese tell themselves about themselves and their society is open to some considerable doubt, and this doubt is based, not on whether his informants were reliable or representative members of Balinese society or not, but rather on the lack of clear and cogent evidence for his conjecture about "the native point of view" of the cockfight.

Such unclarity need not lead of course to general skepticism toward "interpretive anthropology," but it does raise the question of what kinds of critical restraints or regulations must be placed on the activity of "interpreting" cultural "texts" if we are to be able to distinguish clearly between what is "in" the "text" and what is supplied by the "reader," and if we are to be able to have good reasons for believing that particular examples of such interpretations really do capture how other peoples "represent themselves to themselves."

This incomplete and obscure aspect of "interpretive anthropology" deserves the attention of those who endorse Geertz's "interpretive turn" (or his claim that "mainstream social science" methods are inadequate to the job of cultural "translation"). But it should also concern those who agree with him that the need to develop a means of understanding other cultures is not merely a question of which school of social scientific method is correct, but one of practical importance now and in the future, as different political, legal, and moral universes arise and multiply in unforeseen ways through contact with one another, instead of fusing or settling into some predictable pattern of development.

The Silent Majority: Peasants in the Third World

The "modernization" of peasant societies is one of the great themes of contemporary history. It is an urgent issue in Asia and Africa and Latin America. "Peasants"—i.e., self-supporting land laborers and cultivators living in small village communities—make up most of the population in the world's poorest countries. How they are affected by economic and political changes remains inadequately understood, notwithstanding the outpouring of scholarly studies of peasant cultures for the benefit of those who plan "development" and make policy. Peasants have frequently and often violently resisted attempts to change their lives. Most of the Western ideas designed to advance modernization of peasant societies have been sharply criticized by prominent third world and radical intellectuals speaking on behalf of the peasantry.

But they are spokesmen for a largely silent class. What do peasants themselves believe and value or deplore, and what reasons lie behind their reactions to economic and political change? Why have rural development programs for improved farming, small industry, and health services failed so often?

The answers to these questions are much disputed. All that is certain is that peasants have throughout history been a potent political force for both progress and reaction. Their actions have not always met with the approval of either liberal reformers or the revolutionaries who have led them into battle, whether in the sixteenth-century German peasant wars, in the Vendée during the French Revolution, or during the more recent revolutions in Russia and China, Mexico and Cuba, Algeria and Vietnam.

How are we to determine what "peasants' " views really are? James Scott and Samuel Popkin are both Southeast Asia scholars who look to the past in order to support views about what peasants are like, and what they want.[1] They wish to address current problems of peasant politics and rural development. Both of them have written books about Vietnam—not directly about the recent war there but about the effects on the Vietnamese peasants of the centralized bureaucracy and capitalist economy introduced early in the century by the French colonial regime. This experience caused a historical transformation, they would both claim, that contained the seeds of the revolution of 1945 and the ensuing war of "national liberation."

Their common enterprise is a doubly risky one: The peasants of a half-century ago may not be very similar to those in our own era of "transitional societies," straddling the old and the new. Views about what "peasants" are like are usually based on evidence from the distant past and may overlook the variety and constantly evolving character of peasant societies and "borderline" cases like the nomads of Africa, the production brigades of China, and the farmers of Japan who have tractors, washing machines, and refrigerators. More than this, the available information on the particular aspects of precolonial Vietnam with which they are both most concerned is spare and

---

[1]James C. Scott, *The Moral Economy of the Peasant: Rebellion and Subsistence in Southeast Asia* (New Haven, Conn.: Yale University Press, 1976), and Samuel L. Popkin, *The Rational Peasant: The Political Economy of Rural Society in Vietnam* (Berkeley: University of California Press, 1979).

unreliable, so that the reader is not sure how, or on what basis, their views are to be appraised.

James Scott's book is a particularly sophisticated statement of one perspective on peasant institutions that has become something of an orthodoxy. A political scientist and a Quaker, Scott has done field research on peasant politics in Malaysia and Burma; he read widely in the history of Vietnam and Southeast Asia in order to write this book. He recently said that the aim of his work on peasants is "to do justice to a class which seldom speaks for itself, and to its culture and values, which are treated with no small degree of arrogance by Marxist and bourgeois scholars alike." His work is marked by a powerful capacity for understanding what he calls the "moral universes" of others.

"Woven into the tissue of peasant behavior," he writes, "whether in normal local routines or in the violence of an uprising, is the structure of a moral universe." The peasant "as a political actor is more than a statistical abstract of available calories and outgoing rent and tax charges." Scott is preoccupied above all with describing what this universe is like to those who live inside it. Clifford Geertz, who we have noted in the previous chapter is a distinguished contemporary specialist in this kind of research, has written that Scott's work is "extraordinarily original and valuable" and that he believes its "central thesis is correct and compelling."

Scott's thesis is that peasant politics is shaped by the predicament most peasants share—the problem of subsistence, of getting enough to live—and by the distinctive moral outlook that arises among them in response to this predicament. This argument is illustrated in great detail in his study of Vietnam under the French.

Before colonialism, he claims, peasants lived in "closed villages," largely autonomous agricultural communities where social life revolved about the *dinh*, the village meeting house where the effigy of the guardian spirit of the village was kept. This, he says, was a kind of New Deal society, in which an ideology of the survival of the weakest prevailed. A council of elders selected for their age and wisdom periodically leased out communal lands to the more unfortunate peasants who needed them—those whose crops had failed, the helpless and the ill, the aged and the widowed. Tax charges assessed on the village by the local authorities were distributed by the council so as to put the burden on those who were better off; the council members also would give elaborate feasts to spread their wealth among the less fortunate. Peasant landlords would adjust their claims on their tenants according to the yield of the harvest. In bad times, he continues, they would provide tenants with loans, food, medicine, assistance with birth and burial ceremonies. In prosperous times they would demand much more, but this did not strike the peasants as exploitative; they valued stability and security above risk.

How did this mutual assistance network arise? Scott believes the answer lies partly in the unstable agricultural and climatic environment in which the peasants lived. The southern part of Vietnam has a more benign climate than the north, where there are periodic droughts and floods; but the position of the Vietnamese peasant in both regions was for the most part, in the words of R. H. Tawney, cited by Scott, "like that of a man standing permanently up to his neck in water, so that even a ripple might drown him." Peasants were preoccupied with subsistence and so it was reasonable for them to value safety and security above all; they were averse to taking chances and hostile to any changes which interfered with their ways of assuring themselves an adequate living. They had little room for the bourgeois calculus of profit—they wanted to be insulated from risk. A common morality arose among them—the "subsistence ethic," as Scott calls it—that legitimized this desire and affirmed the right of every villager to a bare livelihood; and this served to bring into existence a "moral economy" in which the weakest were protected from ruin.

French colonialism brought improved communications, transport, disease control, education, and roman script. But it also introduced new legal and administrative systems, commercialized agriculture, and cash crops. The peasant provinces, Scott argues, were forcibly transformed into "capillaries of a network of financial arteries leading to the banks of London and Paris," and peasants were brusquely exposed to the flukes and instabilities of markets. The harmonious balance that had existed in the precolonial village was rudely upset: The communal lands and "free" forests and fisheries were nationalized and sold off. The guarantees for the poor—the village's welfare and insurance schemes and the system of feasts—were gradually stripped away. The *colons* introduced a vast bureaucracy and obstructive regulations, together with a host of census takers, surveyors, registrars, road overseers, vaccinators, irrigation experts, forest rangers, veterinary assistants. The French levied head taxes, land taxes, salt taxes, alcohol taxes, tea and drug taxes, fishing taxes, bird taxes, oxen taxes—all on the ground that they represented, as one French official put it, "the manifest benefits of living in an 'organized society' from which all profited."

Not surprisingly, this judgment about public finance seemed wholly capricious from the standpoint of the "subsistence ethic." For in reality the profits of society were not trickling down to the peasant. In the countryside, the richer and more powerful villagers acquired new habits. Instead of honoring flexible and informal agreements and displaying traditional paternalism, they started using the new French courts to enforce what the peasants dreaded most: contracts specifying both rigid terms of tenancy and fixed rents, without regard to the cycles of good and bad harvests. Overnight, large numbers of small-holders fell into the class of the dispossessed as a result of the deed juggling and corruption of landowner and village elders, and enormous inequalities in landholdings followed.

With the double calamity of the world depression and the famines of 1930, during which peasants were forced to eat waterbugs, ant eggs, and bees, and landowners would sprinkle cinders into the edible fertilizer to prevent starving day laborers from surreptitiously eating it,[2] agrarian relations fell apart. The landlords installed grilles on their windows, collected rents through agents, and surrounded themselves with toughs paid with alcohol and opium. The peasants in turn finally exploded in rage, as in the Nghe-Tinh uprisings of 1930. At first, small bands of peasants, armed only with sticks and amulets, petitioned for tax remissions in the submissive and deferential style of the Sinicized culture of Vietnam. Then there followed incidents of overt violence: government officials were assassinated, post offices and schools destroyed, administrative buildings and mandarin residences pillaged, and tax rolls burned. Crowds of 20,000 people were sometimes involved in these incidents and were, on occasion, bombed by French planes.

Scott believes that the particular local causes of such insurrections are complicated, but a main cause was a moral one: The peasants rebelled because their standards of justice and legitimacy were violated by the new economic and political order, and they acted to restore a moral agrarian regime. To do so was not self-deceptive or a matter of "false consciousness," as some Marxists say. The peasants lived, according to Scott, as they had for centuries, in a different "world of meaning" from that of their conquerers—different but genuine all the same, intelligible, rational, based not on some incapacity to see clearly, but on different values.

In Scott's view, those concerned with development in the third world today must take pains to grasp the peasant's "moral universe"; they must attend to experiences quite different from those that economists usually look for. They must see that the life of the peasant takes place within a distinctive moral pattern marking out a territory of conduct over which its dictates have jurisdiction. For planners to provide "incentives" for personal

[2]This information is to be found in Martin J. Murray, *The Development of Capitalism in Colonial Indochina, 1870–1940* (Berkeley: University of California Press, 1981), p. 400. Murray's book—whether or not one believes its central theses—is the most thorough and extensively researched account to be found in English of the misery of the peasantry during the high tide of French colonialism in Indochina.

gain or higher incomes may be beside the point. We will not get far, Scott concludes, by "treating the peasant purely as a kind of marketplace individualist who amorally ransacks his environment so as to reach his personal goal."

Samuel Popkin, a political scientist who studied the Vietnamese peasantry at first hand while doing research on "pacification programs" for the Simulmatics Corporation and for this book from 1966 to 1970, follows the very approach repudiated by Scott, while attacking Scott's findings. Peasants in his view are not very different from small business people in Western countries. Like other "economic actors," they "maximize expected value." Popkin believes the categories of economics can be helpful in explaining human action outside the market as well as within it. His view of peasant society emphasizes the "political economy" and contains many references to "political capital," "selective incentives," "family firms," the "start-up costs" of religions. For Popkin, the most enterprising peasants are "marketplace individualists," and such people do far more to shape peasant institutions than do the moral norms of the group.

How, he asks, does a "moral economist" like Scott know what "ethic" peasants espouse? How could moral standards overcome the everyday economic struggle for resources and ensure them a minimum income? He argues, moreover, that the precolonial Vietnamese villages were not the harmonious communities that Scott describes. The peasants did indeed have subsistence problems and suffered extreme uncertainty—but the result was neither the emergence of a policy of "safety first" nor such mutual assistance schemes as communal insurance and welfare. Instead, the peasants distrusted one another and relied on "private investments" such as animals and having children—a form of old-age insurance. He suggests that it is farfetched to suppose that the same peasants who meticulously calculated the costs and benefits of their decisions about agriculture would blithely surrender their hard-earned surplus products to possibly untrustworthy village elders who might take them for themselves rather than distribute them to the needy. And is it not just as unlikely that the rich and powerful, the notables themselves, would give away their wealth to other peasants, who might just be freeloaders?

Of course, Popkin continues, the problem of the destitute was ever-present, but one common procedure for dealing with those in trouble, he says, was to rename them "nonvillagers" and throw them out. It is true that the rich patrons in peasant villages were sometimes "paternalistic"—but this was part of a "divide and conquer" strategy designed to keep the poor down, to prevent "collective bargaining." The old men on the councils of notables may have been wise, but they used their power and the communal lands to enrich themselves. If the peaceful "collective solidarity" of the moral economists existed at all in the villages, it was imposed from above. The unstable village peace of deadlocked conflict and oligarchic control merely disguised the Hobbesian struggle beneath the surface. And when colonialism arrived, according to Popkin, it was not the commercializing of agriculture or the expansion of markets or new laws and bureaucratic regulations that "eroded" or "penetrated" a united, resistant, antimarket "peasant" ideology or "little tradition." On the contrary, the cleverer peasants themselves initiated alliances with the bureaucrats and manipulated the colonial institutions to their own advantage.

An arresting chapter of Popkin's book tries to explain peasant rebellions such as the "Red Terror" of 1930 by "peasant investment logic." This applies, he claims, not just to agriculture and the village but to "political and religious transformations of society" through collective action. Peasants did not rebel to restore a golden past: They were challenging the political and economic control exercised by elites in order to create new rural institutions which would raise their standard of living. What was needed was someone to organize them. Popkin shows that by the end of the Thirties there was no scarcity of what he calls "political entrepreneurs" who would satisfy this demand by delivering improved institutions in exchange for peasant support.

He gives a fascinating account of some of the groups that

competed with one another—and apparently still do, notwithstanding the domination of the Hanoi government[3]—for control of the peasantry. There was, for example, the Catholic Church, whose priests he calls "quintessential" political entrepreneurs who succeeded in converting many among the countryside "not only because of the appeal of the religion itself, but because of tangible, material benefits—science, cannon, European education—that the priest could offer as proof of the religion's validity." There was also the Cao Dai, a syncretic sect with hundreds of thousands of adherents, many of whom were administrative employees of the French. The Cao Dai were organized on the model of the Catholic Church—they had a pope and a Holy See, a hierarchy of over eleven thousand offices, an armed forces, a welfare branch, together with a pantheon of saints with a "common radical-political streak," including Joan of Arc, Victor Hugo, and Charlie Chaplin. The Cao Dai, as Popkin sees them, sought to revive indigenous pride and political influence in order to have a larger share in Vietnam's wealth.

So did the Hoa Hao, an anticolonial and millenarian religious movement based upon the teachings of the "mad bonze," Huynh Phu So, a charismatic monk who had "differed from other prophets because he knew how to 'mass merchandise' his message" of simplicity, prayer, family obligation, authenticity, and liberation. Huynh Phu So was assassinated at the age of twenty-eight by jealous Communists who subsequently hacked his corpse into three pieces and buried them in separate graves to ensure against his return to life.

Last, of course, there was the Communist Party, which alone was sufficiently expert, according to Popkin, in the sophisticated techniques of leadership and organization to provide a blend of "selective incentives" that could unify the diverse religious, ethnic, ideological, and political groups within the country.

[3]"Who Will Back Vietnam's Rebels?" *Foreign Reports* (London), February 4, 1981.

Popkin, however, does not express an unqualified judgment on the success of the Communist Party. He notes that up to the mid-1950s and the renewal of the French presence after the Second World War, the party enjoyed considerable success in mobilizing peasants to cooperate and get what they wanted, namely raised levels of production and an improved standard of life. This was especially so, he says, in the North, where the Communists could win political control over the tightly integrated villages more easily than in the South, which was prosperous and where the social structure of the peasant communities was looser and less responsive to efforts to reorganize their economy and influence them ideologically. Even in the South, "given the obstacles, the Communists succeeded to an impressive extent." But Popkin also notes that there was frequently serious tension between the Viet Minh and peasants who sought to enter the market on their own by resuming trade with the French and who bitterly resented efforts by the Communists to curtail their market activities for political purposes. Moreover, he does not deal with the acute problems of political control and economic stability that were encountered by the Communists before and after the war with the United States.[4]

All of the movements Popkin describes attracted peasants and increased their resources by using "political skills and bureaucratic connections to give the peasants access to (and leverage against) the institutions that had previously kept them at a disadvantage." In no case, Popkin writes, did they seek to restore "traditional" patterns of life. The moral economist errs in thinking that the uprisings were "defensive" or "reactionary": to suppose so is to suppose that there actually was a golden past before the French arrived. Anyone who believes this has been bamboozled, in Popkin's view, by the less than

[4]The recent situation in the country has been summarized in a comprehensive internal report circulated for "official use" by the World Bank: *Viet Nam: A Socialist Economy in Transition,* Report No. 2503a-VN, East Asia and Pacific Regional Office, The World Bank, March 5, 1980. See also William Shawcross's report, "In a Grim Country," *New York Review of Books,* September 24, 1981.

candid reminiscences of landlords, or by the reconstructions of
the French anthropologist Paul Mus and his students,[5] whose
sentimental vision of Vietnamese life has thrown dust in our
eyes by smoothing over the fierce conflicts that must have been
endemic in precolonial villages.

Popkin thinks that peasants are "not hostile to innovations
from which they expect personal gain." Many attempts to
"modernize" the village "fail (or are not adopted) not because
of a positive regard for tradition or aversion to risk, but because
low-quality leadership and mutual distrust preclude the req-
uisite cost-sharing or coordination among peasants." Contemporary planners must help to build rural institutions that will
encourage peasants to cooperate and believe that "they, rather
than someone else, will enjoy the fruits of their labor."

The charge that peasants have been idealized is not a new
one. Indeed, it seems fair to say that no class or group in society
has ever received such strikingly mixed notices from anthropologists, sociologists, and historians. Romantic German scholars held, as did Rousseau, that the ancient peasant villages
were centers of primitive communism, where, in contrast to
the wicked ways of the town, the fruits of the social product
went to all, and where liberty, fraternity, equality were truly
exemplified—perhaps for the last time. Many other writers
have since depicted the "peasant mind" as "childlike," "un-
contaminated," "nonlinear," "pre-Socratic." Peasants have been
said to be disdainful of buying and selling, acquisition, ambition; the social structure of peasant societies has been described
as solidly grounded in the bonds of blood relations, in imme-
morial and "natural" patterns of marriage and family obligations.

Many Russian populists and Slavophiles—as well as the famous Baron Haxthausen—saw the Russian village, the *mir,* as
a self-sustaining economic unit that would be the salvation of

[5]John T. McAlister, Jr., and Paul Mus, *The Vietnamese and Their Revo-
lution* (New York: Harper & Row, 1970). Frances FitzGerald, *Fire in the
Lake: The Vietnamese and the Americans in Vietnam* (Boston: Atlantic/Little,
Brown, 1972).

the country. Recalling that Marx and others had taught that there are inevitable stages of economic change in society, some of them said that owing to the already existing communistic *mir,* a direct transition to sophisticated communism, without an intermediate stage of industrialization, was possible; the grasping individualism and "atomization" of bourgeois society, they thought, could never arise in the *mir.*

Nineteenth-century travelers to the great British and Dutch colonies—or to the Indian societies of the United States—claimed to observe communities in which a man could always help himself to his neighbor's resources when needy. Georges Sorel wrote that "to the village, not to the town, we must turn for the elucidation of the notion of association in the sense of the Socialist program." A modern writer who quotes Sorel says that "craft and wile alone" could not have brought about the remarkable result that "Marxism sold its first ticket to a peasant, not to an industrial, society."[6] More recently, the University of Chicago anthropologist Robert Redfield described the Mexican peasant society of Tepoztlán as a "smoothly functioning and well-integrated society made up of a contented and well-adjusted people." Clifford Geertz seems to run into peasants who, despite severe economic hardships, cannot be restrained from discussing philosophical problems of the self and freedom of the will.

On the other side stand all those who have found such images unrealistic. Marx and Engels spoke bluntly of rural "idiocy"; in their own time, they said, the peasantry as a class was suffering from the "hallucinations of its death struggle"; peasants were relics, bound to disappear with the growth of capitalism, and they did not mourn the loss. Lenin and Plekhanov attacked the *narodniki* with similar violence for believing in myths about the *mir.* Maxim Gorky asked himself, "But where is the good-natured, thoughtful Russian peasant, indefatigable searcher after truth and justice, who was so convincingly and beautifully de-

---

[6]Nicholas Georgescu Roegen, in Clifton R. Wharton, Jr., ed., *Subsistence Agriculture and Economic Development* (Chicago: Aldine, 1969), pp. 82, 85.

picted in the world of nineteenth-century literature?" He answered that he could not, after much inquiry, find such a man,
discovering instead a man "half-savage, stupid, heavy, . . .
lazily, carelessly, incapably slumped" across the land. He added
that "those who took on themselves the bitter Herculean work
of cleaning the Augean stables of Russian life I cannot consider
'tormentors of the people'; from my point of view they are
rather victims." Oscar Lewis, Edward Banfield, and other social scientists have challenged many of the assumptions of
Redfield and his followers. They came away from peasant communities with impressions of peasants as often fatalistic and
supine, ignorant, dishonest, malicious, rancorous, sunk in ap-
athy and meanness.

The clash between Scott and Popkin is clearly narrower and
less extreme than some of these earlier skirmishes. But what
exactly does the controversy amount to in the case of Vietnam?
As a purely historical debate about the Vietnamese peasantry,
the evidence seems decisive for neither view—and perhaps it
could not be. Both authors rely to a considerable degree on
the same sources, such as the work of the French cultural
geographer Pierre Gourou. Popkin cites him extensively in
support of his bleak picture of the precolonial village, whereas
Scott finds Gourou to be one of the Southeast Asia scholars
who remarked on the "informal social controls which act to
provide for the minimal needs of the village poor." Both views
advanced seem partial, persuasive in different settings. As the
main ethnographic sources mustered by them suggest, there
were striking dissimilarities between the behavior of peasants
and the social structure of peasant villages in North and South
Vietnam.[7] Popkin is certainly right on methodological grounds
to ask precisely how Scott has discovered what peasants find
moral and immoral and to criticize him for his vague claim that

---

[7]See, for example, Terry Rambo, "A Comparison of Peasant Social Sys-
tems of Northern and Southern Vietnam: A Study of Ecological Adaptation,
Social Succession, and Cultural Evolution," Center for Vietnamese Studies,
Southern Illinois University at Carbondale, Monograph Series III, Chapter
II, especially pp. 29–49.

economic circumstances "give rise" to an "ethic" which in turn "shapes" peasant institutions. He is also right to raise the possibility that conflicts within the village may have overwhelmed the influence of such an ethic if it existed.

But much of his attack on the moral economy view overlooks the subtlety of Scott's position: A careful reader will note that he never says that the villages of Vietnam were egalitarian idylls. The issue for him is not whether a "leveling" of wealth took place, but whether a place was provided for the worst off. When Scott writes about the "subsistence ethic," he seems as often as not to be describing peasant ideals, and he does not claim that these preferences were always incarnated in actual institutions. As he writes, "The social strength of this ethic, its protective power for the village poor, varied from village to village, from region to region."

As for the disagreement whether peasant rebellions in Vietnam or elsewhere are "defensive" or "progressive," Scott is mainly concerned with the perspective of the peasant participants: He believes they saw their actions as protecting specific kinds of rights, duties, institutions. This view is not inconsistent with the claim that these same rebellions might have resulted in the extension of peasant rights and privileges or that they were organized by radical elites who thought of the uprisings as designed to achieve this outcome.[8]

Indeed, Popkin's own work would have been stronger had he made some use of the moral economy perspective. He describes peasants so suspicious and distrustful of one another that they could not even agree to create collective irrigation facilities; yet why were they still able to join together to take up the unworldly "incentives" of religious sects like the Hoa Hao? Popkin's repeated appeal to such factors as the "mass merchandising" and "sociopolitical competence" of the sects to explain such behavior needs amplification; but when he provides it, he often refers to precisely the same factors—"reasons

[8]James C. Scott, "Revolution in the Revolution: Peasants and Commissars," *Theory and Society*, vol. 7, nos. 1–2 (March 1979), pp. 97–134.

of duty," "ethic," "moral codes"—stressed by the moral economists.

To take another example, if peasants were indeed eager to sell in the market when they saw the opportunity for personal gain, and were not appreciably constrained by moral beliefs, why then did rebels—as Scott documents—sometimes hand back to the notables and mandarins the portion of seized resources that was left over after they subtracted what they needed for their own subsistence? After one prunes excesses and misinterpretations in this way—and recalls the lack of decisive historical evidence for the central claims at issue—the sides of the "debate" seem far less sharply defined.

Perhaps what animates and sustains the controversy is, finally, a philosophical conflict between the different models or pictures of human nature that are presupposed by the "political economy" and "moral economy" approaches. This is a conflict about which factors—personal gain or moral obligation, economic conditions or cultural traditions—are "more important" in analyzing and explaining human behavior, whether we discuss the agricultural decisions of a peasant or the conduct of a statesman. On this abstract plane, if Scott at times goes too far in emphasizing the peasant's "moral universe," Popkin makes a comparable error: His peasant "economic actors" are too skeletal and predictable. His theory seems to be that since peasants everywhere are latent profit maximizers, some tidy social computation by development planners will bring about a proper organization of self-interest and unleash hitherto subterranean psychological forces. But this is too simple and leaves too much unsaid.

Perhaps "personal gain" lies at the base of all decisions made by "rational economic actors"; but to say so comes close to being a tautology. Popkin provides much useful information when he argues that organizations offering opportunities for self-advancement can be critical factors in economic development. But the concept of "rationality" used by many economists is open to serious criticism, and in any case the Guatemalan cultivator or the Indian untouchable who resists vitamins, vaccinations, or contraceptives, or who does not "co-operate" with other peasants in promoting a "green revolution," might not be a "rational actor." Even if we stipulate that he is, he has a definite set of opinions on what are "gains" and "losses," opinions which are bound up in complicated ways with the rest of his attitudes—say, those concerning worldly ambition, or the value of contemplation, or the afterlife—and these might clash irrevocably with the opinions of other members of his community, let alone with the aims of development planners. Popkin's view is very clear but unconvincing: It does not really provide an explanation of "peasant goals and attitudes"; what he does is to spell out the categories and concepts in which an explanation might be couched. The concept of the moral economy, for all its methodological pitfalls and lack of clarity, still offers a more convincing approach to understanding peasant societies.[9]

Social change itself will not stand still for the debate between these views to be settled, and for many contemporary problems it may not even be necessary to attempt to resolve them at all. But every strategy for development presupposes certain assumptions about the motives and characters of those who are affected by it. What remains to be done in the case of "peasants," perhaps, is more detailed work designed to bring to light and to support realistic assumptions of this kind in specific cases of contemporary "rural development" and "modernization." Understanding the acutely important problems, moral and economic alike, addressed by our authors might be advanced in this way as surely as by the more ambitious and systematic schemes they have constructed.

[9]For further discussion of the debate between Popkin and Scott, see "Peasant Strategies in Asian Societies: Moral and Rational Economic Approaches—A Symposium," *The Journal of Asian Studies,* vol. 42, no. 4 (August 1983). See also James C. Scott's new book, *Weapons of the Weak: Everyday Forms of Peasant Resistance* (New Haven, Conn.: Yale University Press, 1985).

Too Many People? The History of the "Population Explosion"

Between 1949 and 1973 the population of China increased by 64 percent and today it is over one billion. The Deng regime claims that high rates of population growth, lower rates of death caused by modern medicines, and a generally poor and badly educated population have forced China to spend too much on housing, food, and employment. The resources drained for these purposes could be used, Chinese officials argue, to develop and "modernize" the country. To arrest population growth, the regime has created a program of mass "ideological education" and a system of economic incentives to encourage people to have fewer children (in many cases, according to guidelines set by the State Family Planning Commission, just one).

The government has set targets for each province, which in turn allocates birth quotas among its counties. County officials pursue the process down through communes and production teams. Slogans, posters, radio broadcasts, public exhibits, and editorials are used to encourage smaller families; contraceptives and sterilization are provided by the government free. Couples who have only one child are rewarded by supplementary payments, preference in housing, free education for their child, and higher retirement pensions, among other measures. Those couples who have more children than is recommended can become ineligible for job promotion or suffer a reduction in their monthly wages.

Critics of this policy in the United States claim that it is "coercive" and that forced abortions and sterilizations, as well as cases of infanticide, have been condoned by Chinese authorities. The Chinese government has responded that these critics have seized upon isolated instances, reported by the Chinese themselves in their press, of "overzealous" behavior by family planning workers and have treated them as representative of the policy as a whole. They say the key to the Chinese program is "education," and that while there have been mistakes, as might be expected among so large a population, "coercion" could not be responsible for the remarkable declines that have been observed in the Chinese birth rate in recent years. Hundreds of millions of families could not, they say, be forced to have fewer children; they have seen, rather, that it is advantageous for them to do so. Moreover, they say, the success of the Chinese population program has helped the Chinese to enjoy a better standard of living and to devote resources that might have gone to the feeding and training of children to projects that would help the Chinese economy to grow.[1]

There is, however, evidence of increasing opposition to the one-child policy, especially among the rural population. Peasants claim they have a duty to have sons, who continue the male line, contribute to the family economy through work on the land, and support their parents in old age. Under the current policy, fewer than one-half of Chinese couples are likely to have a surviving son.[2] The one-child policy also appears to

---

[1] I am grateful to Jiang Chengzong, counselor at the Chinese embassy in Washington, for helpful discussion on this point.

[2] See John Bongaarts and Susan Greenhalgh, "An Alternative to the One-Child Policy in China," *Population and Development Review,* vol. 11, no. 4 (December 1985).

conflict with state policies allotting the use of land to families on the basis of their size, thereby giving them an incentive to have more children. Corruption and bribery have occurred in enforcing the policy. People tamper with records or move to other parts of the country if they want more children. If the policy is reversed as a result of resistance, China's population could grow considerably once again.

Still, in the United States, critics of Chinese policy persist in their claims. For example, in the autumn of 1985 Senator Jesse Helms disagreed with all of his colleagues on the Senate Foreign Relations Committee and acted to hold up the confirmation of President Reagan's choice for ambassador to China, Winston Lord. According to Helms, by giving money to the United Nations Fund for Population Activities, which supports in part China's population program, the Reagan administration is violating U.S. law, which forbids U.S. support of foreign population programs that permit coercive activities. Helms insists such activities take place in China today, and threatened to filibuster the Senate unless he received assurances from the administration that all funding of such programs would stop. In early November, he apparently received such assurances from President Reagan.

As is evident, such disputes depend in some considerable part on moral values like personal liberty and the "sanctity of life." But they also depend upon difficult empirical questions, the most important of which is whether a rapidly growing population adversely affects human welfare, as the Chinese and many others argue. If this claim is false, then the central reason for creating a population policy is removed and the moral argument against interfering in people's lives by preventing them from having as many children as they wish becomes, if anything, more forceful.

Do additional people cause valuable resources such as land, minerals, and capital to be exhausted, as is widely supposed? Or, on the other hand, should we see children and migrants as good investments because they might more than pay their way in the future? Depending on how one looks at the matter, the "population problem" can be desperate or not a problem at all. One view holds that the problem is serious enough to warrant government intervention in people's decisions to have more children in many parts of the world. Another view—prominently associated with Julian Simon, a professor of economics at the University of Maryland, and P. T. Bauer, most recently affiliated with the London School of Economics, both contributors to an edited transcript of a symposium on world population trends held at the American Enterprise Institute in Washington, D.C., in December 1984[3]—contends that there is no population problem in the world today because a growing population can contribute to the prosperity of a nation, adding as it does not merely more consumers but also more producers.

These views are taken seriously in Washington. Simon and his allies deride efforts by the United States and other rich countries to "impose" on poorer countries the view that their rates of population growth should be reduced through measures that go beyond voluntary family planning. During the past quarter-century, many countries have created family planning programs, which provide information and services so that couples can restrict the size of their families as they wish. Other countries have gone further and encouraged lower birth rates through the use of mass media or through economic incentives, such as payments given to couples who delay having children. In view of this and of the familiarity of the "population explosion" to the general public, the dismissal of the problem by Simon and his followers has been a source of intense controversy.

Such a dispute would hardly have been conceivable during the late Sixties and early Seventies. During the Johnson and Nixon administrations, an alarmist view of population trends was linked to a constellation of popular social concerns, such as conservationism, and backed by powerful institutions such

---

[3] *Are World Population Trends a Problem?* edited, with an introduction, by Ben Wattenberg and Karl Zinsmeister (Washington, D.C.: American Enterprise Institute for Public Policy Research, 1986).

as the World Bank. At the first World Population Conference, held in Bucharest in 1974, the U.S. delegation was the leader of those countries that saw population as a threat to economic growth and improved standards of living. During the past few years, however, Simon's benign view of population growth has gained wide attention, not only for its startling assertions, but also because many of its proponents have endorsed the Reagan administration's political philosophy.

They have, for example, emphasized the family's right to freedom from government interference; they have opposed abortion and argued that government has no business advocating population control but should instead ensure that production can outpace population growth through economic growth. In a striking reversal of its view in 1974, the U.S. delegation at the second World Population Conference in Mexico City in 1984 argued that there is no global population problem and that governments have tended to inhibit people's efforts to better themselves through ill-advised policies; free enterprise and economic development, they argued, will take care of pressures created by increased population.

That the benign view has pushed aside the alarmist one need not be taken as a victory of objective social science. It is, arguably, rather more the achievement of those who used it to promote ideological views having very little to do with the causes or consequences of population growth. But this was also true of the way in which the alarmist view succeeded in capturing the public's imagination in the late Sixties. And in any case, a great many demographers who have studied these questions hold that both views are wrong.

I

A human population may grow because people in it die less quickly, or because new members are added to it when they move from another place, or because people in it have more children. During the late 1950s it was noted by demographers and economists that among the world's many populations modern medicines such as sulfa drugs and antibiotics and modern technology in agriculture (such as the use of insecticides and chemical fertilizers) had led to a fall in mortality. Moreover, in contrast to earlier periods of human history, there was no longer an open frontier—as there was when millions of people left Europe for North and South America and Australia in the nineteenth century—so that people could not relieve the pressures of a greater population by moving to another place. In addition, people in many countries were having more children.

When the population scare began in the Sixties, the global rate of population growth was 2 percent, i.e., 2 percent of the population is added each year to the existing population, which itself consists of the previous year's population enlarged by 2 percent. A population grows at zero rate if it replaces itself, whereas one that grows at a rate of 2 percent doubles in thirty-five years. The global population by the late Sixties was more than 3.5 billion, twice as large as it was at the beginning of the twentieth century.

The prospect that it would double again by the end of the century gave rise to the idea of a population "explosion." Influential spokesmen of the alarmist view such as the ecologist Paul Ehrlich formulated a comprehensive picture of the effect a large increase in population has on existing resources and institutions. They saw themselves as presenting a modern version of the ideas of the nineteenth-century economist Thomas Robert Malthus, who argued that population growth is a major cause of poverty. Human populations, he wrote, reproduce themselves up to the limits set by their environment; the poor, in particular, reproduce and create a surplus of labor, thus forcing wages down, in effect creating their own poverty. "Neo-Malthusians" subscribed to the view that birth control and family-planning programs should be introduced to stem the growth of population in the poorer regions of the world.

As more and more children are born, they wrote, and many more people live longer because of modern medicine, it becomes increasingly difficult to feed them: Food supplies, available croplands, and fisheries are used up more quickly and farmers must make do with smaller and smaller plots. Greater demands are made on energy, fuel, metal ores, and other resources; the demand for firewood, for example, becomes so great that trees are cut down faster than they can be replaced. Moreover, they argued, a greater population leads to crowding, and hence to psychological pathology, to congestion and pollution, and to the degradation of the environment.

A similar argument was used to show that more people impose a strain on political and economic institutions. As more people are born, and later enter the labor force, either productivity per head falls or there is greater unemployment. Furthermore, each new child added to the population lowers the average income of everyone else. As the number of dependent children grows, in this argument, savings are reduced, which in turn reduces the amount available for investment in farms, factories, and housing. Government revenues are spread more thinly on social services like public schooling, hospitals, parks, and police protection.

According to the alarmist view, the number of people in a population is not the sole problem; the way they are distributed is also important. For when there are no jobs or social services, people leave their homes in search of opportunities; in poor countries, especially, people leave the countryside in search of city jobs, creating crowded, polluted concentrations like Shanghai, São Paulo, or Mexico City. Moreover, since people everywhere seem to have a fear of being outnumbered by others belonging to different ethnic, political, or religious groups, the relative size of populations may create tensions, both between and within countries, as seems suggested by the conflict between Christians and Muslims in Nigeria or Lebanon, or the problems created by the growing differences in birth rates between the Jews and Arabs in Israel, or by the growing Muslim minority in Soviet Russia. Poor countries that add millions to their population each year, moreover, may have continually to divert resources they might otherwise have used to improve their economic performance or pay back their debts to rich countries, and must spend them instead on feeding, housing, and schooling additional people. Desperately poor countries, it is sometimes said, might be prompted by the enormous size of their populations to expand their borders by force.

These and other apocalyptic visions were expressed in heated language by alarmists in the Sixties. Julian Simon has collected a number of inflammatory passages in his book *The Ultimate Resource*.[4] Kingsley Davis, a famous sociologist and demographer, for example, claimed that "in subsequent history the Twentieth Century may be called either the century of world wars or the century of the population plague." Robert McNamara, then the head of the World Bank, argued that "excessive population growth is the greatest single obstacle to the economic and social advancement of most societies in the developing world." Simon has even unearthed a pair of authors who claimed that

> at the present rate of world population increase, overpopulation may become *the* major cause of social and political instability. Indeed, the closer man approaches the limit of ultimate density of "carrying capacity" the more probable is nuclear warfare.

By the 1960s, the alarmists had succeeded in persuading the U.S. government to regard population growth as a problem. Under the Johnson administration the State Department's Agency for International Development (AID) began to spend large amounts of money to urge other countries to take their growing populations as a cause for concern. A good deal of this money was channeled through international organizations like the World Bank and the United Nations Fund for Population Activities (UNFPA); other funds came from nongovernmental organizations like the Ford or Rockefeller foundations. The United States has given more money than any other country to efforts of this kind.

Population programs were also considered a cheap and easy way to contribute to economic growth—a view President Johnson expressed when he told the United Nations in 1965 that

[4]Julian L. Simon, *The Ultimate Resource* (Princeton: Princeton University Press, 1981).

"less than five dollars invested in population control is worth a hundred dollars invested in economic growth."[5] By the early Seventies belief in the need to reduce global population growth had become so widespread that, as Simon notes, even Ronald Reagan (then governor of California) said that "unless major efforts are made to reduce population growth, vast numbers of people will face severe famine and misery."

In recent years the alarmist view has been in retreat, in part because of the growing influence of Simon's views, but also because the predictions of the alarmists did not prove true. For example, instead of accelerating further, the global population growth rate fell back from 2 percent to 1.7 percent. There are, however, still many who believe that rapid population growth has serious adverse consequences. The Nobel Prize–winning economist Jan Tinbergen recently wrote that population growth "constitutes a threat to humankind's welfare" and that "it is also highly desirable—in fact inescapable—that population growth be stopped as soon as possible."[6] And Robert Mc-Namara has written that population growth will be stopped by "humane and voluntary measures taken now, or because of the old Malthusian checks. Or perhaps even more likely, in tomorrow's world, it will occur as a result of coercive government sanctions and the recourse by desperate parents to both frequent abortion and clandestine infanticide."[7]

II

Why are Simon and his followers so optimistic? For him, the most important determinants of economic progress are innovations produced by human beings:

[5]Phyllis Tilson Piotrow, *World Population Crisis: The United States Response* (New York: Praeger, 1973).

[6]Jan Tinbergen, in a symposium reviewing *World Development Report 1984,* in *Population and Development Review,* vol. 11, no. 1 (March 1985).

[7]Robert S. McNamara, "Time Bomb or Myth: The Population Problem," *Foreign Affairs* (Summer 1984).

It is your mind that matters economically, as much or more than your mouth or hands. In the long run, the most important economic effect of population size and growth is the contribution of additional people to our stock of useful knowledge. And this contribution is large enough in the long run to overcome all the costs of population growth.

Babies don't create knowledge while still in their cradles; society must pay for the costs of feeding, housing, and educating children until they reach maturity. If we take a "short-term" view, therefore, children are a poor investment, since they are a burden on savings, resources, and social services. But from a more generous perspective, they are not, according to Simon, since innovations may be created by these children when they grow up.

More people mean more minds at work on social problems, he writes, and "it seems reasonable to assume that the amount of improvement depends on the number of people available to use their minds." As in any investment, the short-run costs are necessary if we are to enjoy a larger long-run gain. According to Simon's view, once we recognize the long-run gains of having children, the Malthusian view that our reproductive behavior creates demands for resources that grow faster than nature takes to provide us with these resources is invalidated. These demands may grow rapidly, but the amount of resources in nature is not fixed, since human beings create new resources through their ingenuity.

In part, Simon's argument depends on the statistical claim that a genius who will resolve social problems is more likely to be found in a population of one million than in a population of one thousand. But he also thinks that a greater population creates pressures that impel most human beings to use their ingenuity. For example, he thinks that greater pressure on available land leads to greater effort by farmers to increase their crop yields. People use "successively more 'advanced' but more laborious methods of getting food as population density increases"; they turn from hunting and gathering to "migratory slash-and-burn agriculture, and thence to settled long-fallow agriculture, to short-fallow agriculture, and eventually to the use of fertilizer, irrigation, and multiple cropping." There is no such thing, he thinks, as a "fixed supply of farmland": When people need more land they "make" it by using such techniques as diking, draining, and irrigation, or by using new soil technology. The principle that scarcity induces invention is also true, he says, in the case of resources other than land. When gas or coal runs out, people look for substitutes or invent them.

Moreover, Simon believes that "a larger population implies a larger total demand for goods; with larger demand and higher production come division of labor and specialization, larger plants, larger industries." The presence of more people encourages the creation of more "roads and railways and airlines, which carry agricultural and industrial products as well as persons and messages," more "irrigation and electrical systems, which transport water and power." These are necessary for economic growth, for they allow farmers and businessmen to deliver their products to markets at reasonable cost. It would not, however, be in anyone's interest to create these things for a sparse population separated by great distances. Simon even writes that we should

> welcome the scarcity problems that are caused by increasing population and rising incomes, because if problems do not arise, solutions will not be evoked. And the entire process of scarcity problems arising and then getting solved almost always leaves us better off than if the problems had never arisen.

Even if a greater population could cause a drain on resources, there is no evidence, in Simon's view, that it has done so in history, since "all of the evidence of hundreds and even thousands of years shows natural resources to be getting more available—that is, less costly, even as population has multiplied and resource use has multiplied even faster."

Simon and the late Herman Kahn compiled an enormous

book[8] designed to refute views like that of the *Global 2000 Report*, which was sponsored by the U.S. government and presented to President Carter in 1980. The report to Carter argued that by the end of the century the strain on global resources will deprive many millions of people of "basic needs for food, shelter, health, and jobs, or any hope for betterment," and that "if present trends continue," the world will be "less stable ecologically, and more vulnerable to disruption than the world we live in now."

In their book, Simon and Kahn argue that "mineral resources are becoming less scarce rather than more scarce." The availability of land "will not increasingly constrain world agriculture in coming decades." Although "many people are still hungry," Simon and Kahn claim that "the food supply has been improving since at least World War II, as measured by grain prices, production per consumer, and the famine death rate." One of the contributors to the book cites a 1981 Food and Agriculture Organization (FAO) study which claims that the growth rate of total agricultural production in the world has consistently outpaced population growth rates during the past twenty years. In addition, Simon and Kahn argue that we need not be worried that forests will be depleted soon, or that fisheries will cease to keep up stocks. "Water does not pose a problem of physical scarcity or disappearance," they write, and "threats of air and water pollution have been vastly overblown."

Simon and Kahn argue that "the government should *not* take steps to make the public more 'aware' of issues concerning resources, environment, and population," or "attempt to influence individuals' family-size decision in any fashion." Recommendations to other countries or pressure upon them—such as that made by AID, which spent more than $200 million in 1985 on population programs—to reduce population growth rates are not warranted, for Simon and Kahn, by any facts about

[8]Julian L. Simon and Herman Kahn, *The Resourceful Earth* (London: Basil Blackwell, 1984).

resources and population, and "constitute unjustifiable interference in the activities of other countries, because such policies must necessarily rest upon value judgments." Simon calls his own position "pro-abortion-freedom and pro-population-growth." In his own view, birth control is a "human right" and disseminating birth control methods and information is "one of the great social works of our time." Although he would "vote against any overall U.S. policy that would coerce people not to have children," he is willing to "accord to a community the right to make such a decision if there is a consensus on the matter." But he does not think it is in our "national interest" to promote population control in other countries in part because "there is zero evidence connecting density with the propensity to engage in wars, or even fist fights."

As might be expected, some who are sympathetic to Simon's views have convinced themselves that declines in population, especially in the industrial democracies of the West, pose a greater problem than "overpopulation."

In an article in the American Enterprise Institute symposium mentioned earlier, Ben Wattenberg and Karl Zinsmeister claim that "the geopolitical security and potency of America and its Western allies are likely to be threatened by a variety of population trends now under way around the world."[9] The average number of children born to a couple in the Western nations, for example, is 15 percent below the minimum number of children a couple needs to replace itself. (According to Allen Carlson, a participant in the symposium, "the fertility collapse has hit particularly hard in West Germany, where in the decade after 1966 the number of families with three or more children declined by two-thirds"; in Sweden in 1976, he adds, "deaths actually exceeded native births for the first time.")[10]

Wattenberg and Zinsmeister argue that in the West there may soon be an increasingly aged population and fewer young people to come up with innovations and do hard work, as well

[9]*Public Opinion*, vol. 8, no. 8 (December/January 1986).
[10]*The Washington Post*, April 13, 1986, p. C-1.

as more dependents, fewer workers, and contracting industries and markets. They worry also that countries like the United States may not be able to fulfill their already enormous Social Security obligations. Richard Perle, the assistant secretary of defense for international security, claims in the symposium that "in countries like the Federal Republic of Germany, it is already becoming increasingly difficult to maintain the minimum size military force necessary to provide a reasonable prospect of conventional defense of German and allied territory."

At the same time, Wattenberg and Zinsmeister argue, "the nations of the Soviet bloc" have "higher fertility rates than Western nations" and the "less developed" countries (LDC) are "growing very rapidly." These developments, they say, may soon make it difficult for the United States to maintain what they call its "great-power status." They recommend that the United States continue to provide family planning aid to less developed countries to help bring down high population growth rates in those countries; they also believe that Western nations should accept a larger number of productive immigrants. Steps should also be taken, they say, to reverse the causes of low fertility in the United States and other Western countries. These causes include "delayed marriage, more divorce, legal abortion." In their view more women should stay home and have children instead of competing for jobs. Western governments should consider giving tax credits or exemptions to large families, in order to encourage people to have more children.

Critics of Wattenberg and Zinsmeister's view could respond that while it is true that an aging population is less energetic and less able to learn new technologies, older workers may be more reliable and experienced than younger ones. If their medical care and nutrition are improved, they may be able to work much longer. The negative economic consequences of population declines in Western countries may also be offset by immigration and by greater participation in the labor force by women with smaller families. And even if we accept the arguable conception of "great-power status," it is not clear that the Western democracies are losing that status because of population declines. What declines have already occurred may eventually be reversed by new attitudes toward having children on the part of young couples, as may be occurring in the United States already. Furthermore, in an age of nuclear weapons it seems strained to suggest that military power primarily depends on the number of soldiers.

In the Soviet Union, birth rates have been higher (and declining less rapidly) among its Asian population, so that ethnic Russians may soon no longer be a majority; this may do more to increase conflicts among Russia's different ethnic populations than it will to improve Soviet "great-power status." Moreover, as Murray Feschbach of the Center for Population Research at Georgetown University has argued, in the years between 1964 and 1984 the crude death rate in the Soviet Union increased by over one-half, and life expectancy for males may have declined by as much as six years since the middle 1960s. Even if Wattenberg and Zinsmeister are right that population declines in the West are a serious problem, it is far from clear what to do about them. Policies designed to influence people to have more children have rarely worked, or have worked only where unacceptable means have been used, as when Romania outlawed abortion and banned the import of contraceptives in 1966 and succeeded, if only temporarily, in doubling the birth rate.[11]

III

Simon's "supply-side demography" is not a new view—suggestions of it are found in the work of the seventeenth-century economist Sir William Petty, and in that of recent economists and demographers like Colin Clark, Albert Hirschman, and Ester Boserup. It has helped to show how exaggerated were many of the claims of the alarmists. But Simon's argument is

[11]For further discussion of issues concerning population decline, see Michael Teitelbaum and Jay M. Winter, *The Fear of Population Decline* (New York: Academic Press, 1985).

almost equally exaggerated in its own way. As we saw earlier, he claims that as a population grows in size it is more likely by that fact to contain minds that will solve important "problems of scarcity." But it should be obvious that simply counting the numbers of people in a group is not a reliable way to assess their value as workers or entrepreneurs. Moreover, if (as is true in many parts of the world) people are weakened by diseases like malaria or by protein deficiencies that cause malfunction of the brain and the central nervous system, it seems unlikely that adding new members to their groups will increase the number of ideas. And even if people with the inventiveness of Huygens or Descartes were born into an aboriginal tribe, and happened to hit on a brilliant idea, it would probably be ignored. What we regard as a problem is largely set for us by the society in which we live; the ideas that might be solutions to these problems come to little unless there are institutions— research groups, copyright laws, means of disseminating information—that help us to develop and criticize these ideas in an effective way.

Again, is it true, as Simon claims without qualification, that "additional children influence the LDC economy by inducing people to work longer hours and invest more, as well as by causing an improvement in the social infrastructure, such as better roads and communication systems"? There is no reason to believe that this occurs as a matter of course in poor societies. The National Research Council has recently issued a report on population growth and economic development which claims that "while there are many examples of successful adaptations to high labor/land ratios, there are other examples where intensification of agriculture has apparently led to reduced labor productivity, sometimes accompanied by soil depletion, exhaustion, and even abandonment," as may have been true of Mayan civilization.[12] The report suggests that Bangladesh, for

[12]National Research Council, *Population Growth and Economic Development: Policy Questions* (Washington D.C.: National Academy Press, 1986), pp. 21–22.

example, may not be able to adopt technological innovations in response to population pressures because labor there is already "extremely intensively used."

It therefore seems clear that population growth does not always offer the opportunity to adopt innovations. Nor is it true that people always make use of innovations when the opportunity arises. The Dutch sociologist W. F. Wertheim has given an account of a pioneer settlement in the largely uncultivated island of Sumatra by people from the densely populated rural areas of Java. Far from shifting to extensive agriculture, as their new conditions allowed, they instead constructed precise replicas of their old villages and farms. Their behavior, Wertheim claims, resembled "the ways of colonies of ants who by instinct know how to construct new communities but ignore the outward factors which may endanger existence of the community."[13]

In general Simon assumes that all people respond as "economic agents" in the same way to opportunities. He suggests that people, as rational economic agents, will modify their reproductive habits when it is in their economic self-interest to do so. This implies that people generally want the children they have. But while it is an exaggeration to suppose that there is an enormous untapped demand for contraceptives in the poor countries of Africa and Asia, it is also true that there are unwanted children—for example, those desired only by the father, who insists the mother carry them. When asked, many women around the world claim that they wish to limit the size of their families.

Nor does Simon adequately take into account the institutions that largely determine the way people perceive opportunities. For example, in every society there are common attitudes about who should get married, or the age at which people should have children, or the number of children they should have. In many societies, there are specific institutional arrangements

[13]W. F. Wertheim, "Inter-Island Migration in Indonesia," in *East-West Parallels* (The Hague: Van Hoeve, 1964), p. 205.

that support high or low birth rates, such as property rules, family law, government economic policy. A clear example is the pattern of marriage that prevailed in eighteenth- and nineteenth-century Europe, where most people married only at a late age (and many not at all); newly married couples had to set up their own households and therefore postponed marriage until they were financially independent. This contrasts with the marriage pattern found, say, in many parts of south Asia today, where marrying early and having many children are ways by which women can deal with the insecurities of their lives and where couples can begin married life in the households of the husband's parents.

We need not enter here the dispute whether people are *really* the "rational agents" of economic theory beneath these variances in behavior and social setting; in fact, very little except a definition hinges on the matter. We need only claim that customs, beliefs, and traditions can displace economically self-interested motives, and that they certainly help to define what people think of as a "benefit" and a "cost." In many instances, no doubt, culturally determined attitudes toward children coincide with economically rational behavior. For example, in many rural societies of the world, it not merely conforms to cultural tradition to have many children, but it is economically rational to do so. Children help about the house, deliver meals, bring fodder to draft animals, and when they grow up they provide physical security for their parents and help to support them. They are a kind of old age insurance in societies where pensions and bank accounts do not exist.

It would be an exaggeration to suggest that Simon is unaware of the importance of institutions. When he was asked why, since India and China have the largest populations in the world, they are not much better off than other countries, he replied that their cultural history and institutions were at fault. These, he said, had prevented the problem solvers born into the society from inventing ideas or the society adopting them. But he does not consider the implications of this claim for his own arguments. For one thing, it suggests his argument about the correlation between large populations and useful ideas needs to be seriously qualified. Or consider that while social institutions are only rarely explicitly designed by people, they can be improved by people. Why, then, haven't many large populations not "induced" the problem solvers in them to invent and adopt improvements in their institutions?

IV

Lord Bauer's view that "allegations or apprehensions of adverse or even disastrous results of population growth are unfounded" is closely associated with his claim that conventional development economics has failed to understand how people contribute to economic progress.[14] In most development theory, he has written, people are treated as "homogeneous from an economic point of view." It has been claimed, for example, that economic growth depends on such factors as how much capital or land is available to each person in a society, and indeed this is why many economists have been worried that larger numbers of people might retard economic growth. According to such views, Bauer notes, additional children are treated as a "burden" because they are costly. But this is to overlook that they may pay their way later on; and in any case, Bauer says, most people want the children they have; they do not consider them burdens and would not be happier if the children died.

Apart from such obvious flaws, many general theories of development are vulnerable on other grounds, according to Bauer. For one thing, they often overlook important differences in economic achievement among people and groups. For example, in his own experiences as a visitor to rubber plantations in Southeast Asia, he observed that the "output of the Chinese was usually more than double that of the Indians, with

[14]See P. T. Bauer, *Dissent on Development* (Cambridge, Mass.: Harvard University Press, 1971), and *Equality, the Third World and Economic Delusion* (Cambridge, Mass.: Harvard University Press, 1981).

all of them using the same equipment of tapping knife, latex cup, and latex bucket."[15] The great majority of both the Chinese and the Indians, he says, were uneducated coolies. Differences in educational background or initial capital endowment or other factors regarded as important by many development theories could not be used to explain the differences in output. Bauer believes that these differences can be attributed in considerable, though not quantifiable, part to aspirations and motives, to the resourcefulness, ambition, and energy of the Chinese laborers. The low productivity of many "undeveloped" populations, on the other hand, reflects lack of energy, skill, ambition, industriousness. Even though foreign aid has provided them with initial capital and they often have access to plentiful natural resources, they have not succeeded in marshaling these resources to their advantage. By contrast, most industrious groups (such as those who became prosperous in Europe during the Industrial Revolution) have prospered without foreign aid, capital, or other resources.

For these and other reasons, Bauer does not believe that comprehensive government planning, or foreign aid, is likely to help a country develop, for these do not create the personal qualities that are necessary for such economic advancement and may retard them. Development, he suggests, occurs when people are brought into contact, often through simple activities like trading, with new opportunities and then take advantage of them, as he says many Africans did during the periods when they lived under colonial rule. He particularly deplores the efforts of many less developed countries to impose tariffs, price controls, state monopolies of industries, collectivized farming and other measures that stunt the latent entrepreneurial activities he thinks exist in these countries. For example, many African governments like that of Ghana have used marketing boards to control the flow and the prices of export crops like cocoa and peanuts. These policies were ostensibly designed to

[15]P. T. Bauer, *Reality and Rhetoric: Studies in the Economics of Development* (Cambridge, Mass.: Harvard University Press, 1984), p. 7.

insulate the peasant producers from fluctuations in the world market prices of these products. Their effect, however, was to tax these peasants, thus reducing their incentive to produce more and encouraging them to leave the countryside to compete for scarce jobs in already crowded cities. Policies that retard growth, he thinks, are often pursued by bureaucrats less concerned with the good of the people than with their own enrichment.

As I have noted, Simon's argument appeals to an unrealistic, abstract psychology and to a technological open frontier he thinks is created by human ingenuity. Bauer's work, on the other hand, is full of exceptions to general theories of economic history and splendidly conveys a sense of the diversity of cultures, social institutions, religious attitudes, climates, soil conditions, and other factors that may affect economic progress. Yet when Bauer advances his own view of population he relies on a psychology almost as crude as Simon's and appeals to an unduly narrow conception of what government is ethically permitted to do in altering population trends. Thus, despite his emphasis on the diversity of economic performance among people of different religious, ethnic, and cultural backgrounds, Bauer can write without qualification that "if rapid population growth should substantially threaten living standards, this would induce people to modify their reproductive behavior." This, he says, is true in poor countries as well as rich ones: "In LDCs as elsewhere, people take note of surrounding social and economic conditions in their procreative habits. And if they find that they have as many children as they can support, they will either stop having more or adjust their economic circumstances." This suggests, in effect, that there is no population problem, or at best only temporary bottlenecks as people "adjust" their economic circumstances to make way for the children they choose to have. It is why Bauer writes that "there is no case, either on moral or economic grounds, to induce or press Third World governments officially to promote population control."[16]

---

[16]*Equality, the Third World and Economic Delusion*, pp. 46, 63.

But Bauer's own salutary emphasis on the differing economic performance of different groups clearly implies that we must allow that such problems can exist. For what of those groups who are *not* so far-seeing to "take note of surrounding social and economic conditions in their procreative habits," let alone industrious, resourceful, and ambitious? Or those who do *not* know how to "adjust their economic circumstances"? Might not the addition of large numbers of people create impediments to improving the lives of the existing population in such cases? In many poor countries, children are born into miserable poverty: they are underweight and prone to die from parasitic, diarrheal, and respiratory diseases. Their parents cannot adequately feed or educate them. These seem unsuitable conditions for the development, or expression, of those personal qualities that encourage economic growth. Bauer says little about such groups and implies that, apart from relieving them of misery on humanitarian grounds, they should be left alone.

Bauer's reliance on the economic argument that people modify their reproductive behavior in accordance with economic self-interest suggests that where people do not limit the size of their family they must desire the children they have. But as we have noted earlier, there are unwanted children; it also seems to be the case that at least some women would have fewer children if they knew more about, and had ready access to, modern methods of birth control or means of reducing infant mortality.

Moreover, he devotes much of his argument to criticizing views on population that do not merit serious attention. For example, he argues that population growth does not directly cause poverty or other evils. But no one who believes that there are population problems need disagree, for it is generally only in combination with other factors that population growth could create adverse consequences. Bauer is right to note that land or resources per person is not the key factor in economic development, that life expectancy has been improving in many parts of the world, that many of the statistics on which alarming conclusions about "overpopulation" are based are mistaken. And, as he frequently says, government policies may have contributed greatly in many countries to economic decline. But none of these points overturns the claim that there are problems caused by population trends. Bauer's abstract arguments (like Simon's) show that if people are rational economic agents, then population growth need not hinder economic growth; they fail to present adequate evidence that these motives are indeed held by most poor people across the world.

V

Many subtle and distinguished writers on population who represent the central line of academic thinking on the subject have rejected or have never held either the alarmist or the benign view of population. Such writers, who in the United States include the late Frank Notestein and prominent contemporary demographers like Ansley Coale, do not think that the mere presence of more people is "the cause" of poverty or other evils. Notestein, for example, argued nearly a quarter of a century ago that "extremists who suggest that mortality should not be cut until birth rates are reduced are ignorant of the processes at work as well as immoral." At the same time, he wrote, "those who counsel reliance on the productive powers of modern technology to avoid the necessity of curtailing population growth are giving very dangerous advice." He argued that there was a "need for lower birth rates, not as a substitute for modernization, but as a means of hastening the process of modernization."[17]

Whether a problem of overpopulation or underpopulation exists, according to such writers, can be determined only by carefully examining the balance between births and deaths in

[17]Frank W. Notestein, "Population Growth and Economic Development" a lecture delivered to the Ceylon Association for the Advancement of Science in 1964, reprinted in *Population and Development Review,* vol. 9, no. 2 (June 1983).

a population, the resources available to sustain it (including the skill, energy, and education of its labor force), and the standard of living desired by the population. The issue is not whether new people can be added to the population notwithstanding the costs, or whether doing so will cause a catastrophe. No doubt it is true, as Bauer has argued, that some societies have managed to prosper even though they had high rates of population growth and scarce natural resources and capital. The question, however, is whether it is possible for populations to grow without unduly compromising such social objectives as the improvement of schooling, health, or, more generally, the average standards of living. In this sense there are genuine problems of population in the world today.[18]

According to United Nations projections, population in the world is expanding rapidly in absolute terms even if the rate of growth is declining. In 1980, when the global population was 4.5 billion, 75 million were added; in 1990, nearly 85 million are likely to be added, so that world population is expected to be about 6.1 billion by the year 2000 and more than 8 billion by 2025. According to the UN projections, during the next half-century India will nearly double its current population size and will be much larger than China is now. Mexico will also double in size; Bangladesh will triple in size; and Kenya will grow five times as large as it is now.

Such projections, of course, are not predictions; they only provide the logical implications of assumptions about how people will plan their family size in the future. The assumptions are often based on how people behave now, and, as such, they are fallible and become increasingly so as they concern events in the distant future. Famines, epidemics, or major wars may undermine them. Conversely, population projections may turn out to be wrong if fertility does not decline with the speed that demographers have assumed it will. Still, there is no reason to

[18]See Geoffrey McNicoll, "Consequences of Rapid Population Growth: An Overview and Assessment," *Population and Development Review*, vol. 10, no. 2 (June 1984).

reject such projections in principle. The reduction in the global population growth rate in recent years shows what many have believed all along: There is no universal problem of overpopulation. Indeed, in some parts of the world there might be a need for higher birth rates, as may be the case in Mongolia, for example.

But of course the decline in the global growth rate has not occurred evenly across the world. In the less developed countries of Africa, Latin America, and Asia, there are currently some 3.6 billion people. The population of these regions as a whole is growing at the rate of more than 2 percent. As noted earlier, most of these people are not living in conditions that promote entrepreneurship or Simon's "induced innovations."

For an example of a region in which growing population may be said to pose a genuine problem, consider sub-Saharan Africa. While there are large "underpopulated" regions of the continent, a high proportion of its population is concentrated in the coastal states of West Africa, around Lake Victoria, and in Ethiopia. There is little industry in tropical Africa. On farms, many Africans still use simple tools—axes, machetes, digging sticks—and use of tractors and harvesting machines is unusual. (The plow was unknown in tropical Africa before 1900.) Nor is irrigation extensively used. Across much of the continent there is a lengthy dry season and very high temperatures, which reduce the moisture available to crops, and large regions are infested with the tsetse fly, which transmits trypanosomiasis to cattle and people. In many parts of Africa, AIDS is infecting new populations at a frightening rate.

While the world as a whole has increased its food output faster than population has grown since 1950, food production declined per head in most countries in tropical Africa in the 1960s and 1970s. According to the World Bank's *World Development Report 1984*, the FAO claimed that of forty sub-Saharan countries, fourteen, including Botswana, Uganda, Burundi, and Kenya, "do not have enough land—assuming subsistence level farming—to support on a sustainable basis populations as large as those already reached in 1975."[19] As a group, these countries account for one-third of the land area of sub-Saharan Africa and about half of its 1981 population. Throughout the continent, moreover, food consumption is inadequate, disease is widespread, and life expectancy is low. Average annual GNP declined between 1960 and 1982 in many African countries, including Chad, Zaire, Uganda, Ghana, and Somalia. The region is divided into a large number of small political units, cutting across tribal groupings and often containing feuding ethnic groups; as a result, political and economic organization in many countries is weak and ineffectual. Africa has the poorest people in the world, and as *The Economist* reported, "the average African is now poorer than in 1960."[20]

Africa also has the fastest growing population in the world. Kenya, for example, has an annual population growth rate of 4 percent, a rate that would double the population every seventeen years. Most of the land that has been cleared in Africa is used for subsistence agriculture, which makes use of the labor of children and thus encourages people to have many of them. Moreover, many Africans live in areas with tribal land tenure instead of private property: They therefore seek to acquire wealth through having many children.[21] But the children they have are often diseased, or of the wrong sex, or parents fear they might die prematurely and so they try to have more children. The result is that Africa is expected before the year 2000 to add thirteen persons for each one added to the population of Europe. Very few African countries, moreover, have effective policies explicitly addressing the need to reduce population growth, or even simply supporting family planning. Under such circumstances it is unreasonable to claim that there is no need

[19]The World Bank, *Population Change and Economic Development* (New York: Oxford University Press, 1984), p. 125.

[20]"The Third World Smiles," *The Economist*, April 12, 1986, p. 13.

[21]Ester Boserup, "Economic and Demographic Interrelationships in Sub-Saharan Africa," *Population and Development Review*, vol. 11, no. 3 (September 1985).

for concern about population, or that children born in such circumstances can be relied on to provide the innovations that will solve the problems of poverty.

VI

Still it is not clear what can be done, ethically and effectively, to solve population problems, especially if the local governments are not much concerned about them. Simon is correct to say that both the identification of population trends as a "problem" and the choice of policy to resolve it are a matter of "our values." It cannot be determined in a "value-free" way that population rates are too high or too low or that they pose a threat to human welfare. These claims are evaluative and moral. Even if we could confidently claim on empirical grounds that population growth in a region diverts resources from being used to improve the living standards of the population, this would not in itself be a serious problem unless we also assume that whatever advantages are gained by people having the number of children they want are outweighed by the general benefits of having a greater income per person. Many people and many heads of government make this assumption, but many people who are having children do not.

Again, many of us assume without argument that a government is justified in taking steps to curb population growth if the problem is serious enough. Many couples, we are likely to argue, do not foresee the consequences of their reproductive behavior for society at large. Governments may be justified in taking action because in most modern societies parents do not fully bear the costs of caring for their children—costs measured in the effect these children have on the availability of land, or jobs, or places in schools. There can therefore be a gap between the benefits children bring to their parents and those they bring to society and future generations. In making these claims we tend to assume, however, that the government in question is legitimate and that people can have a voice in determining whether population policies are introduced and what policies will be used. But in most of the countries in which population growth causes problems today citizens have little control over government policies. What is the ethical status of a population policy, however mild, appropriately introduced by a dictator in a country whose economy he has severely damaged through inept and corrupt economic measures, and who has not obtained the "consent" of those affected by this population policy? Or consider, as we have seen, that many people have flatly judged the Chinese limit of one child to a family and other population policies as "unethical" on the ground that they are "coercive"; they also condemn efforts by the United States to persuade poor countries to take steps to lower their population growth rates as "ethically unjustified" (or, once more, "coercive"). Are these claims correct? The answers to such questions are rarely as simple as they have sometimes been made out to be.

To clarify and answer such questions has often been called the business of philosophers. But although in recent years philosophers have tried to rebut the charge that they had lost contact with "practical" concerns, and as a result have produced a whole literature of unreadable papers on moral problems of sports, business, blood banking, the allocation of scarce medical innovations, and other subjects, work on "ethical problems of population" has been sparse. And like much of the recent "applied ethics," it has often been disfigured by false methods and problems.

For example, some philosophers have seen it as their duty to create an ethics specifically devoted to population, a "population ethics." But this is no more reasonable than developing a special moral theory for ethical problems that are suggested by zoning legislation. Other moralists try to "justify" this or that population policy. They do not suppose, however, that these policies are sufficiently justified by describing how they enable the government to promote the public good. Instead, they appeal to an ancient and sterile philosophical tradition according to which a belief or policy is properly justified only if the objections to it of a skeptic are rebutted; this requires, in their view, that a justification appeal to first principles or, more often, to "ultimate values" like freedom, justice, and happiness. Clearly there is a sense in which such values are ultimate, but they shift in importance from one situation to another, so that any permanent or absolute "ranking" of them—according to which, for example, freedom is higher than justice or conversely—is absurd. Moreover, values are not present or absent in a situation in the way a light switch is on or off. They admit of degrees and fall into different species or kinds. For example, there are many kinds of freedom—social, legal, political, metaphysical—and even a variety of political freedoms. To speak of a person being free in a situation is always a matter of identifying a mixture of these kinds of freedoms. Furthermore, the many varieties of freedom or justice or happiness are not harmoniously connected like teeth on a zipper. Nor can they be realized at the same time.

Moreover, some ethical theorists who have studied questions of population have allowed themselves to be charmed by artificial problems. A recent book on morality and population,[22] for example, tries to justify various population policies by a "duty to future generations." The duty is formulated in complicated detail, but it is entirely unconvincing. This is in large part because its practical content is not specified clearly. For example, the author writes that "future generations should not be made worse off than us." But who is "us"? There are enormous differences in wealth, control, access to resources, and power in the present generations living on earth. What complicated formula is to be devised to apportion our generation's responsibility to future generations among people currently living in Upper Volta or Beverly Hills? To which future generations is the duty owed? Our actions have significant effects on generations that will live a thousand years hence (as the actions of the Greeks continue to have effects on us): At what point, and on what basis, do we cut the chain of consequences

---

[22]Michael Bayles, *Morality and Population Policy* (Huntsville: University of Alabama Press, 1980).

of our actions in appraising their effect on future generations? Indeed, on what basis can we discuss the characteristics of these future generations at all? And in what sense can *possible* entities like future persons have *rights* against us?[23]

Is the duty owed to future generations with qualification or only provided they fulfill certain conditions? When giving aid to our children, for example, or writing a will, we often link our gifts to specific conditions. We refuse to leave our money to our children if they use it to promote organized crime or support a drug habit. But, in the case of future generations, how could we ensure that the conditions we specify are observed? Alternatively, who will be the trustee of the resources we lay aside for future generations? What, indeed, if future generations have entirely different values from us, or scorn liberty and justice and behave like beasts?

It is sensible to say that we know altogether too little about future generations to answer these questions. But then why emphasize, as some prominent philosophers have, the question of our duty to future generations? Even though there is a sense in which we must not squander our resources so that people in the future may have some of them,[24] there is too little information at hand to enable us to speak of a "duty" to them. For all we know, future people may be much more resourceful than we are and will be able to develop substitutes for the resources we prize. No case has been made out, in any event, for taking the problem of our duty to future people seriously as it has been formulated by recent philosophers. The same might be said of many other approaches to ethical questions

[23]Some philosophers have tried to deny that all duties have correlative rights (as a contractee has rights correlative to the duty of a contractor to fulfill his part of a contract). They claim that future people—those people who will actually exist—have no rights against us, but we have duties to them. This is a pure fiction designed to keep the problem of our "duties to future generations" alive.

[24]For an elaborate discussion of this point, see Derek Parfit, *Reasons and Persons* (Oxford: Clarendon Press, 1984), Part IV.

of population—for example, that which justifies specific population policies by reference to "human rights."[25]

What is a suitable moral theory for appraising questions of population? John Dewey noted that moral theory "emerges when men are confronted with situations in which different

[25]Although they are frequently discussed, no one has clearly set out what are the "human rights" involved in having children, leaving or entering a sovereign state, or other questions of population. Is it, for example, a human right to be able to bear as many children as one wishes? The very notion of a human right is obscure. A moral right, it is said, is a justified moral claim to specific treatment by others, or to the use or ownership of certain resources; if such a right is made into law, it is a legal as well as a moral right. (Many legal rights, of course, are not moral rights, and conversely.) Human rights are a species of moral rights that apply to *all human beings as such*. But we rarely apply any right in so unrestricted a manner. We deny, for example, the right of life to many human beings, such as a lunatic threatening to blow up a city. We cannot say that he has forfeited his right, since he has not ceased to be a human being. Nor is it clear on what ground human rights are said to exist. They are not derived from the facts of biology or "human nature" or physical truths about the universe. It is therefore unclear in what sense human rights are "human" or "rights." They do not connote something that any known agent has an obligation to provide but at best what he would have an obligation to provide in some ideal society. These rights are best seen as aspirations, imaginative responses to perceived moral imperfections in our social and economic institutions.

In 1968 the Teheran Conference decreed that all couples have the human right "to decide freely and responsibly on the number and spacing of their children." But depending on how one interprets this formulation, it can mean different things. Does it sanction the behavior of women who choose to have twelve children? Yes, it might be said, because they are said to be free to decide with their husbands or mates whether to have them. No, it may equally be said, since the world "responsibly" in the statement of the right implies that they may have only as many children as are compatible with a socially desirable population size. Ambiguous rights of this kind are often found in UN documents on population (and elsewhere), where they are dubiously assumed to be consistent with numerous other rights, including rights to democracy, peace, dignity, and are pompously reaffirmed again and again in proclamations, declarations, covenants, recommendations, and other incantations. See, for example, the *UN Symposium on Human Rights and Population* (New York: United Nations, 1983), the recommendations of a conference held in Vienna, of which—alas—I was the rapporteur.

desires promise opposed goods and in which incompatible courses of action seem to be morally justified."[26] There is no moral life when people are certain of what is wrong and what is right, or when there is no occasion for reflection. Dewey asks us to consider "the case of a citizen of a nation which has just declared war on another country. He is deeply attached to his own State. He has formed habits of loyalty and abiding by its laws, and now one of its decrees is that he shall support war. He feels in addition gratitude and affection for the country which has sheltered and nurtured him. But he believes that this war is unjust, or perhaps he has a conviction that all war is a form of murder and hence wrong. One side of his nature, one set of convictions and habits, leads him to acquiesce in war; another deep part of his being protests. He is torn between two duties: He experiences a conflict between the incompatible values presented to him by his habits of citizenship and by his religious beliefs respectively." He can drift, or accommodate himself to "whatever social pressure is uppermost." But if he faces the conflict he will use whatever moral principles he has at hand—principles he does not question—and if he finds that these do not help him to resolve his conflict, he will be forced to devise what Dewey calls "a reasonable principle by which to decide where the right really lies. In doing so he enters into the domain of moral theory, even if he does so unwittingly."

The problem of the patriotic pacifist is a moral one; and Dewey is right to add that moral "theory" is "a generalized extension of the kind of thinking" in which he must engage. The abstractions of moral theory, in this view, arise from ordinary life. We have wants and desires and we wish to fulfill them; as we grow up, we learn to discriminate among them. We develop conceptions of what is good in general. We also live with others in society, in relations of mutual benefit and antagonism: Out of this shared life arise standards of what is right in conduct. Moral theory describes the kinds of moral

[26]John Dewey, *The Theory of the Moral Life* (New York: Irvington Press, 1960).

conflicts that can arise and states the leading ways in which such problems have been treated by those who have thought about them a good deal. Dewey writes that moral theory seeks to "render personal reflection more systematic and enlightened, suggesting alternatives that might otherwise be overlooked, and stimulating greater consistency in judgment." But he also notes that moral theory "cannot take the place of personal decision, which must be made in every case of moral perplexity." A general principle or rule cannot be a substitute for such choice, for the situations we face in moral life differ greatly; at best, the principles that moral philosophers have invented are factors or considerations to be taken into account.

Nor do our decisions have to be "justified" in the way philosophers have recommended. We do not need to try to fulfill the impossible demand of ensuring that our choices are linked to infallible first principles through logical chains of argument. It is justification enough if our decisions comport with our present values that we take for granted. They are not at issue in the present decision. If they are called into question, then they must be judged against the background of other, more secure values and premises. At no time, however, need all of our moral beliefs stand in need of "justification." If a conflict should arise between us and another person or group, we must try to justify our views. But this justification, once more, is not a deduction of our views from absolutely certain first principles; it is justification of our views *to* these other people, taking for granted values or beliefs they share with us. (If there are no such shared values, of course, then we cannot discuss the matter with them, although we can try to create values of this kind.) Each moral problem, therefore, arises in a specific situation. It is always a problem for someone at some time, and what can be considered as a "solution" to it is always defined by the beliefs, attitudes, and desires of the person or group for whom it arises.

VII

It is clear, then, that the ethical problems that arise in reflection upon population trends cannot be identified in a "value-free" way. We often take for granted procedural and substantive values—a democratic political organization, the desirability of a higher average income or a better education, and other values—in identifying "overpopulation" or "underpopulation." We cannot assume that others will share these values. If they do not, we must try to justify our values *to* them. In general, in considering evaluative questions of population, it seems preferable to begin our inquiry with a consideration of the values and interests of those for whom the problem arises and who must define it and deal with it. We must identify what problem is present, what conflict of values generated it, and how the problem-situation constrains the choice of a solution to the problem.[27]

To give an example of how both procedural and substantive values might enter into the way a population problem is treated, suppose that the population trends of a country are widely regarded to be too high. Population growth can only be reduced in three ways: by raising mortality, encouraging out-migration, or reducing fertility. But since the first two ways are regarded by most governments, though not all, as unacceptable or infeasible, the third way is usually chosen. If a government decides to lower fertility, it may try to do so by one or more of the following methods: It may manipulate public access to methods of fertility control (such as contraceptives or abortions), for example, by distributing them at no cost to users in order to lower fertility. It may try to change the social and economic determinants of high fertility—the way women are perceived in the society, common attitudes toward children, education, causes of infant mortality, income differences. It

[27]For a fuller treatment of this theme, especially as it affects population policy, see Bernard Berelson and Jonathan Lieberson, "Government Efforts to Influence Fertility: The Ethical Issues," *Population and Development Review*, vol. 5, no. 4 (December 1979).

may make propaganda for family planning and birth control; or it may introduce economic incentives and disincentives in order to persuade people to have fewer children. For example, it may offer monetary payments if men have vasectomies, or it may create disincentives to having large families by the adjustment of wage levels, housing allocation, or university admission. It may offer free maternity leave for a couple's first two children but not for the third or subsequent children.[28] Finally, a government may exert social or political pressure or impose direct sanctions to limit family size. For example, Indonesia has successfully introduced a well-organized program whereby population targets are transmitted from the government down to villages and hamlets in Bali and East Java. The program makes use of peer pressure at the local level. In *banjars,* or hamlets, family planning is made a matter of public concern. A map of all the houses in the *banjar* is prominently displayed in the meeting hall, identifying the method of contraception used in each household. Contraceptive practice is discussed at each monthly meeting of household heads and those who do not use contraceptives are asked to justify their behavior before the others. In some of these hamlets, the leader sounds a drum every day to remind women to take their oral contraceptives.

The decision to use one (or more) of these methods has usually depended on how seriously population trends are thought to threaten local values. Charges that strong population policies, such as those pursued by China, are "unethical" may be correct, but they are also frequently flawed by a failure to

---

[28]Some of these measures have been put into effect in Singapore, South Korea, China, and other countries. For example, in 1975 Mrs. Gandhi declared emergency rule in India and set official sterilization targets to reduce population growth. Some six million were sterilized, sometimes forcibly, in the six months between July and December 1976, according to reliable reports. Penalties or disincentives for having children that were used during the Emergency included the denial of food to families with more than three children; in some parts of India, state employees were given a choice between sterilization and the loss of a month's salary.

distinguish among several questions. One of these is whether we have a clear idea of the conditions under which a legitimate government can intervene in people's decisions to have children or other intimate matters affecting reproduction. (How justified, for example, have our own public officials been in imposing a minimum age of marriage or limiting each person to one spouse at a time?) A second question is whether we, or our government, are justified in promoting our view of population trends abroad, and in what way. A third is whether we should help to subsidize or otherwise support the introduction of policies in other countries, if these policies would be regarded as unethical in our own country or if they are introduced by leaders without obtaining the consent of those affected by them.

The recent public debate over abortion in the United States has demonstrated that there is frequently no general agreement about the first question. For example, Representative Jack Kemp of New York and Senator Orrin Hatch of Utah sponsored legislation to stop federal funds from going to family planning clinics where women are advised of the availability of abortion or referred to abortion clinics. Kemp and Hatch wanted to abolish the Family Planning Services and Population Research Act, which allocates about $140 million a year to family planning aid for low-income women. None of this money was supposed to go for abortion, but family planning workers insisted that they must inform their clients of the full range of methods that are legally available for avoiding unwanted children.

Opponents of the Kemp-Hatch bill pointed to the large number of teenage pregnancies that take place in the United States each year—nearly one million in 1985—and claimed that the United States leads all developed countries in pregnancies among girls between the ages of fifteen and nineteen. They noted also that such pregnancies occur most often among very poor girls. According to *Time* magazine, nearly one-half of black females in the United States are pregnant by the age of twenty—a rate of pregnancy in the fifteen-to-nineteen age group that is twice that of white girls—and nearly 90 percent of babies born to blacks in this age group are born out of wedlock. The Reagan administration has supported a constitutional amendment to ban nearly all abortions and has reduced appropriations to provide nutritional supplements to low-income expectant mothers; it has also supported the Kemp-Hatch bill. Despite its efforts, however, opinion surveys reported in *Family Planning Perspectives,* a journal published by the Alan Guttmacher Institute in New York, showed that most Americans do not support a constitutional amendment to ban abortion and believe that women should be able to have one if they choose to do so. Making abortions illegal, they believed, would not prevent them from occurring. Such a ban, they think, would create a black market in abortions, so that only the rich would be able to obtain safe abortions, and would also result in more unwanted children.

Is the government justified in promoting its views or intervening in population problems abroad? Simon believes that the answer to that question is no; as we saw earlier, Simon and Kahn claim that recommendations to other countries to introduce population policies are "unjustifiable" because "such policies must necessarily rest upon value judgments." But it is hardly clear that making recommendations is an "imposition" (unless these are not genuine recommendations, but disguised threats, for example, to withhold aid unless they are accepted), especially if, as is often the case, the United States is requested by other countries to help assess the consequences of population growth in these countries. Even if we should not assume that people or governments abroad share our values, these values remain ours and do not necessarily cease to apply beyond our borders. If we believe a serious population problem (as we define it) to exist in some country or region, and if we believe that problem will affect American economic and political interests, we should not refrain from trying to justify its presence to the people of that country or to officials of its government. But if, as Simon and Kahn suggest, we ceased to promote in other countries any policy based on our "value judgments," we would be barred from doing this. Indeed, we should have no foreign policy at all.

This implies a negative answer to the third question, whether we are justified in supporting population policies abroad that we would find unethical here—or that would be imposed on foreigners without their consent. But much of what passes for moral condemnation of population policies in other countries does not make clear what would be "unethical" if practiced in the United States. No doubt Americans are reluctant to endorse policies like that of the Chinese one-child family as a means of reducing population growth. But judgments such as these often suffer from a kind of moral myopia or failure of imagination. Our eye firmly fixed on what we should regard as ethically unacceptable in our present circumstances, we do not consider what we would regard as unacceptable if our circumstances were radically different.

It is difficult to flatly judge China's policy as "unethical" without projecting ourselves in imagination into their situation and closely considering the reasoning that has led Chinese leaders to adopt their policy. China suffered the largest famine in human history between 1958 and 1962, which took some thirty million lives; Chinese leaders are worried that food production in the country may not be able adequately to cover the needs of the more than one billion people now in China, let alone of hundreds of millions more people. Whether their fears are justified is a complicated judgment that I suspect few who have pronounced the Chinese policy immoral have tried to make. But if they are, then doing nothing and allowing the birth rate to rise in China might be ethically more objectionable than the strong measures to control population growth now being taken.

VIII

It should be clear that there are indeed genuine population problems in parts of the world, and it is not in principle unethical for the United States to support population policies in at least some countries where trends have had adverse results. But it is still not clear what can actually be done to effectively change these trends. I noted earlier that specific policies to encourage population growth have rarely worked. As for policies to limit population growth, since the desire to have children derives not only from biological pressures but also from a wide variety of traditional beliefs and institutional arrangements, distributing contraceptives and information about family planning may be useful but is unlikely to ensure a major change of reproductive behavior unless the beliefs and institutions conducive to high birth rates have previously changed. This has suggested to some observers that the most effective population policies are those that change the people's motives to have many children, not just provide the means of controlling family size. Accordingly, they have said that "economic development" is the best way to reduce population growth.

The reasoning behind this view is known as the theory of the "demographic transition." It has long been known that the decline in mortality that occurred after the Industrial Revolution brought higher incomes to people in the West during the nineteenth century. This was shortly thereafter followed by a decline in birth rates (even though labor unions, churches, and other institutions opposed contraception, and the means used to avert births were often primitive, such as abstinence or abortion). The inference that many demographers have drawn from this and other evidence is that economic development will take care of the problems of population growth because higher incomes and improved levels of living lead to fewer deaths, to "modern" attitudes (since more people aspire to higher incomes or to being better educated), and eventually to the use of birth control.

There are exceptions to this view: In some countries there

has been economic development and no subsequent fertility decline, as in parts of the Soviet Union; in other countries, the birth rate has fallen without previous economic growth.[29] In addition, some social changes that fall short of general economic development might have an effect in lowering fertility, such as an improvement in literacy, or better health, or an increase in female employment. Furthermore, even where the transition occurs, it does not seem to occur in the same way, or at the same pace, in all social settings. In some places, for example, fertility declines before mortality does or follows it only much later, and fertility may even rise again after the transition is completed.

Still, even if the theory of the demographic transition has limited predictive value and cannot be mechanically applied to all countries, it roughly suggests why family planning programs, which often consist of little more than brochures about human reproduction and free diaphragms or pills, are rarely effective except in countries like South Korea, Taiwan, or Singapore, where a decline in fertility has already begun under conditions of rising prosperity, or in countries, like China, which have introduced an expensive, centralized, and militant campaign against population growth that many would find ethically unacceptable. In regions of the world where living conditions have not improved, such as parts of Africa, policies to alter reproductive behavior do not work well. It is often difficult to tell whether this is because people are not interested in birth control or because family planning programs are inefficient. In many poor countries, women must travel too far to find a clinic or

[29]For example, Paul Demeny has pointed out that between 1921 and 1938 the Bulgarian birth rate went down from forty-one per thousand to twenty-one per thousand, a decline that took place even though no modern contraceptive technology was available, no governmental policy advocating lower fertility was in effect, levels of income were low, and income distribution was not egalitarian. See Paul Demeny, "Population Policies," in Just Faaland, ed., *Population and the World Economy in the 21st Century* (New York: St. Martin's, 1982), the proceedings of a Nobel symposium on population growth and world development held in 1981; and also Demeny's comments on pp. 251–252.

wait too long before they are admitted once they get there; the contraceptives they are offered may be too expensive or may have unpleasant side effects. But the central reason for the failure of these programs is undoubtedly that people do not wish to change their decisions to have many children.

The view that "development is the best contraceptive" tells us rather less than we should like to know about what steps to take if population seems too high. It simply repeats the dull truth that if a couple becomes better off—has better housing, a higher income, better health care—it will probably have fewer children than it would when it was poorer. The emphasis on development replaces the problem of population by another which is equally complicated ethically and empirically: how to create economic growth, that is, to increase the total output of goods and services desired by a population in a region or country. The conditions that most economists believe are necessary for such growth are not present in most of the poor countries today. No doubt material advance begins when some people voluntarily take up opportunities that are open to them—for example, through engaging in trade—and when their behavior is imitated by others. Similarly, people have fewer children when they see that it is in their interest to do so. Their way of life and reproductive habits may then be copied by others, thus beginning a decline in fertility in the population at large. The question, of course, is how to get this process started. Decades of social science research on population and development have neither clarified this question very much nor arrived at a solution of it. Not surprisingly, efforts by governments and private groups to create conditions in which people decide to have fewer children have been, and are likely to remain, a matter of improvisation.

About the Author

Jonathan Lieberson is the contributing editor of the *New York Review of Books*. He received a Ph.D. in philosophy of science from Columbia University in 1977 and has taught philosophy at Barnard College since 1981. He has been Andrew Mellon Fellow in the History and Philosophy of Science at the University of Pittsburgh. In 1980 he was made Bernard Berelson Fellow in Population Science at the Population Council in New York, where he is now an associate at the Center for Policy Studies. He has been a contributing editor at *Vanity Fair* and other magazines. His work has appeared in scholarly journals such as the *Journal of Philosophy, Population and Development Review*, and *Social Research*, as well as in such publications as *House and Garden, Harper's Magazine, Encounter*, and *The New York Times Magazine*, as well as the *New York Review of Books*, in which most of the pieces collected in this volume first appeared.